T0330369

The Diplomat in the Corner Office

THE DIPLOMAT IN THE CORNER OFFICE

Corporate Foreign Policy

Timothy L. Fort

STANFORD BUSINESS BOOKS
An Imprint of Stanford University Press
Stanford, California

Stanford University Press
Stanford, California

© 2015 by the Board of Trustees of the Leland Stanford Junior
University. All rights reserved.

Special discounts for bulk quantities of Stanford Business Books
are available to corporations, professional associations, and other
organizations. For details and discount information, contact
the special sales department of Stanford University Press.
Tel: (650) 736-1782, Fax: (650) 736-1784

Printed and bound by CPI Group (UK) Ltd, Croydon, CR0 4YY

Library of Congress Cataloging-in-Publication Data

Fort, Timothy L., author.
   The diplomat in the corner office : corporate foreign policy /
Timothy L. Fort.
      Pages cm
   Includes bibliographical references and index.
   ISBN 978-0-8047-8637-9 (cloth : alk. paper) —
   ISBN 978-0-8047-9660-6 (pbk. : alk. paper)
   1. Peace—Economic aspects. 2. Peace-building—Economic
aspects. 3. Corporations—Moral and ethical aspects.
4. Business ethics. I. Title.
   JZ5538.F668 2015
   303.6'6—dc23
                                      2015010584

ISBN 978-0-8047-9670-5 (electronic)

Typeset by Thompson Type 10.9/13 Adobe Garamond

To KURINA, STEVEN, *and* THEO

In hope that in 2050 they will just shake their heads at what took us so long to figure out—this connection between business and peace

And, always,
to NANCY

Contents

Foreword

"When we say peace, we mean business," a delegate emphatically stated to a global gathering of business leaders, government officials, and other agents of change at the UN Global Compact's inaugural Business for Peace leadership platform in 2013. The newly created initiative aims to foster peace in the workplace, the marketplace and in society. Its creation and support by the global community is part of a growing recognition of the importance of peace to business, and vice versa—the core of the very topic that makes *The Diplomat in the Corner Office* essential reading in a contemporary business environment.

The fact that business, for the most part, is benefiting from peace will not come as a revelation to most, as peace is prosperity. It is the recognition that business can be a powerful *driver* of peace that remains surprising to many. Over the last fifteen years, the role of business in contributing to peace has become the subject of increased interest, and Tim Fort has been in the academic forefront of this exploration, researching and convincingly arguing that a business presence in peace building—through the idea of gentle (ethical) commerce—solves a long-standing anthropological debate of whether human beings have become more or less peaceful over time. Discussing from perspectives of power and trust, Fort lays out a compelling case for the idea that the role of business in fostering peace is neither ancillary nor niche; instead it is germane to the way in which peace and prosperity have developed from the beginning of trade and into the twenty-first century.

As an investment banker and chairman of the Business for Peace Foundation, an international organization vested in promoting a business mind-set and actions supportive to building peace, I was more than in-trigued by Professor Fort's advanced thinking on the topic when we first met several years ago. A long career in business had taught me the value of business relationships and how these often can inspire strong bonds of trust and promote peaceful relations between people, irrespective of culture or background, in the most complex of situations. I had also been reflecting on the rapid penetration of the Internet and how its intercon-nectivity and transparency seemed to be harnessing trust as currency, making us increasingly more ethically connected.

In this changing paradigm, companies should see themselves as in-dependent actors in a global and increasingly transparent and intercon-nected environment. This broadens the scope and complexity of powers with which a business must deal. Fort argues that a business increasingly must act with a sense of corporate "foreign policy," proposing that com-panies can and should anchor themselves in a strategy of fostering peace. Such a strategy begins with attending to one's core constituents (share-holders, customers, and employees) and then extends to crafting a corpo-rate foreign policy that diplomatically supports peace building.

Fort articulates three different approaches of engagement businesses can use to foster peace: peacemaking, peacekeeping, and peace building, with the last holding the most potential for an enduring reduction of violence and the creation of more just societies. Although some businesses entrepreneurially incorporate peace as a business goal, and many others recognize the instrumental value of peace building to their companies, most businesses still have no conscious intention of encouraging peace.

But, as Fort argues, these engagements will constructively contribute to the goal by their ethical and just business actions. These unconscious peace builders tend to be ignored in practice but may provide the bulk of the culture-building practices of companies that can have an impact on peace. Fort convincingly argues that it is commerce that is gentle (ethical) that has the strongest capacity to this end.

It is nevertheless a fact that society's perception of business activities has developed negatively during the last decenniums. Many would character-ize this perception as colored more by distrust than by trust. Increasingly, business has been profiled as a source of conflict, rather than as a force of good. Society has often viewed business as profiting at its expense, rather than contributing to its benefit. Many look on the current business and economic paradigm as unsustainable for humans as well as for nature; they see a rising economic inequality threatening both the sense of fairness in society as well as undermining the postwar decades of prosperity. They observe economic activities as also being culpable for a degradation of our life-depending ecosystem.

How do we explain that business appears to have the capacity of being a force in building trust and peace, although society seems to focus on the opposite? If possible positive capabilities of business activities are conditioned both by *how* one goes about doing business, as well as *what* one is doing, the understanding of what *drives* this behavior will be of importance. How, then, should thinking about the *purpose* of business affect its actions?

Different perspectives of the purpose for being in business might lead to quite different implications. Over the last fifty years, maximizing shareholder value has increasingly been the defining agenda for managing a business. Reflecting on why business has become the villain in the story, and why it is often seen as the cause of conflict, makes me wonder if important parts of the reason can be found in such one-sided financial thinking. Might it be that society's distrust of the greater intentions of business (green-washing, CSR initiatives, and the like) in fact has some truth to it? That financial priorities have led business to profit at the expense of society, and have been conducive to creating conflicts, whether unintended or not? If so, this is short-term thinking. No long-term value can be built if there are not multiple winners.

In business, one can't measure value creation without numbers. But numbers are not the engines driving value creation. What drives performance is inspirational vision, a higher sense of purpose, principles and values guiding the company in its creation of value for others. Forgetting this while maximizing short-term financial value seems to bring downside risk to the business as well as to its relationship to society. Could it be that the negative societal implications of business actions are as poorly reflected on by business, as its capacity for positive contributions seems to be disregarded by society? Might it be that this narrow financial view of the purpose of business causes business leaders to overfocus on the numbers *measuring* success rather than on a spectrum of factors that contribute to the long-term success of a business? Widespread linking of incentives to one-dimensional success measures, rather than what catalyzes success, can create numerous risks and unintended consequences.

Many businesses appear to have lost focus of the broader value they might create. The broader solution and value-creating capacity of business might be much bigger than what a financial focus is able to define. The view of customers and employees as solely means to achieving the end of maximizing shareholder wealth is a myopic view of why a business should exist. The perspective of solving human problems by serving customer needs, and having financial return and jobs as the *outcome*, seems more reflective of the historic rationale for the existence of business and for business as a cornerstone in society.

The implications of the importance of a higher purpose can apply to a businessperson on an individual level as well. Having been an investment banker for many years with maximizing shareholder value as the goal, I know well the daily priority of profits and financial thinking.

As research shows, motivation and organizations thrive if there is inherent meaning to one's work in addition to financial success. Emphasizing positive value creation to society will add to the inspiration and engagement of the organization and its individuals. A higher purpose nourishes the meaning of work as well as strengthening the position of a business to capture more of that value creation financially. We need *both* profit and a higher purpose.

An expanded mind-set in business is called for: a mind-set that can integrate the need for meaning in our work with the need for accentuating a higher purpose that will inspire the broader societal value creating capability of business. Such a mind-set could be working for peace instead of being conducive to conflicts. It would be a mind-set of being worthy of the business of one's customers, employees, community, and society as a whole. It would be a mind-set of what our foundation calls being *businessworthy*.

Those rooted in traditional financial thinking might regard such a mind-set as nice but naïve and unrealistic. Yet it might be that the surprisingly powerful developments within technology are forcing a deeper rethinking of the traditional approach. The exponentially growing capacity of digital technologies is driving fundamental changes in how people communicate and interact. It is changing and equalizing the balance of power within the business ecosystem. At the same time, it's making possible new solutions to human and environmental challenges and needs.

Potentially, it opens a new paradigm in business thinking that is accelerating the upsides of a businessworthy mind-set.

The interconnectivity and transparency of the net are contributing to a reemphasizing of the forces of ethics. When there is nowhere to hide, the common denominators of *how* to behave are accentuated. Over time, one can imagine a gyration toward the promotion of key universally held human values and principles for interaction. Though different cultures might frame these values differently, requiring cultural insight to be managed well, core human values such as dignity, respect, and trust will increasingly be promoted as local businesses connect internationally. To successfully sustain value creation, business will see its interests best served by integrating universally held values of fairness and shared prosperity into how one should go about doing business. The need for a "diplomat in the corner office" seems destined to be increasing.

An implication of our increasingly digital world is a democratization of information. This adds to equalizing the balance of power between business as the seller and consumers as the buyers. Much of the traditional value capturing in business has been a desired consequence of managing the information of scarcity. This is becoming more challenging, as information is democratized and abundant. The penetration of digitization in products and services is accelerated by a marginal cost often being close to zero, forcing more and more businesses to reengineer and become software driven. These consequences of digitization are forcing a rethinking of the traditional underlying business assumptions of managing scarcity. It opens up the perspectives and challenges of managing abundance rather than scarcity.

This paves the way for consumers and society to become interdependent participants in core parts of the value-creating activities of a business. As computer power and connectivity expand, the opportunities also increase for people to move from being purely consumers to being collaborators and participants in the value creating process; as they share or shape information, cocreate, coproduce, codistribute, cofund, or coown with a business. This has been observed time and again through the explosive growth of businesses such as Facebook, Kickstarter, Wikipedia, and others. The significance of this development to traditional business thinking cannot be overstated, as smart connected products increasingly are put on line, contributing to building what over time will evolve as a new global infrastructure. New interdependent business ecosystems are being created in an increasingly interconnected global commons. These ecosystems are defined by their crowds and communities, that is, by society. Their needs and values will increasingly redefine markets, as well as inspiring innovations for fulfilling unmet needs, thus creating new markets.

The implications of these developments are crucial for business thinking and acting. They should promote a broadened and longer-term thinking in business about value creation that is sustainable socially and environmentally as well as economically. Business thinking will increasingly have to reflect what can unify and inspire its ecosystem, promoting a stronger union between business interests and the interests of society. The implications should inspire consciousness about the long-term financial viability of a higher purpose of business, influencing the *how* and the *what* of business activities. Business must become conscious of its social capital, as well as its financial capital.

As the world is becoming increasingly more interconnected, its complexity and interdependence will increase even more. This accentuates the need to seek positive-sum solutions to our problems and challenges as opposed to traditional zero-sum solutions, if society is to be peaceful and prosper. Business's mind-set and capability of seeking to create win-win solutions should be a natural and key contributor and mechanism to this.

The Business for Peace Foundation was established with the mission of *inspiring the higher purpose of business*. The foundation works to promote a *mind-set of being businessworthy*, seeking to reflect key thinking for sustaining successful value creation in the twenty-first century. *Being businessworthy* is defined as ethically and responsibly applying your business energy, with the aim of creating economic value that also creates value for society. Such a mind-set of action aims to promote a better union between business and society and contributes to building trust, prosperity, and peace.

The Foundation searches the world, through its global partners the International Chamber of Commerce, the UN Development Program, and the UN Global Compact, to find the best individual role models for this way of business thinking and acting. An independent Award Committee of Nobel Laureates in Economics and Peace selects the winners, who are named Business for Peace Honourees. The Award is given in the City Hall of Oslo, the venue of the Nobel Peace Prize, and has the ambition to be become generally regarded as the highest recognition a businessperson can achieve.

The discussions on strategy, and the policy recommendations expressed by Tim Fort in *The Diplomat in the Corner Office*, are an inspiration to the thought leadership needed to harness the potential of business to advance a better and more peaceful world.

Per L. Saxegaard
Founder and Chairman, Business For Peace Foundation
Oslo, January 2015

Acknowledgments

I would like to thank the "Team Tim" that made this manuscript possible. Having written it during a time of moving my family from Washington, DC, back to the Midwest and taking on too many projects, I needed a lot of help to write this book. Margo Beth Fleming and her able associate James Holt did a great job of both keeping me on task and providing the understanding and support I needed. Lisa Cornelio, as she has done for me in the past, provided terrific editorial work. I simply would not have been able to write this book without her. Jason Allen did an amazing job with references and cross-references and also contributed his own editorial help as well.

Over the years, I have coauthored with many wonderful scholars. They taught me a great deal and much of that learning finds its way into this book. At the risk of forgetting some great work that was helpful, I want to acknowledge Cindy Schipani, Michelle Westermann-Behaylo, Jennifer Oetzel, Kathleen Rehbein, Jorge Rivera, Charles Koerber, John Forrer, Joan Gabel, Raymond Gilpin, Stephanie Hare, and the late Tom Dunfee. I would also like to acknowledge the work of the U.S. Institute of Peace Task Force on Business and Peace. In coleading it, the interaction with generals, CEOs, ambassadors, professors, and NGO leaders was invaluable as were the interactions I had in two presentations on the topic at the Council of Foreign Relations. Many leaders of peace-related NGOs have been helpful in my thinking, including Keith Reinhard, Michael Strong, Phyllis Blees, Joyce Beck, the late Jeff Klein, John Sullivan, General Dan Christman, Carolyn Woo, Judith Samuelson, Kristian Harvniak, Michael Jarvis, Djordjija Petoski, George Siedel, Javier Aranzadi, and Jerry White.

The experience of coteaching with Federal Reserve Chair Ben Bernanke also provided me with some new perspectives and insights I would not have otherwise had.

A special thanks and acknowledgment to Stephanie Hare and Oxford Analytica for drawing heavily on Stephanie's ideas of corporate foreign policy, which she first introduced to me and which we published an article in Oxford Analytica's *Daily Briefing*. Also a special thanks to Anael Harpaz who provided permission for me to use a long quote/story of hers from the Peace through Commerce website.

Above all, I truly believe that Per Saxegaard should receive the Nobel Peace Prize for his work as founder and president of the Business for Peace Foundation and all the great work Per does through it. I am very grateful for his willingness to write the Foreword for this book.

In addition, there are literally scores of academics to whom I am indebted. Most appear in the footnotes of the book. Others provided me the good grace of making presentations, responding to others, and listening to ideas. I won't try to list all of these folks because I know my forgetfulness will leave out someone of real significance. Hundreds, if not thousands, of students have worked with me on these issues as well. I would particularly like to cite those who wrote such great papers that they gave me new ideas as well. These include Salma Hatem, Marc Lavine, Alexis Levine, Casey Quirk, Smita Trivedi, and Lili Yan. Also my thanks to Jayan Zaman and Kurina Fort for preparing the index.

The aforementioned Michelle Westermann-Behaylo worked with me as a doctoral student and now is a first-class scholar of business and peace work in her own right. She has taught me much about corporate strategy and how it relates to these issues.

As always in this portion of a book, I also must state that all the errors, omissions, and other screwups are my own and not those of these great folks. Such a statement is even more true as applied to me!

Preface

When I started to propose that ethical business behavior might make a contribution to sustainable peace in 1999, I was met with blank stares. Most people in academia, the NGO world, business, and government seemed to be at a loss of what to say, other than they didn't get it. Those folks were the nicer ones. Others asked if I was active in the 1960s hippie movement—though I am a bit young for that—and though no one actually said it, I felt as if they might also wonder if I was a failed contestant for the Miss Universe contest; you know, dreamily hoping for world peace.

While I was floating this idea of businesses' relevance for peace, I continued to pursue business ethics as my scholarly bread and butter. In writing a book for Oxford University Press at that time on what I called a mediating institutions approach to building ethical corporate culture, I had argued that business ethics theories (stakeholder, rights, justice, social contract, virtue, and naturalism) have their greatest impact if corporations are structured so that people work in sizes of groups that match their neurological capabilities. Research suggested that those group sizes were fairly small with rough breaking points around four to six, thirty, and 150. Each time one went above those group sizes, certain communal capabilities became harder to maintain. At 150, it was hard to really know the people one was working with. If one did not internalize the idea that there were consequences to one's actions, then ethical behavior became harder to maintain. People had a greater chance of being ethical on a regular basis if their work entailed a high degree of face-to-face interactions and took place in settings where there was a sense of egalitarian voice; even if decisions were made hierarchically, it made a difference if all employees could speak up.

As I was finishing this book, I came across peace literature studies by anthropologists David Fabbro[1] and Raymond Kelly.[2] Put simply, they, in different ways, focused on the dynamics of human interaction in relatively peaceful or warless societies. In those societies, there was a good deal of face-to-face interaction and egalitarian decision making.[3] Individuals had their own unique identity in the community; when a society grew large, any individual can be substituted for another, especially in the eyes of an enemy.[4] In short, size matters, and so too does voice. One might therefore conclude—as I did—that we need to champion the businesses that are small and engaging, recognizing that the big multinationals and global businesses might be harmful to the cause of peace.

Fabbro's and Kelly's findings struck me as consistent with the proposals I was making for how to build ethical corporate cultures. When I looked around to see what else had been written about the bridge between business and peace, I was surprised that there wasn't much I could find. Jane Nelson had just published *The Business of Peace*, which was a very helpful start.[5] Virginia Haufler had written a book, *A Public Role for the Private Sector*, which also provided fundamentals to build on.[6] Of course, the International Chamber of Commerce[7] had long been established with an aim to serve as a "merchant of peace" akin to Rotary International.[8] In post–World War II Europe, there were commitments that many institutions would contribute to peace.[9] This was a start for considering the role business organizations might play in fostering peace, but, to the extent there was attention paid to issues of, well, money and peace, it occurred at a much more abstract level. Most sustained analysis pertained to large, more macroeconomic issues linking free trade and peace.

Talk of how macroeconomic trade *benefit* peace begged a question: Who would do the heavy lifting? Who would invest? The same holds true for the philosophical renditions of commerce and peace such as from Kant and Montesquieu. Who would create jobs? Who would profit? The answer seems clear: Business. So if there is evidence of a positive relationship between trade and peace, we should focus our attention on the agent that does the trading. What do they do? How do they act? Are there some actions that carry with them attributes of peace? Are there others that do the exact opposite? Moreover, what kinds of businesses most help in fostering peace? The small ones with high degrees of face-to-face interactions or the large ones that dominate global business and that draw the attention of macroeconomic analysis?

When my Michigan colleague Cindy Schipani and I decided to host a two-day conference on the idea of how business fosters peace in 2001, we had difficulty recruiting speakers—until September 11. Although our work was not on terrorism per se, many people wanted to do "something" to respond. Suddenly our speaking roster was full, and so were the seats in the conference room. Our work thus began in earnest: the role of business in world peace.

Curiously, empirical evidence does suggest something seemingly opposite to the Fabbro and Kelly position: that our global, faceless interconnected society is more peaceful than hunter-gatherer days. In this book, a core task for me is to show that both of these arguments are actually right and that what unites them is *gentle commerce*, a term used only in general terms to date but that can be constructively defined as ethical business.

Speaking of definitions, I must pause a moment to define *peace*. To date, I have been content with defining peace as the absence of bloodshed. That remains my primary intention. My argument has been that ethical practices steer us away from bloodshed. Excluding versions of Roman sundering of Carthage, the absence of bloodshed will incorporate justice. Others, for example Gandhi, spoke of peace as social justice and claimed that violence—for example poverty—could occur without bloodshed per se. Well, I'm not going to argue with Gandhi. So I support the notion of injustice—with or without bloodshed—as violent, but for purposes of this book, I am going to continue to primarily emphasize the connection to bloodshed itself. My view is that, though great progress has been made in this field over the past fifteen years, we have enough work to do to get this connection figured out before extending it to the larger questions of social justice.

Research from ethics and anthropology continue to play an anchoring role in this book as they have in my past writings on this topic. In this book, however, I attempt to place the notion of business's role in fostering peace is a more mainstream lens. It seeks to be mainstream in terms of company strategy and what I call corporate foreign policy, mainstream in terms of contemporary political and international relations scholarship, and mainstream in terms of contemporary economic scholarship. In other words, the role of business in fostering peace is neither ancillary nor niche; it is robustly within the way in which peace comes about in the twenty-first century.

That assertion does not mean it is monolithic. Businesses are themselves diverse, and they contribute to peace in different ways. Some do so intentionally because of the commitments of the leaders of the organization. Some do without any awareness that their ethical practices have a positive impact on peace building. Still others, as I will begin with Chapter 1 and end with in Chapter 9, do so as a conduct of smart strategic practice: Corporate Foreign Policy.

PART I

Mainstreaming Business and Peace

1　Corporate Foreign Policy

During the Arab Spring in 2012, Google and Twitter defied the edicts of Egyptian President Hosni Mubarak to create a "speak to tweet" application that allowed protesters to communicate.[1] At the same time, Facebook permitted streaming videos and messages from Cairo's Tahrir Square.[2] Conversely, Vodafone and France Telecom complied with government orders to shut down; when their services were reactivated, the government allowed only pro-Mubarak messages to be sent to customers.[3] Nokia-Siemens and Blackberry, along with Google, Twitter, and others, had previously cooperated with governmental authorities, which led to major news in the summer of 2013 when Edward Snowden revealed the U.S. demands for information from tech companies.[4]

Each company faced a choice. It could align itself with a government in power or defy the government in some way. Aligning oneself with the powers that be hardly seems novel. Companies and people do that all the time. Why make the government, especially one willing to use a gun to punish dissent, angry? Defying a government is a good deal riskier. Moreover, in the cases of Google and Twitter, it did not appear that they were aligning themselves with their own country per se in a way that might be found, for example, in a Cold War standoff between the United States and the Soviet Union. The United States itself seemed torn as to what position to take, balancing its foreign policy between long-time support for a crucial ally (Mubarak) and also sympathizing with a popular effort to secure freedom and protest heavy-handed oppression.

Google and Twitter allied themselves with a set of values associated with free flow of information. Such values are fundamental to democracy, of course, and are also fundamental to their identities as companies. Beyond this question, however, lie other questions: Why do companies find themselves asking them in the first place? What is different about the world in which we live today? What is different about the place of business in the world?

As I will argue throughout this book, one thing that is different is that many companies have their own independent identities that interact with other political and social entities. As they interact, companies form their own foreign policies, forcing them to make choices. Those choices may or may not be as dramatic as the ones Google and Twitter made, but they must make them and draw from some source(s) as to how to do so. Moreover, it is also important to recognize that many companies from many different sectors will be implicated in this. Actually, all companies will be implicated in this, but, to begin to see this, consider other examples of companies with acute needs to address these concerns.

As with sovereign states, the notion of foreign policy in business is to mindfully weave multiple strands of institutional capabilities and best practices into a strategic model that allows a company to respond to crisis and proactively position the company within the shifting balances of power that characterize a "market" comprised of political and moral factors that have a strong impact on the economic bottom line.

Like nation-states, companies must find their way through these complexities with a base that supports them. They may differ as to whether they find that base in the personal commitments of their founders, alliances with their home (or host) government, and/or the loyalty of their shareholders, customers, and employees. In the case of the Arab Spring, Google and Twitter appealed to their shareholders, customers, and employees, whereas Vodafone and France Telecom allied themselves with the Mubarak regime.

Raw material extractors find themselves immersed in the vagaries of geopolitical unrest as well. First Quantum invested heavily in copper and cobalt extraction in the southeastern part of the Democratic Republic of the Congo only to have its license revoked. Freeport-McMoRan Copper and Gold has been known for taking a strong role in working with local populations to achieve living wage standards and protection of human rights, a positive approach that Shell and many other extractives have attempted.[5]

Of course, companies have long practiced lobbying and various kinds of influence-promoting activities, sometimes within legal boundaries and sometimes outside of them. Beyond such activities, companies may proactively attempt to influence constructive change in societies as well. SiThaMu explicitly sets itself out to be one such company, by bringing together competing—sometimes warring—factions in Sri Lanka to work together as fellow employees. Similarly, during the Northern Ireland "Troubles," the Confederation of British Industry actively promoted the cause of peace by demonstrating a peace dividend that would result if the violence stopped; in a gesture similar to SiThaMu's, a nonprofit called FuturWays intentionally populated its workforce with equal numbers of Catholics and Protestants to give them the opportunity to work together.[6] The U.S. secretary of state annually recognizes at least three American companies whose work overseas is so positive that it promotes good relations between the host country and the United States.[7]

Sometimes companies unwittingly find themselves in the middle of controversy. That happened to McDonald's when it changed the formulation of the oil in which they cook their famous french fries from one containing beef tallow to pure vegetable oil and then back to beef tallow. The problem was that they didn't inform the public of the last change, which caused vegetarians to consume beef and for Hindus to unwittingly violate religious precepts. The results were protests and even attacks on McDonald's restaurants in India and elsewhere; one angry protestor even ironically smeared cow dung on the exterior of one of the restaurants.[8]

Some public relations messes take on a bizarre character. Consider the toilet manufacturer that, for some reason, sketched figures of Eastern spiritual deities on the product. Responding to complaints, the company said that it meant no offense; after all, it had a few commodes with the Virgin Mary as well.[9]

Whether they like it or not, companies are judged by more than economic criteria. Nor is it easy to hide these days; between political events and the ability of the Internet to capture corporate, as well as political, behavior, we have a chance of keeping an eye on businesses and politicians. In light of that public attention, what should a company do?

In this book, I will argue that companies can and should anchor themselves in a strategy of fostering peace. Such a strategy begins with attending to one's core constituents (shareholders, customers, and employees) and then extends to crafting a corporate foreign policy that diplomatically supports peace building. With few exceptions, peace and stability are in the best interest of business. Yet it is one thing to benefit from peace; it is another to contribute to it. The former suggests either a pawnlike role for business within a geopolitical balance of power or a free-rider position where businesses simply reap the benefits of others' peace (and ethics) building work. The latter calls for businesses to take on an active role to interact within a balance of power to cocreate a social and corporate interest in peace. A starting point is to understand three forms of power to which companies are subject.

An Introduction to a Three-Pronged Model of Power

International relations expert Walter Mead sets out a framework to explain a matrix of power with which nation-states must deal. It serves as a helpful framework for corporations as well.

Mead differentiates among three kinds of power: sharp power, sticky power, and soft power. Sharp power pertains to military capability. What armaments, personnel, and other physical capability does a country have to be able to impose its will on others? Sticky power is typically economic; it pertains to the trading systems that powerful countries can establish as the infrastructure for conducting commerce. Soft power pertains the realm of ideas and values.[10] Corporate foreign policy (CFP)—an idea first conceptualized and introduced to me by my coauthor Stephanie Hare—must address all three.

Though a defining feature of the nation-state is its monopoly on the use of force, companies do face force-related issues in three ways. The first way relates to the company's dealing with nation-states. In what ways are companies subject to or threatened by the use of force? For instance, is a government threatening to nationalize the industry? Are corporate assets at risk of being redirected toward a country's military efforts?

The second way pertains to how the nation-state's military capabilities can be used for the benefit of the company. At what times and places can such force be relied on (via police or legal enforcement of established rights and interests) by companies?

A third way deals with the autonomy that companies have to use force separate from the government. For example, companies typically use their security forces to remove an unruly visitor, make an initial response to a crime, or even patrol the premises. The extent to which companies can actually wield such power, or do so in conjunction with state security institutions, depends on local laws and agreements. Especially when doing business in conflict-sensitive zones, the issue of sharp power is one of interest to corporate action.[11]

Companies regularly wrestle with issues of sticky power because such power directly pertains to economics. The navigation of trade agreements, export-import laws, regulation, enforcement, competition with other companies, and a myriad of other sticky-power issues arise in CFP. Companies spend considerable time focused on this particular dimension of power, and it draws the attention of practitioners and scholars alike.

Companies, of course, wield their own sticky power as well. Nations need companies to employ people and to pay taxes, which is why governments will go to great lengths to encourage companies to locate in preferred regions. The threat of a company leaving an area can cause considerable disruption for a government. Further, the markets and consumer tastes created by marketing and advertising create webs of buying trends, supply chains, and employment that establish entirely new economic patterns. It seems inconceivable today that human beings navigated life less than thirty years ago with nary a cell phone—obviously manufactured and sold by businesses—in sight.

This naturally leads us to the final dimension of power dimension: soft power, or the power of ideas. Despite the apparent strength of military and economic might, soft power remains the strongest of all. Ideas may be the seeds of new military capabilities and economic markets, but they range much further to touch on the very nature of why and how we live and the institutional arrangements that we rely on as we journey through our lives.

Writings on CFP to date argue that, like sovereign states, companies must face issues of institutional legitimacy, which is the essence of soft power.[12] Corporate social responsibility often focuses on this issue in companies as well. In paying attention to social and moral issues, businesses again parallel the reaction to public demands that governments also face.

Today, even the most authoritarian of states couch their policies in terms of respect for human rights and government programs that are beneficial for the populace. In an exhaustive 900-page book, international affairs and legal scholar Phillip Bobbitt argues that the period from 1914 to 1989 constituted one long war fought among liberalism, communism, and fascism, and each contended—frequently via armed conflict—that it was a superior form of government.[13] Fascism offered efficiency and certainty; communism proposed equality; liberalism touted freedom. How each implemented such notions raises other questions, but among these sets of philosophical alternatives, arguments for legitimacy were central to each ideology's claim to authority.

The same holds true for corporations. If a company is British, it may logically be regarded as an extension of the United Kingdom, but if that company does work in fifty different countries, then its character is less British and more "something else."

To be sure, few suggest that companies should be democratic institutions, though some companies do set themselves up as such.[14] But liberal principles extend beyond the identification of voting rights. They also include issues of voice, human rights, freedom, justice, equal opportunity, and responsibility. Corporate leaders, whether they think these ideals are compelling or not, do trumpet their companies' commitments to such things.

Though sometimes eschewed as public relations window dressing, the fact that CSR consumes a large portion of company time demonstrates that companies recognize the vitality of legitimacy. Indeed, one can examine the actions of Google and Twitter during the Arab Spring as a crucible for adhering to the value of free-flowing information.

Corporate Legitimacy

These notions of corporate legitimacy, appropriate business conduct, and foreign policy provide a different landscape for twenty-first-century business than for twentieth-century business. The topic of corporate social responsibility or business ethics stands in a much different place today than it did thirty years ago. It was once hard to find courses in CSR or ethics in a business school (especially outside the religiously affiliated institutions). Today, every school has one, and the topic has moved from specialty journals to the mainstream.[15] The same holds true for companies. Whether compliance driven, PR (public relations) driven, or driven by leaders who seek to use a business model that makes a social difference, CSR, business ethics, corporate compliance, and sustainability feature prominently in corporate annual reports these days. Whether these corporate efforts are window-dressing or authentic is an important question, but again, even if such efforts are window dressing, companies realize that such things matter to their constituents.[16] As far as the evidence can show, business executives have not experienced a new, spiritual "Great Awakening." Instead, they realize that these issues matter to their businesses.

In the twentieth century, enthusiastic proponents of such issues framed the quest for corporate responsibility as a challenge to the traditional view of business.[17] Yet, the notion of corporate responsibility is quite old, stretching back thousands of years, which now cyclically leads to corporations being independent actors on a global stage.[18] Entrepreneurs may have formed businesses, but they were also citizens who carried civic as well as corporate responsibility on their shoulders.[19] Governments granted significant benefits of limited liability, continuity of life, and transferability of ownership interests to companies through incorporation but typically only when there were public benefits associated with such chartering.[20] Avi-Yonah traces a cycle where, at four separate times in history, this transformation from entrepreneurial to state sanctioned leads to a third stage where companies took on their own, independent identity, history, and culture.[21] This third, real entity, stage is of particular importance in today's world where multinational corporations exist quite apart from any particular set of founding entrepreneurs, straddle multiple domestic and international borders, and transcend any given government charter.

Apart from their founding entrepreneurs and beyond any one chartering government, such institutions practice their own foreign policy and must offer their own rationale for legitimacy. This may repeat a cyclical historical pattern, but the twenty-first century provides its own challenges and opportunities for how that is to be done. In that sense, calls for corporate social responsibility, business ethics, accountable corporate governance, and corporate sustainability are as new as they are old.

This perhaps explains why notions of corporate legitimacy and responsibility draw from philosophical traditions that themselves are as new as they are old. Scholars have argued that a social contract allows companies to come into existence (through chartering, for example) and thus there are reciprocal obligations from companies to the society.[22] A deontological approach has claimed that *any* person or entity should treat others as ends and not as means to an end, thus resulting in a stakeholder approach to ground corporate legitimacy.[23] Communitarians draw from the observation that human beings are social creatures, and so the institutions that they form come with moral sentiments and virtues to which we must attend.[24] Naturalists see corporate existence as a utilitarian extension of evolutionary principles, while cautioning that such principles also entail a web of ecological relationships to which we must attend to sustain economics itself.[25]

In fact, outside of a few libertarian approaches,[26] it is difficult to find arguments that contend for unchecked pursuit of profit. Even Milton Friedman's nauseatingly repeated headline that the only responsibility of business is to increase its profits misstates his actual argument, which recognizes limits in the form of obeying the law and staying within the rules of fair play. His argument also recognizes forms of responsibility, mainly in terms of philanthropy, that benefit the company in the long term as being acceptable.[27] Across the board, thinkers have argued that construing business without moral responsibilities makes business itself incoherent.[28]

This is where notions of peace enter the equation. Talking about how business can affect peace may seem far afield from business practices, but it is not *that* far afield. Just as some have argued that well-run businesses already incorporate solid ethical practices, the same well-run ethical businesses already promote peace. In many ways, advocating that business contribute to peace is to recognize the impact of what ethical businesses already are doing.

What is different about advocating that business contributes to peace is the conscious mindfulness of its impact. Even if ethical businesses do contribute to peace, their leaders may not see this as an objective of the business itself. In this regard, I see the idea of business fostering peace in a place where sustainability was about thirty years ago. The fact that sustainability has had so much success along with other components of corporate responsibility such as CSR, ethics, and governance means, I hope, that it will be easier to establish the idea that business can contribute to peace and, in doing so, integrate notions of corporate legitimacy and responsibility with a conception of corporate foreign policy as a necessity to be effective and profitable in the twenty-first century.

CFP can be defined as a mindful strategic function that uses an array of firm practices, including but not limited to risk management, strategy, corporate political strategy, political corporate responsibility, legal affairs, human resources, compliance, public relations, and business–government relations. That function's aim is to position the company as a distinct, independent entity within a field of play along with other governmental, business, and NGO (nongovernmental organization) institutions. The mission of CFP is to navigate a widely defined market that includes political, social, and moral pressures and opportunities, as well as more traditional economic markets, to ensure the sustainability of the firm and the obligations to which it is subject.

Well, that's fine, one might say, but it doesn't necessarily mean that businesses should pay attention to peace building as a strategy. To draw again on the example of nation-states, a peace-building strategy may be a delightfully Scandinavian approach, but geopolitical superpowers bloodily throw their weight around. Yet I want to suggest that adding to global bellicosity generally advantages two kinds of companies, neither of which really pertain to my argument.

The first kind of company is one that is essentially an extension of the state itself. The company may be a state-owned enterprise (SOE), or it may find itself in a stage of Avi-Yonah's described development so that it really is, at its core, a Chinese, French, or American company. As such, its foreign policy simply follows its home nation, and if that nation's foreign policy aims at military aggressiveness, the company's will follow. For such institutions, no independent CFP really exists; as I have already argued, CFP comes from the point where companies have their own independent identity and culture apart from entrepreneurial founders and the state(s) that chartered them into existence.

The second kind of company is one that profits from war. President Dwight Eisenhower famously warned of the influence of the military-industrial complex in his farewell address to the American people in 1961. Yet, from the standpoint of economic percentages, it has shrunk from 14 percent of gross domestic product (GDP) from when Eisenhower took office in 1953 to 5 percent in 2012.[29] Even if one assumes that all of the companies represented in this military-industrial complex do, in fact, champion war making and/or defense, this still leaves 95 percent of the economy. I have argued that most companies (and people) tend to flourish better when bombs do not drop on their homes and offices.[30]

If most companies benefit more from peace and stability than from war and disruption, then a foreign policy that contributes to those nonviolent goals would seem to fit better within a corporation's self-interest. Moreover, as big as some multinationals may be, they are not political superpowers. Even if Yahoo is bigger than Mongolia, eBay than Madagascar, and Pepsi than Oman, companies have to navigate the geopolitical world more than they bully it.[31] To be sure, smaller countries can be as (or more) violent than superpowers, but multinationals play on a field dominated by superpowers, and they don't tend to play with thermonuclear weapons, drones, and cruise missiles. The confines within which companies will exercise their foreign policy will align far more with peace-building interests than with war-making ones.

A company devoted to peace building will incorporate the major issues of corporate responsibility on which there are significant agreement. To do so, a company will optimally begin with its commitments to a set of core constituents that will anchor its legitimacy. Such commitments will strengthen the sighting of a polestar to guide businesses through the shoals of geopolitical and global economic complexities. A contribution to peace will further strengthen the economic system for the future, which will be good for business itself. In short, a commitment to peace becomes a sturdy strategy for corporate foreign policy.

Mainstreaming Peace

It is well past the time for a serious mainstream examination of businesses' role in fostering peace. Businesses have an enormous impact on our lives, and it makes sense that we take a close look to see if they might have—or could have—an impact on making our lives better. Better, that is, not just because they provide more creature comforts but because they can make our lives less violent.

Investment bankers are having these kinds of discussions.[32] Chief executive officers (CEOs) of PR firms, tourist companies, grocery stores, oil companies, Internet companies, and others have them, too. A 2013 *Forbes* cover story headlines "Peace through Profits" with respect to entrepreneurs in the Middle East.[33] One sees academic and other institutions of civil society holding conferences and developing training programs and initiatives on how business can foster peace.[34] Major government agencies recognize how the actions of corporations improve diplomatic relations.[35] Transnational institutions explicitly promote the role of business in helping to resolve conflict.[36]

Many of these efforts began to spring up at the turn of the millennium, perhaps prompted by the typical kind of resolution making and initiative taking that occurs at the time of a new year, new decade, new century, and new millennium. Others began in the aftermath of the attacks of September 11. Still others, like the International Chamber of Commerce and Rotary International, have histories connecting business and peace that reach back a century.[37] In this book, I will attempt to weave them together.

Three+ Contributions That Business Can Make to Peace

In *The Role of Business in Fostering Peaceful Societies*,[38] Cindy Schipani and I argued that there were four contributions business could make to foster peace. A decade later, I would like to modify that slightly to say that there are three core contributions (that match well with the three-part structure of power) with the fourth contribution that integrates and repurposes the core three.

CREATE JOBS AND SPUR ECONOMIC DEVELOPMENT

Creating jobs and fostering economic development are what businesses do best. Studies from the United Nations[39] and the World Bank[40] show a strong correlation between poverty and corruption. One argument given for this correlation is that the pursuit of resources to sustain life itself within poor countries may be so intense that it spurs violence. The evidence for this claim is ambivalent. Yes, there can be such competition within an impoverished population, but the very poor aren't fighting—they are already dying. It is when people start to obtain material goods, when they have the chance to find a better footing, that fierce arguments break out as to who should get those goods. Though the precise relationship between poverty and corruption may be in dispute, there is a general truth that poverty and violence are linked. More jobs means less poverty, and less poverty means a better chance at peace.

A second explanation, which seems more persuasive, is that high levels of unemployment, as we see in poor countries, leave the unemployed susceptible to overtures from individuals and groups that have an interest in fomenting protest and unrest against a current regime or well-to-do minority. A high level staffer of the U.S. group in charge of bringing economic development to Iraq told me of a man who came into his offices. He was looking for work, but he couldn't find any. Insurgents had offered him $100 to plant a roadside bomb. He didn't want to do it, he said, but he needed a way to feed his family.

Should we be skeptical of such a story? Of course. The man's narrative could be a convincing yarn to get some money on the spot. It also could be a great story by the military to justify its own work: "This country needs us, or else our colleagues will be killed." Although skepticism is warranted, isn't there also a sensibility to the story? If a person has a family to feed and there is no work, exactly what is he supposed to do? Like a modern version of a Victor Hugo novel, the person could keep his integrity and starve or steal (think of *Les Miserables*) or kill (in Iraq) so that his own children don't die.

To the extent that businesses employ people and are profitable so that they can continue to sustain employment, they lower the possibility that the unemployed will fall in with the killing crowd. But, what kind of economic development can accomplish this? What kinds of profitability fuels the employment cycle? To say that employment may provide a stake in an economy that can be built on in a war-torn zone sounds good—it indeed may be good. But will profitability based on corruption, exploitation of child labor, abuse of women, and production of poisonous waste released on an unfavored social minority be considered a social good?

Not just any kind of business will contribute to peace. Not just any kind of economic development will foster peace. It is a particular kind of economic development: one that respectfully treats those with whom it works, buys, sells, and otherwise affects. The quality of business behavior matters. Or, as I will argue later, peace requires not just commerce but gentle commerce.

Many authors link trade and peace, though they often hedge their enthusiasm about trade with some kind of buffering restraint that it must not be exploitative. Scholars identify democracy as a restraint that reigns in rapacious business actions, keeping trade fair, for instance. The reason democracy helps is that it brings to bear another kind of market—a political market—which is infused with values people believe are important but that may not find their way into an economic system per se. Ethical business values simply move the values that make commerce gentler directly into the market apart from the political realm.

An example of this idea comes from the extractive industries, which are a mixed blessing in countries that rely on them for their economic development. Paul Collier has argued that a strong predictor of civil war is if the main export product of a country is an undifferentiated commodity, such as oil, timber, or diamonds.[41] In such a situation, the name of the economic game is control of the territory where those resources are extracted. If one needs to equip a six-year-old child with an AK-47 to control that territory, then, well, that's just the reality of business.

Interestingly, many extractive firms seem to sense this. Twenty years ago, Exxon, Shell, and Chevron were pariahs in human rights circles. Today, they each have considerable programs in corporate social responsibility and human rights. Perhaps these are all window dressing, but, again, even window dressing would mark an awareness that such things matter enough that they have to address these issues in *some* manner.

Similarly, the Kimberly Protocol, created to assure customers of De-Beers, Tiffany's, and others that they are not wearing blood diamonds, was an effort to mitigate the violence frequently associated with diamond mining.[42] The Extractive Industries Transparency Initiative (EITI) also attempts to point extractives toward less troublesome conduct.[43] This suggests that companies themselves have become aware that humanitarian (as well as ecological) forces have an impact on them, and their business models depend on the companies acting to address ethical issues.[44]

Two major technologies also make companies more accountable, cell phones and the Internet. Today, a corporate indiscretion can be captured on a cell phone camera and put on the Internet in about five seconds. What previously might have been an action that would never see the light of day unless an investigative reporter or committed activist unearthed it can now very easily go viral. Companies have to care about this as much as Hosni Mubarak did . . . or should have. Indeed, one of those investment bankers who talks about business and peace, Norway's Per Saxegaard, argues that twenty-first-century companies must conduct themselves in more of a neighborhood setting with their actions under scrutiny. In such a setting, the most valuable currency is trustworthiness.[45]

RULE OF LAW

The notion of "rule of law" simply refers to the idea that a country adheres to consistent legal practices regardless of who is in power. Rather than a country being ruled by men and women, law rules it. A change in presidential leadership might result in a change of national priorities and legislative initiatives, but it does not change the fundamental constitutional structure or ways in which citizens are afforded protections of interests and rights. Central to rule of law tend to be laws that provide for disputes to be resolved. In a country without the rule of law, a dispute might be resolved by vengeance. In a country with a rule of law, disputants have access to a court system or an arbiter; indeed, disputants are strongly encouraged to resolve their disputes through these institutions rather than to settle things violently on their own. Other kinds of rule of law characteristics include protection of private property and contractual rights.

By definition, corruption is anathema to rule of law. If rule of law is about making decisions on the basis of principles and rules rather than on the basis of who the person with power is, then a system in which one obtains contracts or other benefits by bribing will violate the rule of law. Rule of law tends to be associated with peace; corruption tends to be associated with violence. Corporations doing business in countries where there is extensive demand for bribery thus find themselves squarely in the middle of what practices they choose to follow in doing their work.

Moving beyond anecdotes, Professor Schipani and I conducted a simple study in 2002. It showed that those countries that ranked lowest on Transparency International's Corruption Perception Index (that is, that were the most corrupt) were also the countries most likely to resolve disputes by violence, according to the Kosimo Index published by the Heidelberg Institute of Peace Research.[46] The opposite was true as well. Those countries that were the least corrupt were least likely to resolve disputes by violence. Table 1.1 summarizes our findings.[47]

Table 1.1. Correlations of Violence and Corruption

	Top Quartile (least corrupt)	Second Quartile (second least corrupt)	Third Quartile (second most corrupt)	Fourth Quartile (most corrupt)
Percentage of time disputes between governments and organized parties resolved by violence	14%	26%	44%	60%

Source: Fort and Schipani, *The Role of Business.*

For the businesspersons who think that what they do has no connection to peace, the message of this study is simple: It would help if you adopted strong antibribery policies and enforced them. Doing this would contribute to a shifting of a cultural milieu toward peace and away from violence.

Tackling corruption has become a major focus of transnational organizations. The World Bank Institute has a major program devoted to it.[48] The Organisation for Economic Co-operation and Development (OECD) and the G-20 have also spent extensive time and resources on the issue.[49] These efforts emphasize the rule of law and highlight the importance of protecting contract rights and property rights. Building on the idea that strong, noncorrupt economic systems make contributions to peace, the rule of law approach emphasizes that businesses have little incentive to invest and to build in places where they cannot protect their investments.[50] Rule of law practices also extend to the political market where due process, human rights, and the idea of checks and balances become important brakes on any accumulation of excessive power.

Still other studies show links between the presence of effective dispute resolution mechanisms and peace. This of course makes sense: If a country has a way to resolve disputes, there should be less resorting to violent ways of resolving disputes. As with many issues in this field, a problem of circularity does arise: Does corruption cause war, or does war cause corruption? Does lack of property and contract rights lead to violent disputes, or do violent disputes cause governments to dispense with rule of law rights? Does lack of nonviolent dispute mechanism mean that the only way to settle arguments is through violence, or does violent conflict make such judicial institutions anachronistic?

These questions provide an ample supply of research queries for social scientists. While awaiting their answers, it does seem that, whichever comes first, it does little harm and likely much good for businesses to take steps that are associated with peace. Regardless of the chicken-and-egg question about corruption, do we think that a little more bribery will help a war-torn country? Do we think that violating contract rights or seizing property without compensation will help a country? Do we think that undermining fair dispute resolution systems will benefit a society? The answers are clearly no, which suggests that not only should companies avoid corruption, but companies also benefit a country and themselves by providing their own support to those institutions that do provide rule of law practices.

The Communal Dimension

Businesses are not only the locus of transactions. There are politics within a corporation and between the corporation and the outside world. Businesses are social as well. People interact with each other at work; often they become friends with coworkers. Businesses also interact with those outside of the firm as well. In all of these respects, businesses are communities.

The communal dimension of peace recognizes two parts, both of which emphasize ways in which business has the opportunity to create constructive, stable relationships. One part is external—the way that the corporation interacts with the community in which it works. This is basic corporate citizenship or corporate social responsibility and is fairly well understood. Are corporations respectful of local populations, their cultures, and their identities? Are they environmentally responsible? Are they good citizens? These engagements do not call for the business to solve all a local population's ills, but they do require a business not to add to them and generally, to be a decent neighbor.

The second aspect is internal and is more interesting. How is the business organization itself structured? To consider this, we must examine at least four specific factors.

For several decades now, a widespread management model has flourished under various quality-related names: Quality Circles, Total Quality Management, Open Book Management, and Six Sigma, to name a few.[51] One of the central points of each of these versions of quality management is that the most effective way to produce quality goods and services—and thereby to also be more profitable—is for employees up and down the corporate ladder to speak up if they see a product defect *during* its manufacture. If a business waits until the product has been finished to conduct a quality test, it is too late. If it doesn't meet quality standards then, one has a dilemma of either shipping out a defective product or swallowing the cost of remanufacturing, neither of which is attractive.

What are we to make of the requirement to "speak up"? This is an exercise of self-governance, even to some extent of democracy. These *business* strategies recognize the importance of employee voice.

Voice, in turn, has been recognized as having many advantages. If one has a voice, it is much easier to protect one's (and others') human rights; rights themselves correlate with relative peacefulness.[52] If one has voice, one has a better chance at asserting one's needs. Nobel Prize–winning economist Amartya Sen has argued that there has never been a famine in a democratic country, not because such countries are rich but because a poor person with a vote can use it to demand redress of unmet needs.[53]

Carrying this notion of voice further, many studies claim to show that democracies tend to not go to war with each other.[54] In democratic countries, one exercises power through negotiation, and two democratic countries at odds with each other have political cultures that can accept negotiated settlements if they have confidence in the other's democratic traditions. In democratic countries, objections to war itself can more easily be heard.[55]

Another important aspect of internal structuring is gender equity. A practically infallible connection exists between gender equity and peace. The more women are treated equally, the more pacific the results. Here again companies can do something quite directly to actualize this in their employment practices. At the same time, I recognize at least two major concerns raised by this proposal.

Do we think demanding that Saudi Arabian companies provide equal opportunity for women at work will foster peace? Frankly, I think the answer is yes, but, even if it is, getting there isn't an overnight task.

I once taught a group of thirty men from an Asia-based company; in the course of the class, they said that they saw nothing wrong with making it a job requirement for any woman at the company to have sex with her supervisor. I was speechless.

I tried to engage the students in a discussion of why this approach might have a few problems, but it was not an easy conversation. I asked if any of them would want his wife or daughter to be treated in this way, but I got nowhere: "My wife and daughter will be home where they belong." I made more progress by noting that if they wanted to expand to the United States, they should be aware that their practices would trigger costly lawsuits. The best answer came from one of the students, but it was made privately to me after class. He said that he knew what I was getting at. His daughter was graduating from Harvard with her MBA and refused to return home because of exactly what I had just seen in class. My student complained that his country thus lost twice: They lost the talents of a Harvard MBA, and they would likely have to compete against her. I would have loved for the man to make that point to the entire class, but I know he believed that his colleagues weren't ready to hear it yet. Sometimes things take longer than they should.

We shouldn't expect conversations about clashing of cultural norms to be easy. Achieving gender equity may have salutary effects on peace, but the specific corporate contributions to gender equity will be challenged. In some male-dominated societies, like the class I dealt with, those issues may be obvious. More subtle questions about the specific contributions may also arise, and not only from men. For example, in many Muslim societies, women welcome wearing the *hijab* (or burka). It makes them feel safer, freer, and not as prone to sexual objectivity.[56] In advocating for gender equity, these kinds of cultural differences require a heavy dose of Western listening as opposed to Western preaching so that an equity authentic to a given culture is practiced rather than one seen only through Western eyes. The principle, however, of gender equity should remain an objective.

A third aspect brings us back to where I first found myself in seeing the connection between business and peace: business ethics and, in particular, human rights. Are employees' rights respected at work? Is the business exploiting child labor? It is a place where harassment occurs? Are employees safe and protected? These basic aspects of protecting the well-being and safety of employees are not especially controversial, which is not to say that they do not problematically reoccur. In the final analysis, it will be hard to find peace when basic rights are not respected.

Then, there is the fourth aspect, which initially caused me to investigate the business and peace connection to ethics. This fourth aspect is grounded in a combination of normative thought (philosophy and theology) and anthropology. Because the anthropological argument about peace features prominently over the next two chapters, it is worth some elaboration with the key point being that there is peace to be found in mediating institutions.

In natural law, especially in a version championed by Catholic social thought, individuals develop their moral character in mediating institutions.[57] These institutions are relatively small, so that individuals experience consequences to actions. No matter how much your sister may drive you crazy, you still have to find a way to get along with her. Examples of mediating institutions include family, neighborhood, religious organizations, and other voluntary organizations to which one belongs. Over time, individuals develop moral character from the lessons taught in these institutions and, more than from the parental lectures, from the consequences—positive and negative—one experiences from getting in trouble or from doing something praiseworthy.

I have argued that businesses can be a mediating institution as well. In fact, the need for mediating institutions is strong in human beings, so that we will group ourselves into one. This may be true of a local church, but it can also be true of an inner-city youth gang or a rural militia. Individuals have a communal need, a need to have identity and belonging. It can be a good deal more positive. If corporations design their organizations in a way to constructively respond to this need, they can make use of this natural need to help to create ethical corporate culture.[58]

Empirical evidence supports the natural law version of mediating institutions.[59] In his book *Grooming, Gossip, and the Evolution of Language*, Robin Dunbar[60] was trying to figure out why human beings speak better than other creatures. Though this research seems far afield from our topic, it is actually quite relevant. After testing out other possibilities, Dunbar proposed that perhaps the key was the ratio of neocortex size to body mass, which in primates is quite large.[61] Dunbar also noted that primates will live in a certain size of group with a population ceiling. If a group reaches that ceiling, it will break apart into smaller groups and not go above that ceiling. With these data on neocortex ratios and group sizes, Dunbar plotted a relationship to predict a number for human beings. He came up with 150. This is great esoteric stuff; Dunbar tied this research to some very practical examples.[62]

Excluding smartphones, the average number of names in an address book is 150. The same number is the size of the company unit in the military. The Church of England did a study years ago trying to determine the optimum size of a congregation, so that it would not be so big as to lose a sense of identification with the joys and concerns of other members of the congregation. Its number was a bit larger, but not by much: 200. A Christmas Day article in the *New York Times* in 2010 indicated that the average number of Facebook friends is 120 to 130, "leaving room for grandparents" to reach Dunbar's number. Hutterites have made 150 the maximum size of self-sustaining groups for years.[63] Turning to business, the textile manufacturer W. R. Gore will not have a factory size that accommodates more than 150 workers because above that number they lose a sense of team identity.[64]

But 150 is not the only number. Smaller numbers can be found in the range of four to six and then also thirty. These numbers represent sizes of groups that can talk at any one time (four to six) or working together on a regular basis (thirty). They too correspond to neurobiological and/ or evolutionary evidence. If one accepts evolution, these numbers follow logically very well. If 99 percent of human history was lived in hunter-gatherer groups, then it makes sense that our biology would make us most at home in smaller groups.[65] The same is true in work groups the size of thirty, which anthropologists tell us was the average size of hunter-gather groups who lived together nomadically.[66]

The point of this is that people have limited ability to recognize that their actions make a difference to others. If we want corporations to be more ethical—to build ethical cultures—then we should arrange our organizations in such a way as to make it more likely that people will see that their ethics matter. And if we think that ethical business behavior might contribute to peace, then these numbers take on even more importance. Thus, the final way in which corporations can be designed, internally, to be a kind of a community—a kind of mediating institution—that fosters peace is to put these numbers into action.

Of particular interest is that the characteristics of these mediating institutions map well with anthropological characteristics of relatively peaceful societies.[67] What produces ethics seems to also produce peace. A contribution companies can make to peace, then, is to consciously design the work units within their organizations to align with our neurological capabilities of understanding the consequences of our actions. Understanding those consequences helps to make ethics more common in organizations and thereby also makes corporate contributions to peace more likely.

The "Plus" Contribution: Track Two Diplomacy

The fourth way in which business can foster peace is through Track Two Diplomacy. The idea of Track Two Diplomacy pertains to nongovernmental actors interacting with others to create cultural exchanges that provide support for peace between two or more countries that otherwise might be prone to conflict. This is unofficial interaction between the countries, but the dialogue could provide room for leaders of the countries involved to move toward peace. Exchanges between sports teams, the arts, religious organizations, and many others provide examples of this kind of peace-building interaction. Could businesses step into this mediating role too?

The answer is clearly "yes," at several different levels. At one level, there may be no explicit mission to pave the road for peace, but the actions of the company have that result. For example, the U.S. secretary of state gives an award for corporate excellence each year.[68] This award recognizes American companies whose work overseas is so admirable that it contributes to good relations between the United States and that country. These kinds of efforts win friends, which is exactly what Track Two Diplomacy is all about: informally creating the popular support for two or more countries working together that reduces the risk borne by governmental officials when taking more formal peace-building strategies.

Other businesses make it part of their mission to be facilitators of peace. FuturWays in Northern Ireland[69] maintains a workforce that is half Catholic and half Protestant so the two conflicting sides get a chance to work with each other instead of throwing rocks. A tourist company run out of George Mason University provides tours in Israel with its clientele visiting both Palestinian and Israeli-held territory so that tourists hear both sides of the story in that conflict.[70] These examples are explicit, on-the-ground efforts that serve the company with an eye toward diplomacy.

Track Two Diplomacy can occur at even higher levels. India and Pakistan were eyeball to eyeball in a nuclear stalemate in 1998. After Pakistan had detonated a nuclear weapon, executives from General Electric met with leaders of both countries cautioning resolution.[71] Some current U.S. leaders have proposed creating a group of high-level business leaders to advise governments on the benefits of staying out of conflict situations.[72]

Over the years, I have gone back and forth in my own mind as to whether or not Track Two Diplomacy really should be a fourth contribution to peace. After all, businesspeople are not necessarily diplomats. Having them wade into complicated issues replete with nationalism, ideology, ethnic grievances, and property disputes might make things more volatile. At the same time, every business contribution in this book is a version of a business acting as a Track Two diplomat. As such, it may not be so much of a fourth contribution to peace as much as it is an overarching description of how businesses could contribute to peace. Whether it is a fourth, separate contribution or an overarching description, though, the point is simply that businesses can have a positive impact without having to enter into specific peace negotiations, though the times and places where that has happened will be documented in Part II.

The Organization of This Book

Although Part I tends to be more conceptually based and deductive, Part II leans toward an inductive approach. Multiple case studies are presented with an eye toward capturing differentiations that provide evidence that will link Part I's conceptual theorizing to Part III's policy recommendations. In particular, Chapters 5 and 6 use several case studies to demonstrate the differences among peace building, peacemaking, and peacekeeping. The latter two produce clear dilemmas for businesses that are difficult, though not impossible, to overcome. Peace building, however, is an area where many companies, even if not in zones of conflict, can actively participate.

More specifically, Chapter 2 will examine and sketch the causes of war.[73] Some causes of war have little or nothing to do with economics or business, but many theorists do attribute the causes of war directly to economics. Businesses can be drivers for ideological conflict by supplying the economic engine for industrial development that can be translated into war-making materials. This chapter will tie a consideration of political, economic, ideological, and idiosyncratic factors to the contemporary assessments of why war erupts.[74]

Instead of questioning how violence breaks out, Chapter 3 considers how peace breaks out. This chapter captures a battle between interpretations of anthropology that claim that we are either more violent or less violent than what human history once was. In the midst of this debate, I propose that businesses can make contributions to peace that integrate both viewpoints and show a way forward for the foreseeable future.

Chapter 4 connects business and peace issues to larger macroeconomic issues of property and trust. Increasingly, economists attend to the moral foundations of economics. This opens the door to the consideration of a broader range of connections.[75] Corporate misconduct within the financial industry, for example, raises challenges to the trustworthiness of the financial system and the actors within it; for better or for worse, those concerns wash over into questions about central banking as well. In short, this chapter aims to tie business and peace into a larger, more mainstream assessment of central banking, finance, and economics generally. If we get this idea of trust in the economic system right, and if trustworthy behavior is enacted by business institutions and businesspeople, we just may have done something more profound: We will have adapted the financial sector to be a "peace accelerator."

With a conceptual framework established in Part I, Part II shifts to consider cases and examples that offer three kinds of differentiations. Business contributing to peace building is much more likely to occur than businesses making a difference in peacemaking and peacekeeping. Yet, it can happen. Chapter 5 details such examples. This chapter draws on the work of International Alert and the United Nations to chronicle these examples from, for instance Cyprus, El Salvador, and India–Pakistan.

Chapter 6 uses case studies to demonstrate another kind of differentiation. This one examines another kind of corporate purpose: purposefulness in terms of whether companies take on roles as peace entrepreneurs or whether they are more instrumental in their approach. Both can be described as a kind of foreign policy, but the instrumentalist approach is one likely to be more in line with the kinds of decisions and roles companies might play. Then, there is a third, important kind of purposefulness, which belongs to companies that have no conscious orientation to peace at all but may constructively have an impact on peace because of their behaviors. These unconscious peace builders tend to be ignored in practice, but they may provide the bulk of the culture-building practices of companies that can have an impact on peace.

Chapter 7 will examine government policies and recommend changes—nationally and internationally—that would make businesses better contributors to peace. Pursuant to the findings of the U.S. Institute of Peace Task Force on Business and Peace, these recommendations focus on a more reflexive approach to public policy and may relate to tax, immigration, and other specific policies one could imagine being debated in legislatures today.[76]

Chapter 8 looks at civil society, emphasizing the widely shared theological virtue of hospitality to strangers, an ethic that would go a long way in diffusing some of the conflict flash points we see today. Institutions of civil society maintain a love-hate relationship with business, needing their financial support but also frequently criticizing the economic sector.

Although arguing for the maintenance of that critical edge, I also want to suggest ways in which civil society can foster the business contribution to peace.

Chapter 9 serves as a conclusion aimed at the private sector. Simply put, a peace-oriented corporate foreign policy will be a smart twenty-first-century business policy.

Although few people addressed the potential for businesses to contribute to peace at the turn of the millennium, the good news is that many do now. Scholars do so. Government leaders do. Representatives of international organizations do. Businesspeople do as well. There remain many legitimate questions. There remains a dearth of sustained empirical evidence, in part because there has not been a sufficient conceptual differentiation among the purposes and kinds of businesses and the kinds of contributions they can make to peace. My hope is that this book will help to narrow that gap. It's easy to see how a tourist company in Jerusalem that visits both Muslim and Jewish sectors might help to foster understanding and peace. I want to honor and champion such peace entrepreneurs. But I also want to show how a bank in Chicago that has no direct exposure to the Middle East can also make significant contributions to peace even if it has no knowledge of doing so whatsoever. And I also want to show that tough risk-managing global companies make shrewd foreign policies that will benefit their long-term standing by investing in peace practices, an instrumental approach.

2 Causes of War and Lessons
for Balances of Power

Human beings have a tough time being violent. We may bluster and argue, but it's not easy to start whacking people. When it comes to actual violence, we tend not to do much. Even pugilistic youth, one expert says, mostly threaten; they rarely come to actual blows, let alone gunshots. When people do physically fight, such encounters tend to be short and, well, pretty pathetic.[1] The aversion to violence carries over into war itself. In a widely cited study, more than 25 percent of infantrymen in World War II failed to fire their weapon, even in the midst of battle.[2]

These data seem hard to square with the prevalence of war and violence. Violence and war can't be argued away with complaints about media coverage that favors bloodshed. We certainly seem to have quite a bit of violence around us. Yet, the research suggests it is much harder to perpetrate than we might think.

Perhaps the key to understanding this lies in the realization that human beings become quite violent—in an out-of-control, nearly freakish way—when the other side is defenseless. It takes some courage to get into an evenly matched fight and to stay in one. If a brawl turns one-sided, however, or if an aggressor attacks a defenseless victim, bloodshed and even torture are well within our human capacity. Even if we want to be optimistic about our potential to do good, this dark side of human nature is quite real and has to be checked if any person or institution wants to successfully contribute to the good of peace.

The notion that this dark side needs to be checked lies at the heart of perhaps the core concept of any foreign policy: balance of power. Business's role in the calculus of power follows the pattern of other

27

institutions. Like religion or the media, business itself is ambivalent. Religion can fuel violence or take the road of a Ghandi or Martin Luther King Jr. to forcefully oppose it. Media can whip a populace's anger into a frenzy demanding war, or it can expose governmental machinations as a way to deflate a country's reasons for battle. Similarly, business can exacerbate unchecked power, be a victim of it, or act as a check against that dark side of human nature. Business is both affected by balances of power and, increasingly, affects it.

But the notion of balance of power does not reside solely in the analysis provided by international relations theory. It is embedded in our very nature as biological creatures. This means that balance of power notions pervade our individual beings and our business organizations as well as our geopolitical institutions. Although there may never be a "perfect" balancing of interests in ourselves and our organizations, any one of them getting out of whack just might make it more likely that we might, in fact, start whacking others.

The tripartite framework, introduced in the previous chapter, further provides a way to capture the literature describing the causes of war (COW) and a way to relate those causes to the activities—positive and negative—that business conducts.

Value Clusters and Balances of Power

Chapter 1 introduced this tripartite framework in two forms. The first came from international relations expert Walter Mead, who separated power into sharp, sticky, and soft. The second came in the form of contributions businesses can make to peace: following rule of law principles, economic development, and community-supporting actions. Without repeating that discussion here, it is worth repurposing this framework with an aim for describing the deep roots of this tripartite construct and tying it both to peace and to corporate foreign policy.[3]

The starting point is the work of a business ethicist, whose work ranges far outside of what is typically discussed in that field. William Frederick argues that business and its ethics are part of a larger evolutionary story that reaches back to the creation of the universe. As strange as that may sound, Frederick makes the straightforward observation that life on Earth is subject to evolutionary and cosmological forces. Indeed, how could it be otherwise? His unique contribution has been to define those forces in a schematic narrative that allows one to see how such forces extrude—one of Frederick's favorite verbs—into plant, animal, and human (though Frederick would be careful to include humans in the animal world) life and their organizational structures.[4]

He captures these forces in three recurring value clusters. Those three clusters, arising out of evolutionary history, are economizing, ecologizing, and power aggrandizing. As with any ethics scholar drawing on notions of biology, Frederick is aware of the deterministic shadows of sociobiology and has been challenged that his nature-based approach minimizes human autonomy and freedom. He does not, however, fall prey to such dangers, because he argues that part of our human nature is the capability to think, re-create, and recombine these three recurring value clusters. He calls this the human technosymbolic capacity. He also provides for "*x*-factor" values that describe the idiosyncratically occurring values.[5] Thus, three value clusters recur, but humans can repurpose them into new blends and balances appropriate for new times and places. Or, to put it otherwise, we can repurpose these three value clusters to create new balances of power, exactly the task for CFP.

The first value cluster, economizing, refers to the conversion of raw materials into something usable. At its most basic level, this refers to photosynthesis and metabolism. Socially speaking, businesses perform this function as well, converting some substances into goods consumed by the public. In so doing, companies also provide employment, thus making a contribution to peace, as does economic development more generally construed, at least when balanced by the other value clusters.

Power-aggrandizing values are about domination, control, and hierarchy and occur in quests for status in power in businesses just as they do anywhere else. Power aggrandizing can lead directly to violent imposition of domination. Even in less dramatic forms, Frederick is very negative about its place in business because it tends to be neither efficient nor conducive to creating the long-term relationships that sustain business over a long period of time. I have proposed a modification to this value-cluster in the form of the law, which also proceeds from power aggrandizing but, if created and enforced with an eye toward the other value-clusters, can be a firm support of many social goods, including the functioning of business.[6] In that formulation, following the rule of law also supports peace building.

Ecologizing values are about the symbiotic or mutually supporting relationships that can occur among species over long periods of time.

Frederick grounds these examples in mutualisms that occur in nature—animals, for example, that benefit each other, or the complexity of ecosystems where such mutual dependence creates long-term sustainability. Socially, this manifests itself when individuals sacrifice short-term self-interest for the good of a group. Some have argued that religion serves an evolutionary purpose in this regard by showing how a person should sublimate self-interest for the good of the group to achieve long-term rewards, both in terms of membership within a valued community and also, perhaps, in terms of rewards in an afterlife.[7]

These three value clusters correspond very well to those developed in many other nonethics writings,[8] including Mead's sharp, sticky, and soft power.[9] Though not a perfect fit, I believe these two frameworks map well onto each other. The toughness of military projections matches up with a concept of values that is about hierarchy, control, and dominance. Frederick's economizing values and Mead's sticky power also fit well together as dimensions of economic enterprise. Ecologizing values, which recognize more subtle dimensions of community and mutual support, also seem to connect well with the notion of soft power.

Even if the overlap between the two is merely coincidental or convenient, what keeps it directly relevant for what we are looking at is that even hard-nosed balance-of-power realists recognize that these power dimensions are at play in rough-and-tumble politics, as well as in more idealistic, normative discussions. In writing about World War I, for example, Henry Kissinger locates the importance of moral confidence coming from the Americans (think of Woodrow Wilson's high-minded moral approach) as well as from the powers historically connected to the Holy Roman Empire (Russia, Austria-Hungary, and Germany).[10] Stalin may have ridiculed the power of the pope, but a later pope helped to push later Soviets out of Poland. In short, there is more than one kind of power. Economic, political, and moral power has an impact on even the military. Why would we think it doesn't affect corporations?

Causes of War and Their Connection to the Tripartite Framework

Any given conflict will have a specific set of causes that have a unique identity, making an overall assessment difficult.[11] For example, one could describe the commencement of World War I as the shooting of Archduke

Ferdinand of Austria by a Serbian nationalist or as an interlocking of alliances that, once the first obligation of support was triggered, became a conflagration that engulfed Europe and beyond.[12] Both explanations would be correct, and no typology will neatly capture all aspects. My aim is not to attempt a comprehensive analysis of the causes of war—something a business ethicist is likely be in a poor position to do—but instead to capture enough of the literature so that we can relate it to the tripartite structure. That will then allow us to connect the main causes of war to what role, if any, business might play to temper the violence, exacerbate it, or do something in between.

THE OVERARCHING MODEL: BALANCE OF POWER

Some argue that the following three causes of war are the most important: power, economics, and ideology. These three aspects match those of Mead and Frederick and are the negative application of the forces that can lead to peace as well, with "power" mirroring sharp power/power-aggrandizing "economics" the same as sticky power/economizing, and "ideology" paralleling soft power/ecologizing. What makes them warlike sometimes and peaceful at others? Part of the answer is when they are unchecked.

Thucydides said that the Athenians went to war with the Melians because they could.[13] Thus begins a realist school of international politics that sees war as the extension of politics[14] where all countries seek to exert power and do so when they can. A more recent example than the Peloponnesian War would be Saddam Hussein's invasion of Kuwait, which exhibits another feature of balance of power: rational calculations as to what power one has relative to others. Once Hussein believed that he saw a green light to invade from the stronger Western powers, he unhesitatingly crossed the Kuwait border.[15] Such rational calculations of power characterized much of the Cold War.[16]

Unchecked political power rarely leads to good things. This entirely unoriginal idea lay at the heart of the framing of the U.S. Constitution, where the framers sought to make sure that no one branch of government became too powerful. Although the idea of a strongman or, to use a gentler Platonic phrasing, a benevolent dictator has appeal, it prompts adages like Lord Acton's "Power corrupts and absolute power corrupts absolutely."[17]

Even democracy needs to be checked. As Yale Law professor Amy Chua has written, in countries first experiencing democracy there is a tendency for the majority to enact punishing measures against a wealthy minority and thereby ignore any protection of that minority's rights.[18] Traditional elites who have flourished in crony capitalism or in authoritarian regimes where the favored citizens also have favored economic opportunities become the subject of backlash when newly empowered majorities gain political power.[19] Score settling becomes common. Chua argues that pure democracy is no panacea; mature democracies blend the power of the ballot box with constitutional protections (such as the Bill of Rights) so that mob rule does not ensue.

The literature on the causes of war suggests several aspects that need to be checked and balanced and that follow from the models already introduced.

NATURAL AGGRESSION

Human beings argue and compete on many things. We have conflicts. None of those necessarily leads to violence. But, of course, it is also abundantly clear that we do physically fight and that we do kill. One could cite evidence to show that 20 million deaths from warfare in the twentieth century is an improvement from the past,[20] but 20 million deaths are still, well, 20 million people. Violence may be difficult, but we certainly seem to find a way to overcome our inhibitions.

Anthropologists such as Konrad Lorenz have examined the evidence and concluded that human beings were naturally aggressive and, yes, violent.[21] Because his argument is "naturalistic," one would expect that there are other primates who fight a lot, and chimpanzees, one of our closest primate relatives, are a pretty brutal bunch indeed. Others, however, draw more nuanced conclusions. The famous primatologist Frans DeWaal, for example, acknowledges that chimpanzees and monkeys are violent, but he also argues that social harmony is also important to them and documents their very sophisticated peace-making capabilities.[22] Positioning an infant between two squabbling males, another chimp reintroducing the fighters, submission of one chimp to the other, and simple reconciliation all provide ways to restore peace.[23] Based on these studies, DeWaal argues that the peace making is more common than the fighting.[24] Human beings, then, have aggressive tendencies (as well as peace-making attributes) that can result in war. This naturalistic dimension will have impact on each part of the tripartite sectors because remedy for such instincts, per DeWaal, seems to be the presence of the other two value clusters.

ECONOMIC ARGUMENTS

Another argument calls into question the very structure of capitalist societies, suggesting that, by its very nature, capitalism has a negative impact on peace. If true, this should give real pause to the idea of empowering businesses to be peacemakers. According to this argument, the change from hunter-gatherer groupings into agricultural societies made the defense of geographical territory crucial and also generated the economic surpluses that equipped militaries and enabled hierarchical political regimes. These forces generated capabilities and incentives for war making rather than peacekeeping, which intensified further with industrialization. These structural forces not only make peacemaking difficult; they also make the business role in creating and supporting these structural forces more central.

It would be as interesting as it would be daunting to examine whether capitalism—and what form of capitalism—tends to be associated with more violence than other forms of economic organization. Such an analysis would be a book in itself, and scholarship can be found on that topic.[25] There is a robust literature that does argue that capitalism leads to war. Marx made that argument, claiming that capitalism required a consumption of resources that would end in conflict.[26] So too does an anthropological argument that we will delve into more deeply in Chapter 3.

Given the fact that capitalism does organize the world's economic exchanges today, I am less interested in the analysis of how bad it is than I am in which of its traits can be drawn on to make it a force for peace. But I do have to acknowledge this charge of capitalism's and business's problems.

Aside from capitalism, there are other explanations for how economic needs and desires can spark war. The protection of trade routes and the natural resources they lead to, for example, explain much of colonialism.[27] Countries reacting to restrictions on trade access may also trigger conflict, such as Japan vis à vis the United States in the 1940s.[28] Some generals have even said that they had essentially served as "musclemen" for business.[29]

As with aggression, the dark side of economics arises when it remains unchecked and is greedy.

IDEOLOGICAL ISSUES

The third leg of the tripartite description of our public lives[30] considers the notions of community and ideas. How do we live together, and through what values? How do we support each other? Educational institutions are part of this civil society and have a mission of enlightening and educating individuals and institutions. Charitable organizations, such as the Red Cross, Habitat for Humanity, or Doctors Without Borders similarly devote themselves to the cause of humanity. Their efforts, although without guns, can also provide a check against out-of-control economics or politics by calling human beings back to what they are supposed to be about, according to the cultural norms of that society.

Religion factors here as well. Pope John Paul II stared down the Soviets to begin the collapse of communism in Eastern and Central Europe. Martin Luther King Jr. challenged the violent racism of America. Gandhi forced Britain out of India and tried to get Muslims and Hindus to govern together. All three did so without a gun. It is not difficult to find examples of times when religious individuals and their institutions bravely confronted the rich and politically powerful in the cause of justice.[31]

But there is the dark side of religion as well. Religious wars, such as the Crusades, focus on war making to advance a belief in the way the world should be oriented. The European Wars were frequently based around conflicts between Catholics and Protestants (or Orthodox), either explicitly or implicitly.

The critique can be broadened beyond religion. Ideology does not have to be religious to create war. The twentieth century produced two strong, atheistic, ideological movements—communism and fascism—that had as much zealotry as religion is often accused of possessing.[32] What is dangerous is not religion per se but unchallenged (unchecked) ideology. The risk of ideology, religious or atheistic, is that an ultimate utopian good can leave unchecked any means thought helpful to the good. Thus, a jihadist who believes that, by killing, she or he will receive an eternal reward has few inhibitions about doing so.[33]

The balance provided by the other two sectors are needed to make sure that unchecked ideological or religious power does not spin out of control.

THE TECHNOSYMBOLIC AND *X*-FACTOR VARIATIONS

The three value clusters may persist as dimensions of our lives, but, as Frederick reminds us, human beings still marshal them into new forms on a regular basis. We construct organizations and systems that consciously or unconsciously blend these capabilities. On a good day, we do so in a sustainable way that does more harm than good. On a bad day, things don't turn out so well. The same holds true with *x*-factor phenomena as well. Influential leaders and creators can lead people to new heights as well as depths.

PSYCHOLOGICAL FACTORS

Without negating the three aspects of balance of power dynamics, other distinctly human factors can lead to violence as well. Psychological explanations for war can come in two respects. One is grounded in social psychology, whereas the other arises from individually based psychology. The social psychological dimension looks at the frustrations of a population, perhaps from economic decline or from humiliation in global politics. Those frustrations need an outlet, leading to a scapegoat, the attack on which can provide political capital for a leader. The obvious example of this would be Germany after World War I, the rise of Hitler, and the subsequent Holocaust.

In distressed times, a population may desire a strong leader to bring order to a chaotic situation. Once established in power, the individual psychological propensities of such a leader may be the same leadership characteristics that further take a country into war, as with Napoleon.[34]

Both of these factors can be seen in the drumbeat of war. To justify conflict, one party may rouse the population to do battle against an injustice, such as Hitler's complaint about the humiliation of Germany in World War I or his dehumanizing of Jews so that he could scapegoat them. Characterizing an enemy as something less than human also helps to justify the horrors of war.[35]

In a sense, the psychological aspects of war are evidence of Frederick's *x*-factor: the unique behaviors and beliefs of an individual leader, in this case often with bloody consequences. They are also naturalistic aspects given the prevalence of their appearance in war. As we have seen, if violence is difficult, we have to convince ourselves to do battle with the enemy. Self-defense is a rationale for this, as in when we must quell the power of a madman or degenerate group whose existence threatens us. That propaganda frequently raises this threat suggests the naturalness of it. The fact that Napoleons, Hitlers, and Husseins do arise suggests that the threat of the psychological is real as well.

ORGANIZATIONAL DECISION MAKING

Organizational explanations look at the ways in which a decision to pursue war comes from the dynamics of group behavior. Two well-known examples demonstrate this point in different ways. The first comes in the form of small groups, where groupthink, uninterrupted by dissenting critiques, limits options. Graham Allison argued that this dynamic was at work during the Bay of Pigs invasion. Decisions take on their own dynamic, and it takes a great deal of effort and courage to buck the forces of groupthink that push them forward.[36] What's important to see here is that a cause of war is not necessarily aggression per se, or psychological forces, but instead the dynamics of organizations themselves.[37]

Although small group dynamics represent a micro-organizational cause of war, Dwight Eisenhower highlighted a macro issue in his famous warning over the power of the military-industrial complex. When the massive sectors of military want the latest in weaponry advances (and more in their own branch over and above others), the money for that comes from government procurement of industry and its resulting profits, thus cycling back for industry to encourage the military to ask for more and so forth. And, of course, having such advantages requires using them, leading to war and further industrial profit in rearming the military. There is an economic dimension to this cycle, just as there is a small-group dimension of the titans of military, government, and industry. Eisenhower's warning was about a larger, organizational impact that results from a small group dynamic.[38]

This organizational aspect connects well with technosymbolic values, except that rather than these values providing us with the capability to improve human life, the way we design organizations can have a negative impact as well. A hallmark of organizational problems is that they lead to a consequence without anyone ever really intending that consequence. As philosopher Alasdair MacIntyre pointed out, one of the common defenses made in the post–World War II Nuremburg trials was that a given officer would simply claim to have "closed the boxcars" or "run the train" or "processed some paperwork." In such managerial organizations, no one, MacIntyre said, had the responsibility to stop the Holocaust as a whole.[39]

This kind of response is common and predictable in teaching ethics to businesspeople. Although students find large issues of justice, sustainability, human rights, and peace interesting, the scope of what they believe is relevant to their work is quite limited. In one instance, I consulted for a government agency that wanted a yearlong effort on building ethical culture. The team I built to meet this objective introduced topics related to communication, emotional intelligence, strategy, risk management, and some philosophy, with our aim being to equip them with the ongoing capability to discuss ethical issues as they arose, whatever those issues may be. We were fired after the first day because, as the director said to me, "We just want to know whether we can accept a gift from a supplier."

The individuals in this organization were hardly bad people. I found them very intelligent, thoughtful, and respectable. The agency itself was well respected, too. But the sense of managerial responsibility was startlingly narrow. This experience conforms exactly to what MacIntyre criticized and what Graham Allison identified as organizational issues that lead us into situations—including war—that no one ever fully intended.[40]

Thus, whether in the military, government, or business, organizational forces can lead to a decision that no one ever particularly meant to happen.

INTEGRAL CORRELATES

In addition to these causal arguments, there are correlates of war, with data famously dated by the organization of the same name headquartered at the University of Michigan.[41] The correlates of war look at phenomena that recurrently are associated with violence with the concomitant attention to addressing those correlates. Other work on correlates may identify specific factors connected to war couched in broader terms that link war to educational levels or the presence of religious leaders in government.[42] My own arguments on how business can contribute to peace begin in these kinds of correlates, although, as I have argued, I attempt to ground them more deeply in balance of power realities.

If, for example, poverty causes (or consistently correlates with) violence, there should be policies to reduce poverty. If corruption causes (or consistently correlates with) violence, there should be stronger governmental and corporate policies against bribery. One can extend the examples from whatever correlate is identified. The correlates may well arise from balance of power issues, but one can identify more explicit phenomena that link to war that might be directly addressed.

Thus, if there is a correlation between poverty and violence, then there is a role for business in fostering economic development that reduces poverty by creating employment. If there is a correlation between corruption and violence, and with respect to the rule of law, then businesses that avoid bribery and comply with protection of contracts and property and that support nonviolent dispute resolution can play a role in promoting peace. If there is a correlation between justice-related issues such as gender equity, human rights, and individual employee voice,[43] then businesses again can make positive contributions as their work can touch on all of these issues on a daily basis.

Although not relying on the COW per se, most of my arguments on business's contributions to peace share a similar methodology: trying to determine what things correlate with war and then attempting to see if there is a way to limit the correlate, thereby also lessening the likelihood of war. In short, the methodology for studying causes of war has methodological analogies for studying how business can contribute to peace.

The Role of Business

In these causes of war, business typically plays an ambivalent role. It could have an incendiary impact. There could also be a peaceful role business could play, but it doesn't leap to mind as a key diplomat. I want to suggest that one of the reasons for the latter possibility lies not so much in the reality of what business does or doesn't do but in a popular perception that business engages in self-centered activities that often do not connect to the public good.

BUSINESS IS GREEDY

As the agent of capitalism, business tends to carry a lot of baggage. I want to suggest that a reason business is not thought of as an agent of peace is because of a popular perception that it is part of a capitalist system that is perceived to be the work of the devil. Whether that perception is accurate or not, it creates its own reality.

In a 2012 blog, Louis Ryan detailed the disadvantages to capitalism. They include inequality, wastefulness, starvation, antisocial practices, dangers to life (from workplace accidents and unsafe products), undemocratic practices, pollution, the promotion of war making, dictatorial workplaces, and the issuance of propaganda (that is, advertising).[44]

I'm not especially interested in critiquing this blog; I simply want to suggest that many of its statements are heard about capitalism. Of course, there are many supporters of capitalism as well—and different kinds of capitalism, too—but if there is some degree of anxiety about it (again, knowing that capitalism continues to be our economic system because there is also a good deal of support for it), the role of business is even more suspect in popular culture.

Louis Ryan's blog is not an isolated example of the public perceptions about business. Shortly after the mortgage meltdown of 2008, I was invited to be a guest on an NPR program hosted by Kojo Njamnde on the role business school education played in the mortgage meltdown. During the program, Kojo had his producer pipe in the audio from a scene in the film *Back to School* in which successful, irascible businessman Thorton Mellon upbraids a stuffy business school professor for not covering the basics for how to be successful. For Mellon, played by Rodney Dangerfield, that meant talking about bribes, kickbacks, and other unethical actions. Kojo then challenged me with the question, "Isn't this the reality of how business works?"

"Well," I said, "it's the Hollywood rendition of how business conducts itself, and it is an entertaining one, but I don't believe that it actually captures the way most businesses work. Sure, there are a lot of unsavory business actions; if that weren't the case, there would be no need for professors of business ethics! But, in spending a few years as a business attorney and nearly thirty as a business professor, I have found that most business people work hard and try to do the right thing. Do they fail? Of course; so do professors. But I do not believe business deserves the popular perception that it is bad."

Mr. Njamnda was a terrific sport about the entire dialogue, but what is important is that this anecdote reflects a larger theme that business is perceived as greedy and bad. Following our discussion of Hollywood, name three films since 1960 that have painted a positive portrayal of business and that weren't a remake of a pre-1960 film (such as "Father of the Bride").[45] It's not so easy. One could point to Will Smith's *Pursuit of*

Happyness, or Renee Zellweger's *New in Town*, but, on the whole, such a movie is not easy to find. What are easy to find are dark, even demonic portrayals of business from *Wall Street* all the way to kids' films like *Up*, where the bad guys are the greedy real estate developers.

So much is this the case that Ed Freeman, one of the most influential business ethicists, once entitled a speech: "Business Sucks."[46] Freeman pointed out the popular assumption that business is bad. It causes any action taken by business to be perceived as bad or, if good, then window dressing to cover up bad things. It also sends a message to those going into business that they are selling their souls to make a living, impeding their opportunity to see its possibilities. This remains true even in many business ethics courses, where professors often focus on a scandalous case rather than positive ones.

Perception colors reality. If a company seeks to position itself as a peace-building institution, it runs against a strong grain of popular perception. Indeed, in some (perhaps many) instances, such a characterization may be quite accurate. Yet, what is the alternative? Waste the potential business has to make the world more peaceful and safer?

That is, indeed, the opportunity. Businesses could make the world safer and more peaceful if their actions checked power disequilibrium. Moreover, if companies maintained an equilibrium of their own, they might well be a force for peace and might have greater capabilities of recognizing external disequilibrium, as well and acting to correct it. Such actions may be harder to achieve if public perception of business is consistently negative, but perceptions do not need to remain chiseled in stone either.

THE AMBIVALENCE OF THE ECONOMIC AND THEORIES OF WAR

To be sure, businesses clearly can play a role in the causes of war. European colonialism actively used business corporations as both economic and political agents. Yet, businesses can throttle warmongering precisely because of economic interests. For example, in early 2001, China and the United States faced diplomatic tensions when an American spy plane was shot down over Haiyan Island. Bellicose rhetoric, especially from the Chinese, erupted, but reports indicated that multinational businesses—Kmart, to be specific—cautioned high-level officials in both countries to tone down rhetoric. Why? Because everyone would stand to make more money if the conflict were diplomatically resolved. Economic factors can both enhance the likelihood of conflict and dampen it.

Table 2.1. The Ambivalence of Business with Respect to War

	Business relation with government	Business policy possibility apart from engagement with government
Business fostering conflict	Business fueling the powers interested in war	Business as active perpetrator of war
Business distancing itself from conflict	Business as a check on powers interested in war	Business as neutral

Table 2.1 sketches four different ways in which business could be engaged in issues of war.

In the first of these cells, businesses can actively support the policies of government that lead to war. The examples of this are numerous. The most positive of these entail patriotism: a business making sacrifices—reducing profits, keeping factories open longer, putting its resources at the disposal of the state—in a loyal effort to defeat an enemy. This was particularly prevalent in the United States during World Wars I and II.[47] A less attractive second example is for war to erupt because of the joint interests of business and government, such as the Iraq wars, where oil supplies were of interest both to extractives and to government.[48]

A second possible interaction is where business is the active instigator of war. Cornelius Vanderbilt built both an economic and a military capability before the Civil War and offered some of his ships to fight Confederates. He rejected attempts to rein in his aggressiveness with the retort, "Taint I got the power?"[49] Today, illicit black market businesses tend to flourish when sovereign borders are porous. Absent serious governmental regulation, which is harder to enforce with the ease of transportation and communication, boom markets have developed in the arms trade, the sex/slave trade, drug trafficking, and money laundering.[50]

A third course of action is for business to act as a check on a political power interested in declaring war, as with the actions of Kmart and other business interests to dampen the dispute between China and the United States. Other than the (not insignificant) war-making and rebuilding industry, most businesses do not thrive with bombs falling on them, and business leaders have a vested interest in wanting commerce to thrive in peaceful—or at least stable—environments.

A final course of action is a Swiss-like neutrality approach. This is where business simply tries to stay out of any political dispute. During a presentation at the Council of Foreign Relations in Washington, a questioner from a major business indicated that this exactly was their approach. The company did business in more than 150 countries whether the company thought highly of the regime in power or not. The question said that the company had no political engagement. When I redescribed it to him as a Swiss-like neutrality, he thought that was a better framing: The company simply wanted to do business and not get involved in anything political.

The Impact on Corporate Foreign Policy

Companies seem to thus find themselves in a conundrum. Businesses are powerful forces that shape economics and politics. Ninety-five percent of businesses benefit from peace and stability rather than war and disruption. There may even be contributions that businesses can make to peace, but the perception of business can be so negative that little beneficial public relations value may accrue to its efforts. If my argument is that companies should design a corporate foreign policy with an aim toward peace, then exactly why should companies bother?

One reason might be that that contributing to a scenario where it is less likely that a child will be killed remains a good thing, regardless of whether the company gets a big public relations boost. Another is that the future may hold more potential for recognizing the corporate role in fostering peace. This is the argument of Norwegian investment banker Per Saxegaard. Saxegaard argues that the Internet changes everything because it allows for greater awareness of what companies actually do.[51] Just as there is more emphasis on compliance, governance, CSR, and ethics than there was twenty years ago, business's role in fostering peace may increase in the future, creating public expectations of business's contributions.

A second reason is because by aiming for a good, such as peace, the business culture is likely to orient itself in a way that has been shown to be more economically productive. The way people are treated within the organizations vary. Such differences often matter in terms of economic performance. Indeed, improving corporate culture is a popular topic among businesses today. Interestingly, the remedies offered for improving corporate culture tend to emphasize the need for moving away from hierarchical (that is, power aggrandizing) and economically obsessed (that is, economizing) toward a more balanced integration of those dimensions of corporate culture and soft power dimensions attending to caring among individuals (ecologizing) in the culture and entrepreneurial re-creation of models to solve problems (technosymbolic and *x*-factor).

If cultures that balance various kinds of power aggrandizing, economizing, ecologizing, and technosymbolic tendencies find themselves more successful and competitive in the economic market, why would we not think that similar kinds of balances of power might make a difference to the character of their actions in other realms? If balances of power are important politically, perhaps a balance of power within corporations might help businesses conduct foreign policies with an eye toward peace.

In their influential book *Diagnosing and Changing Organizational Culture*,[52] Kim Cameron and Cameron Quinn provide a methodological template that they call "the Competing Values Framework." One might just as well call it a balance of power framework because it shows that corporate cultures result from the same pressures and values that exist within individual beings as well as nation states and geopolitical systems. Cameron and Quinn's research shows that there are four main types of corporate cultures: clan, hierarchy, adhocracy, and market.

The clan culture has the feeling of an extended family, with the leaders of the firm seen as mentors or even parents.[53] Employees share a good deal of personal information at work, and this carries over to a strong sensitivity to customers.[54] Human resources focuses on long-term development, with resulting qualities of loyalty, cohesion, morale, teamwork, participation, and consensus.[55] Employee empowerment and open communications become crucial in this familial environment.[56]

The hierarchical culture, on the other hand, is very formalized and structured.[57] Smooth, long-term, efficient performance is valued, with leaders being viewed as coordinators and organizers.[58] Procedures, formal rules, and policies hold the organization together, and attention to employees focuses on secure employment and predictability.[59]

The market culture is a competitive, results-oriented organization that tends to feature toughness, a demanding load, drive, and competitiveness.[60] Winning motivates the participants, with success being defined in tangible measures of performance and market penetration; leaders are hard-driving competitors.[61]

The adhocracy culture tends to be entrepreneurial and creative.[62] Leaders are innovators and risk takers and encourage such traits in employees.[63]

What binds members of the organization together are a commitment to innovation and a desire to be cutting edge, with success measured in the creation of new unique products and services.[64] Creating new standards and finding creative new approaches become hallmark strategies.[65]

This reconceptualization fits well with the tripartite model we have sketched.[66] In this reconceptualization, hierarchy would map with legal and compliance notions of business; market would map onto the economic; and clan would map with a moral dimension. Moreover, I would argue that this model further accords Frederick's schematic and that of Mead as well.

Cameron and Quinn note that companies tend to "gravitate toward an emphasis on hierarchy and market culture types. . . . Once their culture profiles become dominated by those . . . quadrants, . . . it takes a great deal of effort and leadership to make the change to a clan or adhocracy culture."[67] Or, to phrase otherwise: There needs to be more balance among the values rather than any one of them becoming too dominant. A company attuned to realms of values and ideas will likely be better positioned to contribute to notions of ethics and peace in the political world than one concerned solely with profit and avoidance of legal sanctions.

The Need for Integration

The conscious integration of elements benefits the effectiveness of corporate culture. This aspect of soft power/ecologizing/affective crucially benefits the work of companies themselves as well as providing a way to contribute to the global good of peace and stability. Even if such efforts do not garner public applause, they can garner internal benefits that would provide a strong foundation for corporate foreign policy regardless of public perception. If the public can see these benefits, then so much the better.

This insight adds to an otherwise missing element of a business-peace model that goes beyond the hard-to-replicate General Electric kind of intervention with political leaders. Businesspeople and their organizations can choose a pacific route in many other ways short of helping to avert a nuclear showdown. They may do so by interacting with any of the aforementioned causes of war, primarily by checking a power prone to attacking another country or people. They may similarly check the powers that can spin out of control within their own organizations by integrating a peace-building motivation into the daily work of the company.

The next two chapters drive more deeply into understanding how the current economic system can (or cannot) facilitate peace. If corporate foreign policy maintains that peace is beneficial for a company, then seeing how the system can foster this goal will help to strategically align the company's practices. Further, regardless of whether good public relations result from a firm's commitment to peace and stability, a positive, affective goal benefits the company's culture, leading to a more effective institution.

To be sure, there are different sectors in society. One should not expect a part of the economic sector to necessarily lead civil society. Different sectors have different roles. But that is not to say that each sector does well by ignoring the values and powers that exist ubiquitously. Governments may be about power, but they have to attend to their own funding, and they typically are also about the power of ideas. Civil society may be about championing ideas, education, and beliefs, but its institutions still have to match revenue and expenses, and, as Stalin's successor realized about the pope, civil society can have political power as well. Businesses may be about "the bottom line," but their well-being also depends on internal policies as well as enough moral values so as to sustain trading relationships.

The following two chapters sketch these notions of balances of power, especially with respect to the economic system in a way that provides a platform for businesses to be an actor that can foster peace and do so in a way that is smart corporate foreign policy. Indeed, crucial to mitigating these causes of war is for today's (arguably) most powerful sector—business—to play a role in the building of peaceful relationships and for it to be done in the presence of the balancing forces of soft power in the form of ethical ideals.

3 Could Peace Break Out in This Day and Age?

Are human beings becoming more violent than we were in our ancient past, or are we becoming more peaceful? Although some anthropologists view us as innately aggressive,[1] some primatologists claim that our genetic heritage places great emphasis on peacemaking.[2] Certain scholars conclude that time's arrow points to an increase in violence, noting that the creation of large formal institutions (economically and politically) led to less peace because they "swept aside valuable modes of association that had evolved in their respective cultures while creating a framework for even larger polarizations."[3] Yet other scholars claim that large organizations actually dampen the fires of violence.[4]

Much is at stake in this debate. If human beings were once more peaceful, then we should look to the past to determine what attributes and practices they used to reduce the amount of violence in the world. If human beings are more peaceful now, then we should spend less time attempting to replicate the past and instead see how modern forces have mediated our violent nature to continue a march toward peacefulness.

Much is at stake for business as well. Simply from a regulatory posture, the more our past suggests peacefulness, then the more laws should be passed to replicate those peaceful practices that tend toward egalitarianism, small sizes of institutions, and protection of individual voice. The more large-scale global commerce links to peace, then laws should promote freer trade, more lenient immigration policies, and fewer restraints to large-scale corporations. Moreover, what if both positions are correct? What would that suggest for public policy? As I will show in this chapter and the next, there are implications for economics and ethics with respect to this question as well. In short, although much of this chapter dives into some esoteric issues of anthropology, primatology, and sociology, some very real business issues arise from the discussion.

In this chapter, I want to focus on the ways in which war and violence are situated within an evolutionary narrative. The causes of war and the ways in which peace breaks out help us to consider the practices conducive to establishing peace in the twenty-first century. Because principles for contemporary corporate responsibility, we need to understand human behavior and recognize the evolutionary pressures that have given rise to our basic nature as people.[5] Moreover, I argue that Chapter 2's concluding combination of business and ethics is *exactly* essential to twenty-first-century peace.

I'll start by focusing on two very different impressive scholars, Donald Fry and Steven Pinker, both of whom try to explain human violence and warfare by reaching back thousands of years. Pinker says we have become less violent, whereas Fry argues that we need to reclaim the past to reduce violence. Although they disagree about almost all the evidence they rely on, the solutions they propose for reducing violence and enhancing peace are quite compatible and coalesce around the way in which gentle commerce can foster peace.

Fry: *Beyond War*

In *Beyond War*, anthropologist Douglas Fry sets out a case for how human beings can draw on deep history to create peace.[6] Fry objects to the idea that human beings are prone to warfare, saying that the idea of "man the warrior," central in Western thinking, really rests on very limited evidence.[7] Our contemporary assumptions about the violent nature of human beings, he argues, come from at least two sources.

One of those is scholarly research itself, the analysis of which consumes much of Fry's book. To give a flavor of Fry's concern, consider his critique of the book *Demonic Males*.[8] Fry rejects as "simply false" the claim that there is no evidence of a truly peaceful society. In the authors' enthusiasm to paint the demonic portrait of men (who Fry agrees are more violent than women), they deny that all the complex hunter-gatherers and equestrian hunter-gatherers make war while also overlooking the fact that a majority of the simple (nomadic) hunter-gatherers do not.[9] So, finding evidence of peaceful societies is possible, especially if we look toward nomadic hunter-gatherers.[10] But that evidence requires going back into deep human history.

The second assumption about how violent we are comes from "violence-saturated programming [that] can contribute to a false, unrealistically violent picture of the world."[11] Frankly, peace is kind of boring. Action films, war stories, cowboy movies, and science fiction adventures all thrive on violence. The same limitations of the screen also spill over into television, especially the nightly news, which seems to follow the old adage, "If it bleeds, it leads."

Fry's task is not to combat Hollywood per se but rather to provide an account of the evidence for war and peace drawing heavily on prehistory. By looking too recently in human history and by projecting violence onto evidence that would objectively lead us to see ourselves as peaceful had led scholars to conclude, incorrectly according to Fry, that humanity is naturally violent.

In addition to not looking back far enough into human history, Fry believes that researchers confuse violence with war. He makes note of a voluminous treatise that claims 5 percent of societies lacked warfare (that is, no military and no weapons) and 59 percent engaged in only mild warfare. The author of this study labels all the societies warlike. Why? Because societies in the 5 percent category would be warlike inasmuch as they would (presumably) engage in a defensive war; those in the 59 percent category, he claims, would engage in "social war" which was a mix of feuding, duels, and the like. Fry offers another interpretation of this same data: Sixty-four percent of the sample was relatively peaceful. The rest of the societies in the studies engaged in war for economic (29 percent) or political (7 percent) purposes.[12] In other words, the data themselves are subject to a glass half empty or half full interpretation. If we start with an assumption that humans are violent, then we interpret the data as reinforcing our assumptions. Fry pushes back against that interpretation.

To further substantiate his point, Fry considers a study noting that warfare was absent or rare in 28 percent of societies, with "rare" meaning less than once in ten years for those "pacified" by a colonial or national government and only 9 percent if nonpacified. Feuding or revenge killings were included in the definition of war for the remaining 73 percent of the study, which constitutes a very broad definition of warfare because it would include the actions of a single person against an enemy group.[13]

Even with this broad definition of war, the study shows that war is absent or rare in a significant percentage of the population.[14]

From this analysis, we might well conclude that, when reaching deep into human history, especially if we keep violence and war as separate categories, human beings demonstrate quite a bit of peacefulness. All of this, of course, begs the question of how to define war. Fry relies on a definition with widespread support:

> A group activity, carried on by members of one community against members of another community, in which it is the primary purpose to inflict serious injury or death on multiple nonspecified members of that community, or in which the primary purpose makes it highly likely that serious injury or death will be inflicted on multiple nonspecified members of that community in the accomplishment of that purpose.[15]

This excludes individual homicides and feuding and clarifies that war is "impersonal lethal aggression between communities."[16] A degree of anonymity marks war. A person is not getting even with someone; instead, a group is aiming to kill a category of individuals who comprise something "other." It doesn't make a difference who that person is; each person is the same as anyone else from that tribe/country, and so on.

This is exactly what terrorism is about: killing 3,000 "Americans" on September 11, 2001, not because of a grudge against those specific people but because they simply were assumed to be Americans. And although there may have been nineteen terrorists hijacking planes that day, there have been plenty of other single-actor terrorists who would fit a broad definition of warfare.

With respect to peace, Fry is cautiously optimistic. Sweden has not been to war in 170 years, Switzerland for over 200, and Iceland for over 700.[17] Of course, there will be conflicts between people, but usually without violence.[18] Aggression—the infliction of harm, pain, or injury on other individuals—is not synonymous with conflict.[19] Yet, the large arc of warfare among nation-states along with a global economic system stand as the antithesis of nomadic hunter-gatherers and provides the caution for the optimism Fry expresses. He is optimistic because of his hope that we can learn from the practices of nomadic hunter-gatherers. He is cautious because the arc of large nation-states and globalization risk catastrophic warfare.

Fry's argument strikes me as carefully wrought in terms of precisely identifying when humans were peaceful and in what ways. Today, nomadic hunter-gatherers comprise less than a thimbleful of the human population today, and it is important not to overreach; it is not that nomadic hunter-gatherers are never violent but that they are far less so than humans living in other social organizations. If the quest for peace depends on us all becoming nomadic hunter-gatherers again, prospects seem dim. Moreover, if a central part of the war-making tendency is an economic system that runs from agricultural to industrial, we might view business as inevitably part of the problem. Fortunately, that doesn't seem to be the case. The surprise is that Fry's solutions, even given his concerns about modernity, are quite compatible with those of another scholar whose work is almost completely at odds with his anthropological account.

Pinker: *The Better Angels of Our Nature*

Apart from the fact that Steven Pinker, a Harvard psychology professor, is also optimistic about the human potential for peace, his narrative is the inversion of Fry's. For Pinker, human beings were naturally aggressive and violent and have become more peaceful precisely because of large governmental organizations, commerce, and limiting ideology.

He may seem off base today when people often feel there is a greater likelihood of violence than in the past, in large part because of terrorism. Pinker, however, places this threat in context:

> Every year more than 40,000 Americans are killed in traffic accidents, 20,000 in falls, 18,000 in homicides, 3,000 by drowning (including 300 in bathtubs), 3,000 in fires, 24,000 from accidental poisoning, 2,500 from complications of surgery, 300 from suffocation in bed, 200 from inhalation of gastric contents, and 17,000 by "other and unspecified nontransport accidents and their sequelae": In fact, in every year from 1995 and 2011, more Americans were killed by lightning, deer, peanut allergies, bee stings and "ignition or melting of nightwear" than by terrorist attacks.[20]

In arguing that we are less violent, he does not claim that there is *no* violence. As he colorfully puts it, "In earlier decades, a man's willingness to use his fists in response to an insult was the sign of respectability. Today it is the sign of a boor, a symptom of impulse control disorder, a ticket to anger management therapy."[21] More broadly, Pinker argues that a civilizing process that stems from the creation of the central state, commerce, and a diminution of ideology tamed our aggressive nature. He makes note of the violence of chimps to support his claim that aggression is rooted deeply within our genetic heritage. Recognizing that some argue that bonobos are significantly more pacific than chimps, he answers that the human gene line does not trace to them.[22] Even kids are not let off the hook: Pinker shows that the single most violent time is the terrible twos.[23]

Whereas Fry raises concern about the centralization of human society, Pinker champions it. The emergence of the central state, he argues, crucially transformed human society from nomadic hunter-gatherer bands to sedentary bands, to tribes to chiefdoms to petty states and then to large states.[24] Again counter to Fry, Pinker does not disentangle war from violence. He specifically attacks the notion that tribal battles don't harm many people and argues that rates of death are higher than imagined and also that "the sneaky raids" are more lethal than noisy battles.[25] Moreover, his anthropological starting point is that of sedentary horticulturalists rather than Fry's nomadic hunter-gatherers.[26]

Things changed. In England, between the thirteenth and twentieth centuries, homicide rates dropped by a factor of one hundred; the rest of Europe, too, saw major reductions.[27] Pinker argues that a civilizing process made human beings less gross, foul, and poorly mannered and dramatically affected the way human beings conducted themselves. That included violence. Pinker notes that, in the Middle Ages, everyone was quick to draw knives at the slightest offense.[28] They relieved themselves in public, had sex in public view, and blew their noses on tablecloths.[29] From the eleventh century on, upper-class Europeans began to inhibit their impulses and anticipate the consequences of their actions, a shift that trickled down to the lower classes.[30]

During this time, a market system developed that encouraged people to treat others decently in order to trade with them rather than to attack them. The second half of the eighteenth century saw a rise of humanitarianism, coinciding with a reduction of torture, cruelty to animals, slavery, and capital punishment—all prompted by the growth of literacy and writing.[31]

The results of this process have been impressive. Western and Central Europe (with a gradient of lawlessness extending to Eastern Europe and the Balkans)[32] are the least violent locations globally, along with former English colonies and some Asian countries such as Japan, Singapore, and

Hong Kong (all of which adopted Western models).[33] The most crime-prone areas are Russia, sub-Saharan Africa, and parts of Latin America.[34]

Though we are prone to think of the twentieth century as an exceptionally violent time with two major world wars, Pinker places this violence in a new context. Examining a chart that assesses rates of death in major wars (given populations at the time), World War II is number 9 and World War I is number 16.[35] Older wars had higher death tolls. The bottom line, from Pinker's perspective, is that humans are not as violent as we once were.

Further, he acknowledges that although great powers do participate in major wars, no one has used a nuclear weapon since 1945, the superpowers have not fought, and with rare exception (Hungary in 1956 and Russia in 2014), European countries (at least) do not invade and conquer others.[36] Peace has broken out in Europe. Pinker attributes this welcome news to the rise of democracy,[37] trade,[38] and the United Nations.[39] Democracy does not reduce the number of wars, but it does reduce their severity, he says. Moreover, openness to global economy appears to drive down the likelihood and severity of civil conflict.[40]

One response to Pinker's argument is that he has run afoul of Fry's insistence on separating violence from warfare. Indeed, Pinker regularly moves back and forth between the two and further draws on starting points that Fry would complain come too recently in human history. In that regard, Pinker's argument seems incomplete: Are we really more peaceful than we were as nomadic hunter-gatherers? If there is something about the nomadic experience we can learn from, then omitting it may overlook a way for humans to become more peaceful in coming years.

At the same time, Pinker appears to be onto something quite profound. His data show that peace is breaking out because of practices like constitutional democracies, rule of law, empathy, humanitarianism, civilizing behaviors, and economic trade. Perhaps we can't see this because of media attention on violence, but, beyond those lead stories, seeing how peace is breaking out helps us know how to foster that development.

Making Sense of the Differences and Similarities

When one looks at the Fry and Pinker differences, recalling that they merely represent a much longer and widespread debate, an obvious conclusion is that they are irreconcilable. At a fundamental level they are. But if one thinks about them more in terms of balance of power, the directions they point to are not so different.

In this case, ethical business behavior will be central to this narrative of continued peace. I see no reason why Pinker and Fry would disagree. Pinker only hints at that contribution through his choice of words; he champions "gentle commerce" without much of an understanding of what the adjective "gentle" adds to commerce. In fact, it adds a lot. Business per se is entirely absent from Fry's position, but the thrust of his argument is that we need some of the dispute-resolving practices and empathy-building cultura; practices that can be drawn from the example of nomadic hunter-gathers. Indeed, those practices and cultures are exactly what define ethical business practices that are simultaneously peace builders.

"Abolishing war in the twenty-first century is not only realistic in the sense that it is possible, but also realistically necessary for human survival and [well-being]. The flexible peacemaking primate has the capacity to do so."[41] This perspective stresses the importance of avoiding war, promoting tolerance, negotiating, and teaching ways for people to settle their own disputes. Fry also advocates for a more juridical settling of disputes by third parties, including mediation and arbitration strategies, as well as repressive peacemaking in which a significant power exercises its influence to prevent war.[42] Finally, and crucially, he wants to tame the ills of contemporary economic and political governance to create transnational institutions for dispute resolution, such as those within democratic societies. The risk to peace in the current "war system" is that itself perpetuates more violent self-redress: If I am angry with you, I get even.[43] Higher forms of judicial authority, such as an international body, would be a step in the direction of resolving disputes peacefully.

From this view, our interdependent global world also provides opportunities for building peace by fostering crosscutting ties to reduce an "us versus them" mentality[44] and further develop interdependence and cooperation.[45] We may be Americans or Chinese or Ethiopians, but, in today's world, we also might find ourselves coworkers and Facebook friends in a way unprecedented in world history. Someone who might otherwise just be "Chinese" becomes "friend," complicating the choices an "American friend" or "Ethiopian friend" has in the event of conflict between the two nations. Moreover, humans can reduce violence by fostering of a set of common values, attitudes, and beliefs.[46]

Would Pinker or any of the others who argue for the benefits of the modern nation-state disagree? It is hard to see how they would. Indeed, those championing the importance of the contemporary liberal systems spout a long argument about the benefits of the large state, "gentle commerce," and international associations (such as the United Nations). Throughout his work, Pinker stresses the importance of self-control and emphasizing long-term interests over short term interests; of exercising restraint over indulgence.[47] In addition to historical evidence, he notes lessons that have been derived from game theory, where the most effective survival strategy is not simply tit for tat but to build on qualities like forgiveness, which produce long-term relationships beneficial for everyone.[48]

One might think that Pinker would turn to traditional forms of institutions and approaches that emphasize long-term strategies. But, in fact, his argument draws on a very long-term, incremental civilizing process that changed the way Europeans think and act. Literacy and printing were part of the fabric of the change that enabled the masses to read and to think about long-term consequences rather than defaulting to immediate needs. Institutions like these are far from the governing bodies that might immediately leap to mind. What is the pedagogy that would help us think long term today?

Religion might be a candidate. It has been defined by many as reducing indulgence and short-term interests in exchange for long-term membership in a community.[49] Why give alms? It doesn't help the alms giver in the short term, but it is something one does to be a good member of a community. Being part of a community does have long-term benefits. What religions teach is to sacrifice short-term benefits (such as hoarding money) and instead look out for others, at least those who share one's beliefs. Without claiming that all such sacrifices and all such loyalties to a religious tradition are good things, being a member of a religious tradition teaches the importance of the long term.

But Pinker, as well as many others, sees religion as a problem. He recognizes that it is always with us, and he is careful not to demonize believers. At the same time, he is very critical of the violence religion can perpetrate. This is true enough, but if religion is indeed always with us, then it might be better to engage with it and steer it toward peace building than to ignore it and hope it goes away.

Business actually stands as a candidate. Businesses bring people of different backgrounds together, and if business is conducted in ways that create economic development, adhere to rule of law practices, build good relationships with external stakeholders, and respect the rights of internal constituents, it will have an organizational culture that could also allow for constructive dialogue, collaboration, and a higher level of civilization.[50]

Another suggestion Pinker makes is to cultivate empathy, which plays an important role because it gets people to think of others rather than themselves and shifts people away from short-term self-interest. Even though Pinker agrees that empathy has a positive role, he argues that the decrease in violence owes more to prudence, reason, fairness, self-control, norms and taboos, and human rights.[51] Similarly, morality typically attempts to rein in short-term indulgences in favor of principles that orient individuals to a longer term, but Pinker says that the world has too much morality; morals tend to get universalized and then can be used to punish others.[52]

In making these observations, Pinker strikes me as inconsistent. How are norms, taboos, human rights, fairness, self-control, prudence, and reason not part of morality and ethics? Aren't they the very stuff of such things? And who teaches them? Pinker is wary of religion. But won't spiritual traditions be central to teaching ethical norms and human rights? To be sure, religion has a checkered history, but it is checkered rather than evil; although misguided religious zealots might slaughter and torture, other religious leaders include Ghandi and Martin Luther King Jr.

What, then, is Pinker's hope for continuing the shift of attitudes toward peace building? Part is the continuation of the state's ability to suppress violence and to find ways to resolve disputes through governmental and transgovernmental institutions. In this, he ends up differing little from Fry. Both also want to see attitudes continue to evolve toward peace. Pinker's preference for the shifting of attitudes, however, relies on softer things such as humor and satire,[53] which he views as ways to challenge orthodoxy and call citizens and their leaders to see new ways of resolving international disputes. Yes, *Saturday Night Live* and *Comedy Central* have a role in peace building!

So Jimmy Fallon and Jon Stewart may be peace builders, but who owns the shows and the infrastructure, especially on a worldwide basis? NBC Universal and other corporations. A key mechanism for peace building must then feature corporations willing to at least put such humor and satire on the air. Why would NBC Universal do this? Well, to make money,

of course. Although there may be some commitment from the corporation to values such as free speech, humor, and satire, the corporate dimension raises the notion of gentle commerce; that is not just that business
might create a larger economic pie, but that the way business operates
makes a difference. Ethical businesses make stronger contributions to
peace than unethical ones.

Suffice it to say that commerce presents a challenge for Fry, and I believe it is more of a challenge to Pinker than he lets on. Neither will
endorse colonialism as a good. Neither will endorse a commercial system that exploits children and women and violates other human rights.
Neither will find a commercial world that fosters unfairness, short-term
gratification, and out-of-control greed attractive, nor would they argue
that such unethical conduct would be likely to lead to peace.

We can integrate Fry and Pinker in a way that makes business into a
peace-building force. In short, it would appear that the sweet spot that
aligns Fry and Pinker are the arguments Schipani and I have championed:
those businesses that are economically productive, that abide by overarching rules of just law, and that build prudent, responsible communities
that respect human rights, gender equity, voice, and approach issues on a
long-term rather than a short-term basis. As I will show in the following
chapter, more and more, economics itself demands this integration.

Gentle Commerce as Crucial for Peace to Break Out

Including, but moving beyond, our key thinkers in this chapter, there's
a whole body of research that suggests peace may emerge from specific
geographical locations, such as in South America or across North American borders via hegemony, common heritages, and economics. It has broken out in Europe because of the revulsion from world wars. It might also
stem from an equilibrium resulting from balances of power. As I have
already begun to suggest, I want to propose that there is a strong place for
economics in this process.

Indeed, some scholars provide an argument for a "capitalist peace." This
research notes a dramatic drop in deaths with the establishment of greater
prevalence of capitalism.[54] This research also identifies a relationship between politics and economics but tends to place more stress on the economic aspects that create increasing integration that makes it much more
expensive to resort to violence to resolve disputes.[55]

Erik Gartzke, political science professor at the University of California at San Diego, notes three attributes of mature capitalist countries that temper the prospects for war. The first is that land is less important in today's economy; competition today occurs more through markets than in territorial expansion, and therefore war is not as effective a strategy as it once may have been. A second is that there is more overlap in foreign policy goals of developed nations post–World War II in terms of coordinating an integrated market system. Third, global markets provide more new ways to compete—to obtain influence—than what might have been the case in the past.[56]

If capitalism provides a lever for peace, then who does the heavy lifting of capitalism? The answer is business. Businesses provide the jobs for economic development, make the investments, marshal the resources, employ people, and market the products. Capitalism—or at least a certain kind of capitalism—may be linked to peace, but the instruments of peace are corporations. Those businesses are not simply transactional ciphers; they are comprised of men and women with cultures and histories that act in many different ways—exploitatively and responsibly—that form attitudes and dispositions. They represent not only a Gartzke capitalism or a Pinker gentle commerce but also the face-to-face interaction of people akin to Fry's hunter-gatherers.

Yet many claim that this confidence in economics is too fast and neat. Instead of making economics primary, some argue that economics is secondary to resolution of political disputes. Economic development does not settle political disputes; instead, once disputes are settled politically, economic development then steps in to secure and extend peace.[57]

Ian Morris, for instance, recently published a book claiming that war was a good thing. Morris is no bloodthirsty troublemaker. Citing many scholars, including Pinker and Fry, he argues that the modern nation-state has made us more peaceful and richer because of economic development and that states were created through war. Although a "lesser of two evils," war has made us more peaceful and safer, thus earning some degree of goodness and laying the conditions for more economic growth.

Morris goes on to say that war has put itself out of business.[58] Our capability to kill has become so effective that we can't risk doing it any more. This means that governments have even more pressure to find ways to resolve disputes, short of unleashing the jackals of war. But in a world where the Internet and globalization increasingly place pressures on governments to control their own borders and claim their own sovereignty, can we possibly delegate peace solely to the state? The answer is no, we can't, and we don't have to because business and economics are in exactly the place where they can shoulder part of this burden. Indeed, Fry and Pinker's arguments ultimately lead us to the trajectory of economics, capitalism, and peace—and the integration of ethics with each of these pillars.

Commercial integration does not need to take a backseat to political diplomacy, nor does diplomacy become in any way irrelevant. One could note that many historical studies of "peace breaking out," are pre-1989, and many of them are decades or even centuries old. Perhaps the Internet-driven global market is different from the commercial integrations of the past. Such an Internet-era difference might support Gartkze's argument further.

Economics and diplomacy surely are both important. My argument is that an ethically infused economics—a gentle commerce—simultaneously is diplomatic and builds the economic basis for peace. Gentle commerce carries with it economic vibrancy and with it peace building. Its gentleness contributes to a track two style of allowing public diplomacy to be carried out. In serving both functions, it also contributes to the factors Pinker advocates while doing so in a way that insists on the importance of values Fry finds in peaceable nomadic hunter-gatherers. We need to further explore how this inherently integrative activity works.

4 The Economics-Ethics-Trust-Prosperity-Peace Matrix

The good news is that the notion of gentle commerce that I've suggested is now well supported by a matrix that integrates economics, ethics, trust, prosperity, and peace. No longer should these be thought of as anitipodal. To be sure, there remains tension among them, but a twenty-first-century quest for peace depends on their integration, and that is an integration that is happening in today's scholarship as well as in practice.

A free market, after all, is based on some degree of trust that the game of the market will be played fairly. Following from the tripartite structure from earlier chapters, there is a role for government, for business itself, and for character-forming institutions, such as religious, educational, and other nongovernmental organizations. When the market lopsidedly veers to too much speculation, too little spending, too much excess, too much illegality, too much competition, things get out of whack, and the market, as well as the stakeholders affected by the market, suffers.

Laws do address these excesses—for example, Sarbanes-Oxley after the Enron-WorldCom kinds of problems or Dodd-Frank after the mortgage meltdowns. Egregious behavior can occasionally be handled within the industry itself or imposed on the market by popular protests. The Occupy Movement's protest over the bailouts of large corporations—an accentuating of moral hazards if there ever was one—may not lead to violent action, but the perception of an economic system existing only for the benefit of the rich and powerful and not to the entirety of society was exactly the grounds for the appeal of Marxism.

Of course, an investment bank may decide that it should gore its own customers, but this approach is both shortsighted and free riding. To be sure, businesses—as economic institutions—are primarily interested in economic success. One may have additional noneconomic objectives in going into business, but making money is going to be at the top or very close to it for any businessperson, and impaling one's own customers surely is a wrongheaded strategy to employ. Businesses do not have the obligation to save the world from war, hunger, and disease, but it might help if they also didn't act with the moral maturity of a two-year-old, a standard of corporate foreign policy that seems doomed in the long run.

Scholars have demonstrated how companies and societies hold "shared values" that allow both to flourish.[1] It is an insight long held within the field of corporate responsibility and one that is increasingly shared by major economic institutions who have a profound interest both in maintaining trust in the financial and economic system and in fostering peace and stability rather than providing the desperate breeding grounds for violence that economic collapse can create.

For example, the Federal Reserve is one institution that recognizes a need for intervention in the market system when excess dominates. In 2013, Federal Reserve Chairman Ben S. Bernanke gave a series of lectures to my class at George Washington University about the Fed that included economics but also considered the Fed's place in society from the perspectives of law, political science, sociology, consumer protection, and ethics.[2] In his first lecture, Bernanke examined the early experience of the Federal Reserve in dealing with the Great Depression, which honed the Fed's responsibility in tending to the economy through monetary policy and acting as a lender of last resort.

Bernanke argued that the Fed had not used its tools to live up to these responsibilities. His analysis guided him during the financial crisis in 2007–2008. While Bernanke focused on the Fed and its mission, what he was really talking about is how the Federal Reserve's job is to create and maintain trust in the financial sector. With trust as an ultimate goal, trust-debilitating actions become relevant to issues of peace and stability throughout the financial sector. What became clear in listening to Bernanke and the lecturers who followed was that the notion of checks and balances works best when it exists within each institution so that some perspective is gained as to how to govern complex institutions over the long term.

What happens when there isn't financial and economic stability? What happens when there is no lender of last resort to save desperate runs on banks or when there are high interest rates that undermine savings and salaries? History shows that great unrest ensues. If governments cannot provide a level of economic stability, protests can turn deadly. Moreover, it is at these times when a country may be weakest and thus most vulnerable to attack. Alternatively, it may be that a government uses the rallying cry of war to get a country out of recession; some have said that entering into World War II brought America out of the Great Depression.[3] A leader in such times can blame the country's economic troubles on a scapegoat with ensuing persecution of that population, which is exactly what enabled Hitler to ascend.[4] In short, central banking has a direct impact on the conditions that cause war.

Main Street versus Wall Street

Prior to the creation of the Fed as we know it, there were two previous attempts to create a central bank. Both attempts failed because of a disagreement between what today we would call Main Street and Wall Street. The folks on Main Street—farmers, for example—feared that the central bank would be mainly an instrument of the moneyed interests in New York and Philadelphia and would not represent the entire country and be a *national central* bank.

This unease continues today and raises some important questions, not only in terms of economic fairness but also about how this edifice of powerful government and gentle commerce (along with multilateral work) will maintain the trust of the people governed by it and necessary to support it. Or, to phrase it otherwise, to place the adjective *gentle* in front of *commerce* so that gentle commerce becomes a trust-building glue that holds ethics, economics, and trust together with an outcome of peace.

The consensus we identified in the disparate work of Fry and Pinker relies on support from people who believe that there is some degree of fairness in the system. In that regard, Main Street values become important for the system and for peace as well. There is no one definition of "Main Street values," but I would suggest that any definition would emphasize a strong ethical content and make commerce gentle. As a business ethicist, my job has been to propose such moral taming of what can otherwise be a rapacious form of capitalism.

Although there will always be crooks and shady businesspeople, good, solid business ethics and citizenship in the community are both old school and the wave of the future. The explosion of industrialism, large business interests, the primacy of a business form—the corporation—that truly has no soul (good or bad), and privatization of moral views led to a century or so when businesses could often get away with what they wished. Add to that liquid markets and the sophistication of quantitative models poorly equipped for elusive notions of morality, and the forces for ignoring ethical business conduct presented themselves quite well.

Those forces have been noted by many Americans, including one of my students in Bernanke's lectures. She told the chairman he had done a great job demystifying the Fed but that she was still uneasy as to how the work of today's financial markets connected with the values of Main Street America.

"Given how unpopular bank bailouts were among many Americans struggling to pay their mortgages who don't really understand the importance of financial stability," she asked, "do you ever see Americans reconciling these differences?"

Bernanke acknowledged that the Fed has done outreach to try to explain what it did and what it is doing. It is inherently difficult because the Fed is a complicated institution and these are not simple issues.

"But all we can do," Bernanke said, "is to do our best and hope that our educators, our media, and so on will begin to carry the story and help people understand better. It is a difficult challenge and it does reflect a tension in American feelings about central banks ever since the beginning."[5]

The fear of Main Street that the moneyed interests, buoyed by a central bank, will act only in their own interests and have little regard for the well-being of even their own customers is real and significant. And it stems from the experience of small town accountability that can be hard to find in today's big box store culture.

As the son of the local lawyer who grew up just outside a town of fewer than 800 people, I had a firsthand glimpse of Main Street business behavior. Businesspeople were not perfect, but many had a very strong sense of personal integrity, and all of them had a keen understanding that their businesses were enmeshed with the well-being of the community and its citizens. The businesspeople were the town's activists, supporting local charities, leading community betterment efforts, and partnering with the government. Today, we hear a good deal of the newfangled "public–private partnerships." Such things have been alive and well in small towns for centuries.

I don't believe there was anything particularly unique about my hometown. The sign marked "Café" looks the same as it does most any place else, in a small town or in an urban neighborhood. Main Street looks about the same as any other Main Street. I doubt if the residents of my hometown were any more moral than people anywhere else. Central was the fact that the children of the local bank president were coached by the teller or a customer. The owner of the car dealership sat in the pew in church between a customer and a competitor. One's sense of right and wrong can change when one has personal contact, interaction, and relationship with the business's "stakeholder."

The key factor here is the personal nature of the business. Russ Davison's name was on the Ford dealership; Clarence Neff's was at the farm implement dealership, and Ivan Jacob's was at the hardware store. When business, name, and the very person are on the line, things like personal integrity matter a great deal. And with businesses often passing down from generation to generation, a long-term perspective is important. Incorporation doesn't necessarily change this. Many businesses in small towns are incorporated, but the "incorporated" doesn't stand in the way of the enmeshed identity with Russ, Clarence, or Ivan.

Large corporations, however, are another story. The larger the business, the harder it is to keep a core mission and identity that matters to all the people who work there. This can be true when there is a separation between family ownership and nonfamily workers; once there's a separation between ownership with distant stockholders and professional managers, the challenge becomes great. Many competing agendas tend to crowd out core missions of a company.

If a company stays private, it may be able to continue a historical identity and mission, especially if, when a company goes public, it announces its mission and credo. This explains the history of a company like Johnson & Johnson.[6] When it went public in the 1940s, it published its famous Corporate Credo, which prioritized those using its products, followed by its employees, suppliers, the community, and government.[7] After all of these were taken care of, the Credo states that shareholders will then receive a fair return on their investments. The company readily pulled Tylenol off the shelves after someone tampered with the product because of its commitment to this mission.[8]

The more a company becomes fully public, though, the more the common denominator of shareholder interests becomes return on investment only. Such companies also often feature thousands of employees, making it difficult for any one employee to believe that his or her actions make a difference. If actions don't have consequences, then the temptation not to act ethically increases, and employees are more likely to try to make sure they don't get caught doing something they shouldn't.

The corporate form is also less likely to be ethical because of its central feature: limited liability of investment. This invention spurred the risk taking that paved the road for the Industrial Revolution and the globalization that followed. It also increased employment and began the process of international communication, without which there would be scant opportunity for peaceful conflict resolution. Among other negatives, however, it also created an immediate ongoing moral hazard: divorcing liability from actions. Tort lawyers may try their best to pierce the corporate veil and make investors financially liable for their actions, but, on the whole, they've had little success.[9]

With all these factors, responsibility within companies tends to revolve around dutifully carrying out one's job description. As to the overall responsibilities of the company, those defy gravity and move upward to the C suite. But when shareholders ultimately decide who sits in the C suite, executives do not have the range of actions one might expect. Moreover, in a public company with thousands, even millions, of shareholders, responsibility further diffuses. The result is a conundrum where no one seems to be responsible for corporate actions.[10]

Yet corporate responsibility does have a payoff. Studies generally show that ethical business behavior (or corporate social performance) tends to correlate with increased profitability.[11] That is, on the whole, businesses usually do better financially if they are behaving ethically. Of course, one can make money illicitly and unethically too. Indeed, the authors of these studies conclude, the empirical evidence does not show that one must be ethical to be profitable. But, on the whole, it's a smart strategic move with a payoff. Moreover, the studies do show that one does not have to be a crook to be profitable.[12] In the end, there is enough of a correlation to be valid but not a strong enough one to mandate that ethics and business must go together.

But these studies focus on the long term. The reality of a liquid market—where an investor could buy and sell a position in a company a dozen times (or more) a day—is that executives are often evaluated on a very short-term basis. Even an executive who wants to manage for the long term may not get the chance if short-term performance is bad. Further, while accountants calculate values of things like reputation, such notions are notoriously difficult to quantify in the short term.[13]

Not only do short-term approaches undermine moral values, but some argue that not practicing moral values undermines trust in the market, which connects ethical conduct in the market and the integrity of the market itself. The market works when individuals believe that their property and contract interests can be protected from theft, breach, and other misappropriation of goods and services. The economic market, however, doesn't necessarily teach such virtues.[14]

Trust-building behavior will be essential for any successful business in the twenty-first century precisely because "the Internet changes everything."[15] In this way, my nostalgic meanderings about Main Street are both relevant and actionable for the twenty-first century. If Main Street values rely on a core awareness of connectedness and if the Internet and other modern communications capabilities can refashion reputation as an important business asset—which I believe it is already doing—then the Main Street versus Wall Street divide might be lessened. I don't believe that technology can do all the work, but it is central and plays into an understanding of how ethics, economics, trust, and peace hang together in a multisectoral matrix.

Gentle Commerce?

Does predatory, exploitative commerce produce gentle commerce? Do we care about conduct, or do we care solely about the bottom line? Investors and CEOs certainly do care about the bottom line, but what I am considering is whether, in that final analysis, employees, customers, communities and other stakeholders simply care about a bottom line or the way in which that bottom line was reached. As much as people complain about how Wal-Mart drives out small shopkeepers, people flock to the megastore because of the inexpensive prices and variety of products.

Of course we want higher salaries, cheaper products, and bigger 401K balances. But I also believe we are interested in the "gentleness" of commerce itself. Pinker, among others, champions commerce as a peace builder, but commerce can be conducted in different ways. Wouldn't we think that respectful conduct would more likely produce more peaceful results than would exploitative moneymaking? Respectful and fair commerce surely is more civilized and civilizing than culturally insensitive and corrupt business conduct. Business conduct can be made more civilized in the same way as Pinker and Elias described more generally. In their account, boorish, self-centered, childlike, indulgent behavior was overcome by a rational civilizing process governed by self-control and more oriented to long-term considerations. If we want to capture the full peace-building benefits of commerce, we need a similar civilizing process—one that integrates ethics and fairness with economics.

That's not to say that ethical business conduct is easy. Big businesses have (or can have) the moral maturity of a two-year-old because the market rewards them for acting like one.[16] The short-term liquid market with thousands of small-stake shareholders creates incentives for businesses to satisfy short-term desires and bully if necessary, with little regard for impact unless some authority stops them. There is little internal, rational, long-term process that evaluates choices. If only the behavior of businesses and economics could be reoriented in the same way that human behavior has been.

In the last ten years, some firms actively preyed on the poor with predatory lending practices, others sold investment vehicles while simultaneously not only selling them short but attempting to create that market downfall, and, all the while, both profitable and the not-so-profitable companies were paying large salaries to corporate executives.[17] This conduct raises challenges to the trustworthiness of the financial system and the actors within it.

In discussing these issues, business ethicists and economists share much with philosophers such as Adam Smith. At the core of Smith's writings was a moral understanding not only of free markets but of the behaviors necessary for free markets to flourish. Smith also believed that when individuals focused on their own self-interest, it created a market where everyone is better off. But what is the "self" whose interest is being promoted? Smith is no Buddhist; he doesn't see us all connected like a grove of aspen trees, but he does see human beings as part of a community in which there are obligations toward each other and toward the well-being of the community as a whole.

Most of Smith's work was about morality,[18] and his *Wealth of Nations* is best seen in the light of this body of ethical work. In Smith's work, economics rests on a foundation of moral sentiments and not the other way around.[19] If economics rests on a foundation of ethics, then good business must be good ethics. The two are not separate. If one can be ethical only after one is economically successful, then economics is foundational and ethics simply is after the fact: It becomes philanthropic, additional, rather than constitutive. Although the defining line between corporate social responsibility (CSR) and business ethics is arbitrary and slim, scholars who work in CSR tend to eschew philosophical or legal foundations for their work. For many of them, CSR traveled a path of being about corporate philanthropy, which is largely dependent on whether the stock market is doing well enough for corporations to pay attention to it. Consequently, CSR has endured many criticisms.[20]

Yet a strong strain of CSR literature has reclaimed a strategic perspective: CSR is not about philanthropy but about recognizing that being a responsible citizen tends to pay off, especially in the long term.[21] This is a stronger position to take, especially because empirical studies tend to confirm the assertion that corporate social performance either helps corporate financial performance or at least is a viable financial strategy to pursue. There remain those who would argue that if CSR is simply about strategy, then we don't need CSR at all; we just need more strategy.[22] That argument, of course, can be made by any academic discipline: We don't need anything else but our own, whether coming from economics, strategy, ethics, or whatever.

Rather than trying to determine which is foundational and which is secondary, the more fruitful path might be to recognize that different disciplines can provide supporting insights and frameworks that help each other. In that sense, ethics and economics can be mutually supportive allies. Further, they are particularly supportive allies when it comes to the creation of a business model that contributes positively to peace, precisely because their complementariness creates a commerce that integrates economics and ethics.[23]

F. A. Hayek, a key figure of the Austrian school of economics, which is much more dependent on a set of social institutions and supports that also emphasize notions of fairness, is no fan of CSR. But Hayek did see a rich relationship among ethics, trade, economics, and even religion and peace. Hayek argued that trade was based on relationships. It was simply more efficient for people to be able to trust each other than to expensively police all activity.

Trust, of course, depends on the practice of certain ethical virtues, such as promise keeping and production of high-quality goods and services, which enables economic exchange and trade to flourish. Indeed, trade provides a way for new relationships to develop, even internationally, so that Hayek argues that trade is key to global peace itself. That peace—and trade—however, relies on the practice of ethical virtues, what I have called the practice of gentle commerce.[24] Gentle commerce has a character to it; it is not just money making but is instead *a way in which money is made.* This sense of gentle commerce goes further than Pinker's notion—though I suspect Pinker would be supportive of the extension—and happily connects with a long-standing free-market school of thought that integrates ethics and economics.

Indeed, Hayek anticipated this step. Unlike a moral philosopher such as Smith, Hayek does not claim that there is anything intrinsically worthy about integrity-based virtues; they simply lubricate and underpin trade. Though I would be more aligned with Smith in terms of the intrinsic value of virtues, Hayek's instrumentally grounded valuing of these virtues provides a place to start for those who see no particular worth to moral values. Even with this limited instrumental orientation, however, Hayek, an agnostic, further claims that institutions that teach moral values of honesty and promise keeping are valuable because it is more efficient for people to learn and believe the value of ethics as independent goods.[25]

Thus, from Adam Smith one finds the intrinsic importance of moral values on which the edifice of economic exchange can be constructed. From Hayek, moral values may not be intrinsically important, but they are fundamental to the flourishing of economics, especially when people sincerely believe that ethics are intrinsically important. Clearly, ethics and economics are richly related, and they are most clearly related when we think of how, when joined, they lead to peace.

That we can find support from a long-standing school of economic thought is even more enhanced by the fact that contemporary economics increasingly argues for the importance of ethics to economics. Writing about developmental economics, David C. Rose argues that the neoclassical economic model worked well for many years, then petered out, as evidence accumulated that social institutions mattered in creating prosperous economies.[26] Yet as Rose points out, there are plenty of copies of the U.S. Constitution floating around in Argentina, but the template of that institutional model does not create a similar, operating constitutional republic there. What's missing are the morals, the tastes, and the aesthetics that underlie any given neoclassical or institutional model and which make it work or not.

Rose emphasizes the trust created by "moral restraint."[27] Any economic system relies, at some point, not just on rewards and punishments but also on values that restrain the opportunism often painted as an attribute of human nature. Much like Pinker, Rose is talking about a civilizing process that causes people—here economic actors—to restrain certain kinds of behavior and relies on social institutions to make some behaviors uncouth. Hayek might rely on religion and educational institutions here; Pinker might instead look to the arts (for example, satire and humor) or government.

This kind of use of ethics is deontological; that is, we have certain duties, either as laws or social customs that we should not violate. Though I tend not to be a deontological ethicist, I am a lawyer, and putting my lawyer's hat on, I do believe that there need to be prescribed duties—again, that can either be legally or customarily grounded—necessary for a flourishing society that leads to peace. Ethical business behavior fosters trust and can transform the financial sector into a peace accelerator.

The Peace Accelerator: Corporate Foreign Policy

In Steven Pinker's work, commerce is gentle because it trades, so to speak, on exchange rather than appropriation. Rather than invading, conquering, killing, and pillaging, commerce revolves around getting what you want and need by giving up something for it. Trade tends to offer a lot of advantages over bloody conquest and certainly poses fewer health risks.

In this way, commerce becomes a way for people to obtain what they want in a gentler fashion; economists agree that a certain level of moral integrity helps trade flourish. Moral virtues make trade more sustainable. Trade is gentler than bloody appropriation, and an ethically based approach is similarly gentler than an exploitative one. A civilizing process gave rise to a way of acting that, among other things, resolved conflict without war.

If commerce generates peace and if some degree of moral integrity enhances commerce, then a further integration of ethics into business should make commerce an even more potent peace-making force. The challenge is that nostalgic notions of business support this idea, but corporations have no souls. Although an individual may gain moral maturity through aging, education, and experience, a corporation has no such cognitive capability. Indeed, as creatures of the law to foster economic growth, corporations tend to have the moral maturity of two-year-olds; acquisitions are naturally desired and thwarted only by pressure from law, public opinion, or competition. Yet the potential of a capitalist peace hinges not just on markets but on their gentleness.

Just as the integration of ethics and economics happily coincides with Hayek, it also coincides with one of the giants of philosophy and ethics: Immanuel Kant. If Kant's ideas serve as a grounding philosophy for economic peace, remember that Kant, like Adam Smith, was a moral philosopher whose work on the political and the economic brought with it moral duties that held that people should be treated as ends rather than means to an end.[28] Kant's categorical imperative is categorical because it applies universally so that any stakeholder—defined as someone affected by a corporate action—must be taken into account in making business decisions.[29]

In *Perpetual Peace*, Kant relied on a three elements to create peace: constitutional (democratic) republics, economic interdependence, and a civil society of nations akin to a League of Nations or United Nations.[30] If businesses acted as poorly as many have in recent years, Kant would have a difficult time arguing that economic interdependence would foster peace. Indeed, Kant and others have argued quite carefully that not just any democracy but a constitutional republic with its own set of checks and balances to prevent excesses inherent with majority rule fosters peace. Democracy does mean that citizens have a voice in their government, but a republican version of democracy means that there are also checks against majority excesses such as the rights to speak freely or practice one's religion even when either runs against majoritarian sentiments.

Why would we think that the economic sector is different? Why would we believe that markets can be as fully free as they theoretically might be unless checked by government or public opinion? Without discounting the importance of such checks, the economic sector fits into Kant's *Perpetual Peace* best by having a set of internal restraints that check its excesses, including how individuals (and businesses) conduct themselves in economic markets.

Research further validates this point. Earlier, I reported studies that show that the most violent countries are the most prone to corruption and the least violent, the least corrupt.[31] The very term *corruption* implies a moral deficit, but, prose aside, bribery has been outlawed in every country and condemned by every religion,[32] strongly suggesting that there is something morally amiss with it. If one looks at other studies, one finds that lack of gender equity, human rights, robust educational standards, and democracy itself strongly correlates with violence, and the presence of those elements correlates with a lack of violence. Democracy also correlates with countries avoiding famine[33] and peace itself, whether associated with contemporary capitalism or not.[34]

There are mechanisms within economics that most closely correlate to peace. Trade, in particular, is the process most often noted as advantageous by economics and political scientists, but it's less important than economic development, financial markets, and monetary policy coordination, all of which carry with them normative dimensions.

What is important to see is that all of these things are of a piece but not so disparate to prevent strategic coordination and alliances. Constitutional republics, capitalist peace, transnational institutions—the pillars of Kant's *Perpetual Peace*—act as checks and balances on each other. But because they also function optimally with a strong foundation in moral sentiments and values, each sector would do well to attend more carefully to these normative principles and aspirations. In doing so, they will reinforce the peacemaking potential of each sector. As each sector interacts with other sectors, an optimal peace-building dynamic would ensue.

The economic side of that matrix dynamic has been at the heart of this chapter. To bring the moral dimension to life and make it more contributive to peace building requires ethical business behavior. The same behavior one might term "Main Street" also makes today's corporate conduct more trustworthy and may be, surprisingly, within our reach given arguments on how the Internet makes business reputation more crucial. Accepting this point of view is not easy, because the notion of an interdisciplinary, intersectoral matrix requires people (economists, political scientists, philosophers) to go beyond their normal focus or for actors (politicians, businesspeople, civil society advocates) to ally with those who otherwise may seem to be sectorally adversarial. But such work, integration, and alliances are crucial for peace building.

In his pre-Fed academic career, Ben Bernanke argued that policy initiatives encounter friction in the market; the perception and actions of individual bankers accelerate financial stress. Right credit reduces the value of collateral, further blocking issuance of credit. Bernanke argued that policy makers must factor in the concrete actions of institutions that ultimately distribute credit. Similarly, Federal Reserve monetary policy does not enact behavioral changes by fiat. A central bank may want to increase credit flow, but in a crisis lenders will demand more collateral to protect themselves exactly when collateral values are declining. This leads to tighter credit, which in turns tends to devalue collateral, and the downward spiral of lending and deflation continues. With trade policy (which includes central banks) that means real honest-to-goodness business people and businesses who trade heavily on trust and ethics and act in a virtuous cycle that enhances prosperity.

With this conceptual connection among ethics, economics, and peace in mind, Part II turns to case studies and specific instances that provide examples of the ways in which businesses can practice not just commerce, but gentle commerce, and contribute to peace. Part III will then further integrate Part I's conceptual focus and Part II's examples to propose a way forward and why it is smart business—smart corporate foreign policy—to contribute to peace.

PART II

Cases in Point

5 Peacemaking, Peacekeeping, and Peace Building

The environmental movement had not yet taken hold in the public consciousness when I was a young boy in the 1960s. There were, though, some initial efforts to sensitize the public about littering. In one famous commercial jingle, children sang, "Please, please don't be a litterbug, 'cause every litterbug hurts." At five or six, this struck me as compelling, so I complained when I saw people throw paper or gum out of the car, something that happened with an astonishing degree of regularity.

One day, two older friends eventually had enough of my complaining (and singing). They convinced our driver to stop the car then walked into a grassy area and firmly placed their used gum on the ground, defiantly saying, "See, it doesn't make any difference."

"Well, if everyone did it," I told them, "we'd have gum pollution." With this comment, I both annoyed them and anticipated an argument that continued in the environmental debate for decades.

In business and peace, it's easy to ask what difference certain efforts make. At times it can seem that the actions of any one business will be too small to have any measurable impact. In today's business and academic worlds, if one can't measure something, it doesn't count. Thus, a response to business and peace advocates tends to be that contributing to peace is akin to that piece of gum; even if businesses do contribute to peace, one can't quantify the difference any one company makes.

Yet we have already seen that there are good reasons economically for businesses to adopt ethical and even peace-related practices. An ethical approach to commerce often contributes socially and politically to a reduction of violence. By ethical, I mean being economically productive and thereby fulfilling shareholders' expectations; avoiding corruption; respecting contract and property rights and promoting fair dispute resolution; being a good corporate citizen; treating employees well, especially in terms of gender equity, voice, human rights, and empowerment; and placing them in teams small enough to see consequences of their actions. Measuring the impact, however, of any of these is akin to that one piece of chewed gum and pretty difficult. The harassment of female employees matters to peace as little as my little piece of gum to the environment. Except that it *does* matter, of course.

A 2011 report looked at how the private sector can have an impact on peace, distinguishing between peacemaking, peacekeeping, and peace building.[1] Businesses involved in *peacemaking* try to separate the warring parties and find ways for them to work out their disagreements. *Peacekeeping* revolves around maintaining truces among factions after a peace accord has been adopted. *Peace building* addresses the various social and economic causes that can give rise to grievances—or dampen them—and thereby create an atmosphere for disputes to be resolved in ways that avoid violence.

Neat dividing lines among these three contributions to peace are hard to maintain, yet these categories enable us to understand the choices a company faces in devising and implementing a foreign policy. Is its work to settle a dispute or to incrementally build a more stable system? The categories further allow us to group companies in a way so that we don't fall into the trap of thinking that only companies in zones of conflict deal with peace issues.

Most business contributions to peace tend not to overtly involve peacemaking or peacekeeping.[2] To have the opportunity to support peacemaking or peacekeeping efforts, a business needs to be in a zone of conflict. A company providing tours in Jerusalem so that tourists visit both Israeli and Palestinian-held areas surely is in a zone of conflict, and its business contributes to both peacekeeping and peacemaking. How about the tourist bus in Bloomington, Indiana? As far as I have been able to tell, there is no such impact on peacekeeping or peacemaking because Bloomington is not a zone of conflict (except, perhaps, when Purdue comes to town).

But just as the fumes released by the bus contribute to environmental issues, so too does an entire industry contribute to the products, ideas, services, practices, communications, and infrastructures of how tourism is conducted. Best practices spread. Best technologies spread. If tourism practices evolve so that tourists are able to obtain better information in a better experience—through better microphones on the bus, through introductory videos, through learning when people need to stop sitting on the bus and instead move through the geography—then billions of us contribute to peace building, though in an incremental way like that piece of gum you disposed of properly or that soda pop can you recycled last night.

Though my bigger concern is to shed light on the gum-picker-uppers that build peace, first I want to examine those companies that wade into the thick of conflict to promote peace and the organizations that support and recognize their work.

Peacemaking and Peacekeeping

Some NGOs focus a good deal of their attention on the ways in which businesses engage in peacemaking and peacekeeping. In 2006, International Alert detailed the ways in which businesses could play a significant role in conflict-ridden places.[3] The UN project on companies operating in conflict-prone areas also examines and guides businesses so that they may foster peace.[4]

INDIA–PAKISTAN

Perhaps the most often cited example of a business directly involved in preventing a dispute from becoming violent occurred in 1998. Pakistan had just tested its first nuclear device, sending shivers through the world's existing nuclear powers, especially Pakistan's longtime rival, India. The two countries engaged in increasingly acerbic verbal exchanges and began to mobilize armed forces.

As reported by the *New York Times*, executives from General Electric met with leaders from both countries and urged each country to tone down its rhetoric and find a solution. Further, the executives explained that an eruption of violence would significantly harm the economic vitality of each country and threatened to pull G.E. ventures out of the countries.[5]

This incident rose to prominence because of the exposure gained by *New York Times* coverage and the fact that the dispute involved nuclear weapons. Though the conflict between India and Pakistan has been

Table 5.1. Business Actions Promoting Peace in Selected Countries

COLOMBIA

- Business plays a high-profile role in the Pastrana administration's peace process with the armed group FARC
- The energy company Interconexión Eléctrica S.A. creates the Programa de Desarollo para la Paz, an initiative that tackles the root causes of conflict at the community level
- Compañía Envasadora del Atlántico, in collaboration with the UNDP, helps organize farmer associations that produce passion fruit for its export business, providing them with livelihood alternatives to coca plantation
- Allianzas Red works to involve the private sector in reintegration initiatives that offer training and employment opportunities to IDPs
- The national Federation of Chambers of Commerce initiative Empresas por la Paz combines conflict resolution training at the microlevel with business start-up support to participants

DEMOCRATIC REPUBLIC OF CONGO

- Local businesses in eastern Congo employ ex-combatants and cooperate with MONUC to strengthen stability at the community level and engage in policy dialogue at the national level

EL SALVADOR

- The business community actively participates in the peace process and negotiations, shaping the final agreement
- Business leaders are involved in the citizens' initiative Patriotic Movement Against Crime, advocating for and carrying out a weapons collection scheme

ISRAEL/PALESTINE

- Israeli fruit and vegetable export company Agrexco partners with five Gaza-based growers' associations to export their crops to European Union (EU) markets and sets up a separate brand to promote Palestinian produce
- Logistics zones at border crossings between Israel and Palestine are set up to overcome access problems and facilitate continued cross-border flow of merchandise and economic cooperation between businesses

long-standing, the nuclear standoff represented a discrete issue where one can see how a specific company—G.E.—had a direct impact, showing leaders of both countries why they would benefit from standing down in a specific situation.

There are of course countless other examples in which businesses played a significant role in creating or maintaining peace. Table 5.1, drawn from *Local Business, Local Peace*, summarizes the multitude of ways businesses worked to dampen conflict situations. The contributions range widely, from harmonization of banking regulations to maintaining funds for un-

Table 5.1. Business Actions Promoting Peace in Selected Countries (*continued*)

ISRAEL/PALESTINE (CONTINUED)

- Pre-Intifada plans for cooperation in the information technology (IT) sector resurface in the aftermath of Israeli withdrawal from the Gaza Strip and hold the potential for future joint ventures
- Tourism is harnessed to promote greater cooperation between Palestinian and Israeli tour operators to maximize mutual benefit from tourism to the region
- The Alternative Tourism Group promotes "justice tourism" to ensure that Palestinian communities benefit from tourism to the region, at the same time educating visitors about the political and conflict context
- The Peres Center for Peace and the Center for Jewish-Arab Economic Development fosters business linkages through various initiatives reaching out to Israeli and Arab business communities

NORTHERN IRELAND

- The Confederation of British Industry (CBI) engages in advocacy and support to the peace process, emphasizing the benefits of a "peace dividend"
- Together with other business associations, CBI establishes the Group of Seven, which urges a settlement to the conflict through public campaigns and media statements at critical junctures during the peace process, as well as direct engagement with all parties to the conflict

SOUTH AFRICA

- The Consultative Business Movement (CBM) combines efforts with others to consult with the different parties to the conflict to facilitate an inclusive peace process; it subsequently gets invited to provide secretariat and administrative functions for the Convention for a Democratic South Africa process that brings about a new constitution
- After the first elections, CBM and the Urban Foundation form the National Business Initiative to channel business support and work in partnership with government to tackle systemic problems hampering social and economic development
- Business leaders set up Business Against Crime, a nonprofit organization to partner with the government to tackle threats to security
- A separate business trust is set up to deal with the problem of unemployment, in particular focusing on job creation in the tourism industry

---

employment to actively participating in the peace process. From reading this overview of cases it would appear that businesses can contribute to peace in a number of ways, limited only by their own imagination.

To get to the heart of the reasons for which businesses might engage in peacemaking and peacekeeping, let's examine a few less publicized cases.

EL SALVADOR

The way in which business partnered with the government of El Salvador to settle disputes stands as an example of Gartzke's theory that the changing assets deployed in commerce make a difference in the opportunities for businesses to contribute to peace. Although wealth in El Salvador had traditionally stemmed from real estate holdings, the growth of trade and finance encouraged companies to cultivate relationships with other nations such as the United States and the EU, which demanded resolution of the disputes.

El Salvador had been under military rule since 1931, a rule that often was charged with torture and murder as well as rigged elections to retain power. Violence convulsed the country from 1980 to 1992, and it suffered from poverty as well as stark differences in wealth. The resentment against the military reached a flash point when Archbishop Monsignor Oscar Romeo gave a homily in which he appealed to soldiers to refuse orders to torture or murder.

The next day, while celebrating mass, Romero was assassinated. The military was later found responsible, and at Romero's funeral a few days later, the military attacked a crowd estimated to be as large as 250,000. Forty people were trampled to death in the panic. From that point, formal opposition formed against the military and continued for the next twelve years. During that time, there were numerous reports of people "disappearing"; according to the United Nations, 75,000 people died from the violence.

Although businesses initially refrained from participating in peacebuilding efforts due to their opposition to the redistribution policies of President Jose Napoleon Duarte, by the end of the 1980s businesses became increasingly interested in stopping the violence.[6] Two kinds of business efforts—one structural and the other overt—affected the quest for peace during these years.

New forms of business changed the structure of the Salvadoran economy, transforming wealth that had been built mainly from land holdings to a wealth that included large components of trade and finance. At the same time, global economic opportunities and development offered ties to trade, financial services, and agribusiness.[7] Emerging out of this structural change were new business leaders such as Alfredo Cristiani, who later became the leader of the probusiness Alianza Republicana Nacional, which won the presidency in 1989. Cristiani and his allies recognized that conflict cost the country—and its new businesses—money; in fact, more than $1 billion, with tremendous loss of infrastructure and investment. In addition, those in the business community were also the target of kidnapping and extortion, which further encouraged businesses to become involved in a peace process.[8]

The business community supported Cristiani's efforts to resolve the conflict, which included dialogue with the primary opposition group, and in return the community was included in the decision-making process and obtained physical protection. In addition, the tides of lost foreign investment, capital flight, and destruction of infrastructure were all stemmed. This created a strong business–government partnership, though it did not create strong policies for reform, especially with respect to labor unions.[9] It did, however, produce both stability and economic growth.

Is El Salvador an example of gentle commerce? Somewhat. To be sure, stamping out violence and combating kidnapping and extortion should be commended. Doing so through negotiations rather than violence counts as an ethical good, too. By creating greater stability, commerce flourished, with an increase in jobs, development, and growth, all important ways businesses can contribute to peace. That the governmental agreements did not include labor, however, raises questions as to whether stability was balanced on the backs of El Salvador's workers. Nor is there evidence of attention to other valuable contributions such as gender equity, corporate citizenship, or environmental sustainability.

Business and government did cooperate to make and keep peace, which is worth celebrating, but while it qualifies as commerce, it does not qualify as gentle commerce. A higher standard that would further build peace, even though such contributions may feel like gum-in-the-grass, would be even more commendable.

To be clear, I am not suggesting that the El Salvadoran example should be criticized. In creating peace, one rarely will be able to secure stability perfectly. That is true with El Salvador's example of peacemaking and peacekeeping. Yet just as Pinker and Fry have pointed to the need to continue to make progress—even if we are more peaceful now than what we have been historically—it is important to recognize a positive event while holding out the possibility for even better resolutions.

COLOMBIA

Colombia has long struggled with the impact of its involvement in the drug trade. In particular, the Revolutionary Armed Forces of Colombia ("FARC," after the Spanish acronym Fuerzas Armadas Revolucionarias de Colombia), had established a powerful and disruptive presence in the country since at least 1964. They attacked energy-related structures, kidnapped hostages and held them for ransom, and of course participated in the illegal drug trade, which has been widely blamed for the persistence and deadliness of the conflict.[10]

A constitutional democracy for most of the twentieth century that has not had a war with a neighboring country since 1932, Colombia lacks both significant ethnic animosity within the country and toward its neighbors, as well as extreme poverty. Yet building resentment against an informal agreement between the two leading parties led guerilla groups such as FARC (Fuerzas Armadas Revolucianaries de Colombia) and ELN (Ejercito de Liberacion Nacional) to campaign for a socialist system of government that would address increasing economic inequality.[11]

In the 1980s, FARC began to tax, and ultimately control, the coca used to make cocaine. FARC grew this "business" from 40,000 hectares in 1990 to 169,800 in 2001, when it controlled 76 percent of the world coca market. This provided the funds to equip paramilitary organizations that further disrupted the Colombian political and economic system through kidnappings, extortion, and other attacks. FARC forces increased from a few thousand fighters in the early 1980s to as many as 18,000 a decade later, a number that continued to hold through 2002;[12] FLN and others grew to similar numbers.[13]

Until the late 1990s, the private sector stayed out of the conflict, as it was centered in rural areas and didn't affect most businesses. Business leaders also believed that issues of war and peace were the province of government and not the private sector, which felt it bore little responsibility for issues of peace and justice.[14] The government estimated that, between 2000 and 2005, the country suffered $6 billion in lost revenue, damage to infrastructure, and spending on the conflict itself. Unemployment reached 20 percent, and internal displacement of Colombians who had lost their homes or whose homes had become central to the fighting reached nearly 280,000 people per year.

Resolving the conflict took years. A turning point occurred two days after the inauguration of Ernesto Samper in 1994. Audiotapes revealed that he had accepted $6 million in contributions from the Cali drug mafia. The negative fallout from this revelation raised the stakes for Colombian businesses.[15] The Colombia Business Council, described as a "semiformal union of the fifteen most important business associations," proposed that Samper resign after his campaign manager admitted the allegations were true.[16] When Samper refused, traditional business associations continued to oppose him, but some, known as *grupos*, faced a more delicate balancing act.[17]

Grupos were networks of independent firms held together through mutual shareholding or family ownership under a common group name. The most prominent four groups owned one-fourth of the largest 100 (public and private) companies in Colombia, six of the ten largest private companies, and 12.5 percent of Colombia's GDP.[18] These four organizations controlled 21 percent of the financial sector, 33 percent of the sugar-refining sector, 50 percent of the soft drink industry, a near monopoly on the beer industry, and large holdings in insurance, cement, and food.[19] The companies grew to their position through credit subsidized by the government, which brought with it regulatory oversight.[20]

Thus, opposing the government posed serious risk to these influential businesses and effectively undermined any chance of a monolithic business position that might result from members of the business sector joining forces. Contributions to the campaigns of potential leaders were considered good business investments.[21] At the same time, *grupos* maintained strong relations with the Samper government and with business associations that opposed him but were favored by the United States, because negative action by the United States would harm them.[22] At the same time, they established contacts with the FLN to find a way to reach a settlement to the conflict.[23] Just like a government tiptoeing through a diplomatic minefield, the *grupos* engaged in a corporate foreign policy that attempted to gain favor with both sides while protecting their own interests.

Such corporate efforts protected the interest of each of the *grupos* but made it difficult for the business sector to present a unified front. As opposed to a check and balance of business against government, the business–political dynamic was one of dozens of moving and influencing institutions. Indeed, the Colombia situation provides a microcosm of what we see on the world stage. Google, Shell, and Marriott will not content themselves to have their interests articulated by the International Chamber of Commerce or Rotary International; the businesses act as independent institutions, powerful in their own right, rather than through association with the business community per se.

Once Samper left office, his successor Andres Pastrano named a commission to spearhead outreach to FARC; business was heavily represented on the government's negotiating team, including the president of one of the largest firms in the financial sector as well as one of the largest *grupos* in Colombia. A cattlemen's association offered to donate land and financing as a way to achieve demobilization, another group of business leaders formed a think tank to assist with building support for negotiations and to raise awareness of entrepreneurial responsibility for the common good, and several business initiatives for peace were proposed.[24]

Though these efforts did not result in an immediate settlement, businesses continued to participate in peace-related efforts after 2000, with philanthropic programs that addressed issues of poverty, inequality, human rights, social exclusion, democracy, and unemployment.[25] The private sector has also participated in peace and development programs and searched for crop substitution. Group Empresarial Antioqueno has helped structure institutions that reintegrate former combatants while corporate-funded foundations have supported the work of local authorities and NGOs in fostering peace.[26]

Recognition of the costs associated with conflicts, the increased engagement of international donors in the country, and a growing awareness and acceptance of corporate social responsibility norms help to explain why businesses would be willing to engage in peacemaking and peacekeeping in Colombia. The influence of progressive multinationals, NGO advocacy, and the UN Global Compact are also essential factors.[27]

Does the Colombia example represent gentle commerce? Again, somewhat. As in El Salvador, violence was stopped via negotiations, with business leaders taking a prominent role in peacemaking and peacekeeping. There were good business reasons for companies to take a strong role. Little is known of the conduct of any of the businesses, though, so it's unclear how various corporate stakeholders were treated. And because FARC grew out of perceived voicelessness and alienation, one wonders if the seeds of resentment will sprout again if powerful Colombians dominate society once more.

History will reveal the results, but, apart from what is hoped to be a positive story, the Colombian example further demonstrates that, more and more, business is not monolithic because individual businesses are powerful in their own right and can triangulate their foreign policies apart from traditional business associations. Individual businesses matter.

If they do stand out, their conduct is more visible, and they can no longer be lumped together in an amorphous monolithic business community. If that is true—if one can hold Grupo X accountable for its actions as opposed to "Colombia businesses"—then it will be easier to assess just how gentle any given business's commerce is.

Indeed, it's difficult when scholars are unable to clearly see the ethical actions of a particular business. In the past, we have simply thought of businesses as monolithic and not individually accountable. But through technology, public records, and other information, we can make businesses accountable for their actions in ways impossible centuries or even decades ago. As a result, they are more likely to contribute to peace.

NORTHERN IRELAND

"You can't keep a business going when rocks are flying," the host of a home I visited in Northern Ireland in 1978 told me. "People don't want to come here, and the smart ones want to leave," he continued, saying Catholics and Protestants could and needed to work together, which I took as a general statement of cooperation. "Everyone would be better off economically if that would happen."

In 1994, *The Peace Dividend Paper* echoed the comments of my host. *The Paper* also claimed that if the violence ended, Northern Ireland would capture a $1.42 billion savings. Indeed, once the fighting ceased in 1998 (with some sporadic violence thereafter), Northern Ireland's unemployment rate dropped and its tourism increased, as did other investments.[28]

The Troubles, however, did not go away easily. Cease-fires temporarily stopped altercations, but those truces did not last long. Local voices calling for peace were missing. The government was locked in its own disputes with Northern Ireland Protestants, a minority in the country that desperately wanted to stay under the sovereign leadership of the United Kingdom, and with Catholics, whose affinity leaned toward Ireland. On occasion, such as in El Salvador, the Church might be a voice for peace, but religion itself was the focal point of the violence in Northern Ireland. Outside countries, such as the United States and much of the British Commonwealth, called for the disputants to settle their differences, but inside voices were lacking. What institutions, then, could call for negotiations, reason, and a way forward? Business became one important voice at that moment.

In 1996, the Northern Ireland Confederation of British Industry (CBI) joined with six other trade and business groups to create the Group of Seven (GoS) that championed the need for peace and outlined the cost of violence on the entire country. The GoS convened meetings with all nine political parties to argue that violence must stop and that a peace dividend would ensue if it did. In 1998, the GoS intervened in the Dumcree Standoff and later, when bombings resumed, condemned the violence and called on its members to observe a moment of silence. The GoS continued statements in support of peacemaking all the way through the establishment of a new government—transferring power from London to Belfast—in 1999 and cautioning of some of the persistent discriminatory factors embedded in the Troubles.[29]

Northern Ireland's businesses had an impact on the peace process very differently than had businesses in El Salvador and Colombia. Much as Pope John Paul II peacefully challenged Soviet leadership in the late 1980s, businesses of Northern Ireland acted as honest brokers to try to mend the conflict. That role provided them with a moral stature that had an even stronger impact when they spoke out against violence and in support of the need for social and political changes. The pope was not equipped with weapons, but he did have the moral authority to embolden his fellow Poles, then others. This helped to bring down the Soviet empire. The unified voices of the businesses of Northern Ireland, just a few short years later, were similarly crucial in sounding the message of peace. Voices matter; in Northern Ireland, the voice of business articulating the need for peace helped achieve it.

SOUTH AFRICA

Two issues of corporate responsibility predominated campus talk when I was a student at the University of Notre Dame in the late 1970s: a boycott of Nestle for its promotion of infant formula in developing nations and calls for corporate divestment in South Africa because of apartheid. Reverend Leon Sullivan, who served on the board of directors of General Motors, demanded that businesses that chose to stay in South Africa work to uphold ethical standards, including those of inclusion and equality. The Sullivan Principles, promulgated in 1977, became a statement of corporate responsibility conduct committed to equal treatment of racial groups, promotion of blacks in leadership capacities, and nonsegregation. Eventually 125 companies endorsed the principles.[30]

Debate has long ensued as to how effective the Sullivan Principles were; even Sullivan stated that they did not go far enough. But they became an introit into a larger role of business as apartheid ended and free elections were held. Business leaders quietly built relationships with existing political parties so that, by the late 1980s, the business leaders were in a position to take concrete actions, some of which were peacemaking, but also examples of peacekeeping, given their duration and presence in ongoing power transfer.

In 1988, The Consultative Business Movement (CBM) was formed, and, together with the South African Council of Churches, the CBM was able to break the political impasse between F. W. de Klerk and Nelson Mandela that had been preventing the creation of an inclusive peace process.[31] In 1992, the CBM helped secure international mediation, which led to an agreement that enabled the first democratic elections in the country. A year later, the CBM created the Business Election Fund, which championed free and fair elections in a nonpartisan way and also supported a voter-education program in rural areas.[32]

The CBM's work continued as South Africa found its way toward a new political regime. In 1995, CBM partnered with the Urban Foundation to form the National Business Initiative (NBI), which was committed to a democratically led reconstruction and development effort.[33] The organization Business Against Crime (BAC) formed in 1996 and consulted with Nelson Mandela to work with the government to combat crime, taking a major lead in creating and managing the technological infrastructure for crime fighting. In the same year, the South African Department of Housing partnered with NBI to improve the management systems relating to housing availability, increasing subsidies to first-time homeowners fivefold by 1999. The NBI also helped to mobilize support for education and training of South Africans to meet the needs of businesses.[34]

Businesses engage in peacemaking and peacekeeping because of commitments to society as a whole, or because conflict-ridden areas provide poor prospects for business. Violence disrupts business. Talented people leave to work elsewhere. Investment dries up, relocating to places where it is more secure. The costs of conflict lock up resources that could be used for further investment, education, and growth. These are but a few reasons why business would actively engage in peacemaking and peacekeeping in South Africa and elsewhere.

Indeed, in each of these preceding examples, countries faced an immediate need to end violence. Businesses took several roles to achieve this. In El Salvador, new business associations enabled a new president to step outside of traditional battles and, with business allies, find negotiated settlements. Similar negotiated settlements occurred in Colombia, which highlights the nuanced diplomatic role that businesses play in protecting their own interests as separate institutions. Both cases show a peaceful dimension of commerce, but then in Northern Ireland and in South Africa businesses did not simply join in peacemaking to end violence and achieve stability. They began making moral arguments as to the benefits of peace and used their own stature to achieve it. In integrating moral objectives, they began the creation of gentle commerce that has more to it than economics; it also has the ethical dimension that, as we saw in Chapter 4, tends to ground efficacious economics itself.

Ethical economics, though, is gum-in-the-grass. It doesn't stick its head up in the midst of bullets to demand peace. It is based on longer-term considerations that extend beyond peacemaking and peacekeeping and might be better categorized as peace building. For example, in South Africa, recognizing the potential of the tourism industry, a group of business leaders partnered in 1998 to create a $156.7 million fund to create the "Business Trust" that focused on employment opportunities within the tourism industry.[35] Does something like this make peace? No. Does it keep the peace? A bit. But what it really does is to incrementally create the conditions so that peace is the norm. It is gum-in-the-grass peace building.

Peace Building

The U.S. Secretary of State Award for Corporate Excellence (ACE), established by the State Department in 1999, recognizes the important role U.S. businesses play abroad as good corporate citizens.[36] The award sends a strong signal of the department's commitment to further corporate social responsibility, innovation, exemplary practices, and democratic values worldwide and helps define America as a positive force in the world. It highlights our increasing outreach to the business community, our public–private partnerships, and our public diplomacy efforts.

The ACE also recognizes the contributions business makes to improving lives at home and abroad. One would be hard pressed, though, to argue that any of these award winners' actions were crucial to making peace in the country where they are doing business. Each business makes an incremental contribution to a better society in ways very consistent with the model Schipani and I sketched that emphasized economic development, following rule of law practices (especially with respect to avoiding corruption), being a good corporate citizen, and creating an ethical business organization.

Past winners include both multinational and small- to medium-size enterprises and include Cisco Systems, Mars, Motorola, and Procter & Gamble, which I will focus on either because they have won ACE recognition multiple times or because their work has been recognized by other organizations as well. The full list (located in the appendix) is useful to see the range of companies and industries that have received awards. The range of peacemakers and peacekeepers will almost always be more limited. A company needs to be in a zone of conflict to have much of a chance to have an impact on peacemaking and peacekeeping. Anyone, though, can be a peace builder.

CISCO SYSTEMS

In 2013, *Forbes* profiled the work of Cisco Systems in Palestine, where Cisco is incubating a relationship between Israeli Jews and Palestinian Arabs to boost the tech industry. Cisco, along with Intel, has trained Palestinians to create businesses in the tech world under the tutelage of Jewish trainers. The Palestinian groups, called *tamkeen* (which translates as empowerment or enablement), meet with Cisco subcontractors under the name PosiTeam. As of July 2013, the PosiTeam, comprised of Israeli Jewish instructors, had conducted over 100 training sessions for seventy Palestinians from twenty-four different companies. In five years of the Cisco project and others like it, the contribution of the tech sector to Palestine's GDP has grown from 1 to over 6 percent.[37]

The investment came as a result of a meeting between Cisco CEO John Chambers and Palestinian President Mahmoud Abbas in which Chambers promised $10 million to help develop Palestine's tech sector. Businesspeople in that sector were more interested in learning skills that would allow the sector to grow than in philanthropic contributions.[38] The initiative grows out of Cisco's previous engagement in the area. Indeed, for its work, Cisco won a U.S Secretary of State Award for Corporate

Excellence in 2010, which recognized Cisco's investments, including an engineering project collaboration between Cisco Israel and Palestinian software development companies as well as other venture capital investments in small businesses and training programs. This demonstrates Cisco's work in commerce, work that will build peace. But the company engages in gentle commerce, too. The company's CSR commitment in Israel focuses on supporting women and youth in underserved communities and integrating minorities into Israeli society.[39]

In addition to project collaboration and supporting women and youth, Cisco's attention to legal issues also promotes peace. In Schipani's and my framework, rule of law is crucial; companies obeying just laws help to create peaceful societies. That is true whether it is by respecting property and contract rights; supporting peaceful dispute resolution institutions, such as courts, arbitration, and mediation; or avoiding corruption and being transparent about activities. Societies with these attributes tend to be more peaceful. As actors in such societies—and often powerful actors at that—businesses that follow these practices strengthen the same peaceful attributes of the society, further reinforcing their peaceful stability.

A small provision in the 2010 Dodd–Frank legislation required that companies extracting certain minerals used in many high-tech products such as smartphones disclose their sourcing. The law was aimed at the mining activities in the Democratic Republic of Congo and surrounding countries and went into effect in 2014, when Cisco announced that it would comply with the law through its work through the Electronic Industry Citizenship Coalition and Global e-Sustainability Initiative. In addition, Cisco stated that it would work to assure that not only would it disclose any sourcing of materials in the Congo and adjacent regions but it would also disclose sourcing in areas free of conflict.[40]

This kind of certification program became increasingly popular after the establishment of the 2003 Kimberley Protocol, an attempt to address the issue of "blood diamonds," or diamonds that originate in conflict-sensitive areas. Warlords often control the areas and mines where diamonds are located and force children as young as six years old to fight with semiautomatic weapons. If they refuse, limbs are amputated. Outrage over this revelation placed pressure on companies such as Tiffany & Company and DeBeers to assure their customers that their jewelry did not stem from such atrocities.

As a result, an international agreement was reached that provided for sourcing transparency in the diamond industry to allow for conflict-free certification that companies could then tout with their customers. Results of the Kimberley Protocol have been mixed. Some NGOs, such as Global Witness, have withdrawn support because of continued human rights violations and child abuse in countries such as Zimbabwe and the Ivory Coast.[41] The idea behind the model has, however, endured in efforts to create partnerships that would trace supply chains to pinpoint and root out human rights abuses. The Dodd–Frank Conflict Minerals Law is one such law meant to achieve those goals. Many other voluntary mechanisms exist as well.

Cisco might have some impact on peacemaking and peacekeeping in the Middle East, but, at least to date, it is a hard claim to sustain. Its work is more incremental and, even though it was featured in *Forbes*, less flashy. Cisco's intent is not to get public attention or to threaten boycotts of companies that don't comply with principles. It is not involved in measures to help the government combat kidnapping of Cisco's executives, which occurred in Colombia. It is slow, step-by-step empowerment and training, incremental good citizenship, and following legal processes directly aimed at stamping out human rights violation. It is peace building. It is gentle commerce. It's getting gum out of the grass.

MARS

Cocoa farmers face many risks in their work such as marginal production, unsustainable production practices, and low prices. They grow cocoa in countries (such as the Ivory Coast and Ghana) with unpredictable social and economic infrastructures; they have little access to quality education; hazardous labor conditions for children and adults alike; limited water and sanitation; poor nutrition as well as HIV/AIDS, tuberculosis, and malaria challenges; and lack of other crop options. Mars partnered with several groups to create the "Mars Partnership for Africa Cocoa-Communities of Tomorrow ("iMPACT").[42]

The project was aimed at the Ivory Coast, which holds 40 percent of the world cocoa product, and Ghana, which holds another 23 percent. The three-year goal of the project is to "contribute to the development of cocoa farming in West Africa as a profitable, socially rewarding, and environmentally sustainable livelihood for families."[43] More specifically, this public-private partnership seeks to:

- Empower local communities to understand the various developmental needs of its members
- Set up "farmer field schools" to better agricultural practices
- Build the capacity of intermediary organizations in professionalizing their services to farmer
- Strengthen farmers' skills to diversify their crops
- Improve the communities' financial management skills
- Support the communities to adopt sustainable land management practices
- Implement literacy programs and improve schools
- Sensitize the communities to health issues and prevention
- Support the communities to identify and eliminate abusive labor practices, especially those involving children[44]

For this work, especially with respect to Ghana, Mars received an ACE Award in 2010. To enforce these initiatives and set an example for the industry, Mars committed to certifying its entire cocoa supply.[45]

As with Cisco, it is possible that some of these aims might help establish peace and keep it, particularly if a farmer decided to turn the proverbial sword into a plowshare. If true, the same practices might also help keep the farmer in the field and out of a military unit. But literacy training and sensitizing the community to preventative health issues is more of a long-term incremental attempt to build a community in which citizens have a vested interest in stability as well as in how they are treated, protected, and empowered. This is gentle commerce and peace building along the lines of the long-term incremental civilizing process Pinker champions in making the world as a whole more peaceful.

MOTOROLA

Motorola has twice won the ACE Award. In 2000, the company won the award for its work in Malaysia, where it helped develop that country's technology industry through $1 billion worth of investment, using local Malay businesses as suppliers and providing managerial training for running effective businesses. Motorola transferred managerial as well as technological know-how, which spilled over as knowledge into Malaysia.[46]

This example is one that Schipani and I relied on in creating our four contributions business can make to peace. Like that of Cisco and Mars, Motorola's work is incremental peace building. Recall from Chapter 1 that one of the best predictors for a civil war is when a country's main export product is an undifferentiated commodity such as oil, timber, diamonds, or coal. By bringing $1 billion worth of technology along with requiring suppliers to adopt state-of-the-art management practices, Motorola automatically differentiates the economy. This step itself is peace building.

Better management practices certainly are not going to stop a war, but they can build a more vibrant economy that is less prone to violence by being differentiated. Motorola's economic model is not extracting a mineral but making it into a consumer device. Indeed, what Motorola contributes is exactly what Gartzke traces, moving a country from land-based wealth to a free market based on innovation, intellectual property, and trade.

Motorola has long been one of the leaders not only in ethical business practices worker training but in training academic business ethicists themselves, taking a very strong public stand on the importance of ethical conduct. To encourage the understanding and teaching of business ethics, Motorola has hosted many ethicists at the Motorola Academy to learn how companies can inculcate ethics into corporate culture. Without deifying the company—it makes its mistakes and is no longer independently owned—its work in Malaysia followed the ethical business practices that are the essence of gentle commerce.

In 2004, Motorola won the award for its work in Brazil, where it partnered with local agencies to strengthen public safety programs, increase environmental protection, heighten industrial research and development, promote youth and early childhood development, and generate greater employment in both Brazil and the United States.[47] Motorola worked with Brazilian police chiefs, providing them and other citizens with vehicles and radios to fight crime. The company invested more than $230 million in an industrial and technological campus in Sao Paolo, creating jobs for more than 4,000 Brazilians.[48]

Here again, Motorola's work extends beyond basic business. It is a company engaged in building good communities, supporting children, and reinforcing law enforcement. The efforts are similar to the company's work in Malaysia and peace building more than peacekeeping or peacemaking.

PROCTOR & GAMBLE

In 2012, Proctor & Gamble became the first company to win an ACE Award for its work in two countries in one year. In 2010, extensive flooding hit Pakistan. P&G partnered with other organizations in the country and provided clean drinking water, food, medicine, clothes, and hygiene products to 1.9 million people. It also worked with local human resources offices to support orphanages and schools as well as collaborate around sustainability practices. The company has been in Pakistan for twenty years and had sponsored CSR programs such as Pampers mobile clinics, educational programs, and assisting with the delivery of more than 500 million liters of clean drinking water. The company's employees volunteer in various community programs as well.

In Nigeria, P&G supported children in need through P&G Live, Learn and Thrive, which includes branded initiatives such as the Always Hygiene and Puberty Education Program that reaches 700,000 girls every year. It also started a Pampers hospital program and mobile clinics that touch the lives of 1.5 million mothers and babies annually, as well as the Pampers-UNICEF program that has provided 7.5 million tetanus vaccines to mothers and their babies.[49]

P&G's actions are yet more examples of this section's themes. P&G is a big company; when it invests overseas, it brings economic development, jobs, and other monetary benefits with it. That's commerce. But P&G's commerce is not one of colonialism or exploitation. It's a commerce heavy with CSR efforts. Like Motorola, P&G has a long tradition of being recognized as a highly ethical company and knows that its brand is associated with more than just its products, so its foreign policy emphasizes values as well as profit. This is the true meaning of gentle commerce.

Buying diapers has never been noted as a factor in stopping a war or preventing one from kicking back up. Yet this incremental long-term community-building and business-building effort is important for P&G and for peace. If you were to zone in on any one of P&G's efforts, it would be gum-in-the-grass. Yet major companies today know that gum matters, and it matters to peace.

To be clear, I celebrate peacemaking and peacekeeping. Companies that make these contributions do so in zones of conflict; wading into those conflicts calls for courage and conviction. Actions documented in this chapter from El Salvador, Colombia, Northern Ireland, South Africa, and elsewhere have saved lives and made societies safer and more prosperous. NGOs that focus on this work also do a good service by showing how such businesses have helped foster peace. Thus, it is worth celebrating the work of the United Nations, International Alert, and others that shine their civil society light on these constructive corporate actions.

My interest, however, lies more in peace building and those incremental, gum-in-the-grass actions that are akin to Pinker's and Elias's civilizing improvements that change the cultures of businesses and countries. We have seen the actions of Motorola, P&G, Cisco, and others recognized, though it is difficult to know precisely how much impact a company's action has had on peace building. Yet these incremental contributions add up and may be more sweeping than wading into a zone of conflict. Thus, without minimizing the importance of peacemaking and peacekeeping, I want to focus more on peace building, especially in the next chapter, where I will look at three ways in which companies might incrementally build peace.

6 Peace Entrepreneurs, Instrumental Corporate Foreign Policy, and Unconscious Peace Building

"I'm just coming to work every day, doing the best I can to make a buck. I'm now responsible for world peace too? I don't think so."

That was the pinnacle of a conversation I had with a high-ranking executive at General Motors shortly after the turn of the millennium. I had been writing about business's impact on peace for a few years and was beginning to introduce it into the corporate environment. My conversation partner's reaction may have been an offhand remark over a cup of coffee, but it represents something much deeper.

Why should a person—or a company—concern him- or herself with anything to do with peace? Sure, the reasons presented in the previous chapter all make sense, but they are very macro oriented. Business and peace seems too pie-in-the-sky and far too grandiose for any given person who goes to work. Those of us who advocate for business to contribute to peace need to be clear as to what motivates a person or company to make such a contribution. In this chapter, I propose three reasons.

It should not be surprising that there are different reasons. People go into business itself for different reasons. John Mackey, the founder and CEO of Whole Foods, claims that he has never met an entrepreneur who went into business solely to make money. There was always some "other" reason, perhaps to show the entrepreneur's parents that she could be just as successful in business as a sibling. Perhaps the entrepreneur was a difficult person and couldn't work with supervisors, so he solved the problem by becoming his own boss. Perhaps it was something more profound, such as wanting to achieve a social good in conjunction with the business.[1] Although some attention has recently been given to new laws in the United States that more clearly allow for such social entrepreneurial businesses,[2] the corporate structure has always been open to the pursuit of noneconomic as well as economic goals, as long as the shareholders condoned the activity.

One reason, then, that people might seek peace as part of their business is because they have a deep motivation to do so. They simply use the business form as a way to achieve both social and business goals. These are *peace entrepreneurs*, exactly the term used in the International Alert report. As with those businesses that seek to achieve quality or sustainability as well as profits, these entrepreneurs may have a challenging landscape with which to deal, but they also may set new standards, expectations, and models for what becomes mainstream business.

A second reason businesspeople or companies might seek peace is as an instrumental benefit to their company's self-interest, what I have been calling their corporate foreign policy. When businesses see themselves as entities with identities separate from nation-states, their interactions with the rest of the world are akin to a country conducting foreign policy. These individuals and entities may hold altruistic aspirations, just as countries may seek to protect democracy and human rights, and they tend to draw the most attention from researchers looking for motivations and explanations for corporate involvement, especially in conflict-sensitive environments.

Finally, if ethical business behavior contributes to a milieu of peace exactly because it supports and/or replicates the attributes of nonviolent societies, then companies may also contribute to peace without any conscious ambition or calculation. That is particularly true of companies engaged in peace building rather than peacemaking or peacekeeping. Peace building companies may not have a goal of peace in mind at all; they may be more interested in avoiding bribery or respecting the rights of women, for instance, simply because they believe that both ethical commitments are valuable in their own right. In doing so, however, they *are* contributing to peace.

This chapter sets out these three motivations for contributing to peace. In the final section, I provide a bridge between the motivational factors and the policies and practices of institutions throughout society that can make it easier for businesses to envision the significant contributions to peace they could make but have yet to attempt.

The Peace Entrepreneur

The quest for peace may stem from a desire for stability or equilibrium. It is tempting to analyze such a balance in terms of data, military might, and social pressure. These ascertainable measures fit contemporary academic scholarship well and remain crucial to any assessment of how peace might be successfully pursued.

Yet peace is something that inspires so it should not be a surprise that those who seek peace—including those in the business realm—may be motivated by inspiring things; in other words, things spiritual. Though not affiliated with any particular religious perspective, the Austin, Texas–based NGO Peace Through Commerce works directly with business entrepreneurs who bring spiritual, inspirational motivations to their work. The following story demonstrates the deep spiritual motivation that can inspire a peace entrepreneur:

> I grew up hating Arabs and Germans. I am ashamed to admit, but the Black Africans were mere shadows who never entered my consciousness, who took care of my every need without my knowing anything of their background, their lives and their suffering!
>
> In 1967, a few months after the victorious Six Day War, our school offered a trip to Israel for three months in order to connect with our Jewish roots, tour the country and learn the language. I was enamored by the palpable energy of victory and every soldier was my hero. All I wanted to do was leave school, live in Israel, become a soldier and kill the Arab enemy! I had been obsessed with the holocaust as a teenager, reading every available book and the need to protect our people was very much alive in me.
>
> My parents insisted I finish school and soon after, all the family moved to the Promised Land. Not once had we been made aware that this land had also been promised to another people. I was a product of a secular, cultural conditioning. I came to Israel, studied the language on a kibbutz, became a kindergarten teacher, and a soldier; thank goodness I was never near combat. I then married the cream of the crop, a pilot in the Israeli Air force. What a great gift for my Zionist father.
>
> My personal journey and my country's journey were at a time of reconciliation and it appeared that peace was just around the bend for both of us. Suddenly, tensions rose, Rabin was killed and soon after, the second Intifada was upon us. Thirteen young Arab men were killed near where I lived in the Galilee. I was devastated and traveled to a peace tent that had been set up in an open field in a nearby village. We sat in circle, passing an olive branch as a

talking stick, Jews and Arabs, shocked over the carnage. Though my husband objected strenuously and with great anger, I joined the group to pay respect to three of the Arab families whose sons had been killed. Quaking with fear over the memory of a retaliatory killing in Ramallah that very day, I determined that it was my destiny to visit these families.

At the home of young victim, Assil Asli, I had to hold myself back from screaming out in pain as I saw his pictures and the loving environment of his home. Asil's parents believed in co-existence so he went to a Jewish kindergarten. Assil was a peace lover who chose to go to a peace camp called Seeds of Peace. He wrote poetry, was recognized as a future leader, and was shot in the back, his Seeds of Peace T shirt bloodied.

That day I looked up to the heavens and told God that I was getting off the fence. "You find the way for me to serve." A wise friend suggested that it was time for me to focus on the youth of our country. I was offered the opportunity to do a peace camp and in 2003, Creativity for Peace was born.

After nine years of co-founding Creativity for Peace, I knew that I had to continue on my journey. I remembered that years before, while chatting with the Palestinian co-facilitator, I had an idea to create a peace pillow. I knew that the only person in the world to do this with me was Valerie Valentine, who had been the art director at camp for five years. Her immediate reaction was "why not add a book to it?"

My vision is that before kids go to sleep they will draw or write their intentions on their peace pillowslip and fall asleep with positive thoughts, irrespective of their outer circumstances. My hope is to be supported to create a path for those with resources to donate to those who lack resources so that children worldwide learn that we are responsible for each other, to have compassion for each other and thus create a better future for our grandchildren. (Anael Harpaz, cofounder of Creativity for Peace)[3]

Since 2003, Harpaz's nonprofit, Creativity for Peace, has trained more than 200 Palestinian and Israeli women on how to partner with each other and advocate for peace in the region. Through summer camps, in-country training, and collaboration, the organization hopes to equip young women with the skills to transform—step by step—the protracted conflict from one of violence and instability into one of partnership and peace.[4]

The problems of the Middle East have spurred other peace entrepreneurs as well. William Ury, author of *Getting to Yes*, organized a tour business aimed at the common heritage of the Abrahamic traditions— Judaism, Christianity, and Islam. He created *The Path of Abraham*, which consists of a tour along the long-distance trail from northern Turkey to southern Israel that follows the sites visited by Abraham and revered in all three religious traditions, documented in the Torah and Koran. The goals of the business are to spark economic development, to enable people interested in the Middle East to meet, and to provide a space for the stories that mark the culture and heritage of the region.[5]

A third example has been previously mentioned: the MEDJI Tours of George Mason University, during which tourists visit both Israeli and Palestinian parts of Jerusalem with tour guides from each of the populations to hear both sides of the story of that conflict.[6]

Each of these examples draws heavily on an inspired desire to use business as a way to foster peace. One arises directly from religious belief; the other uses religion to highlight a common experience; and the third recognizes the conflicts associated with religion and tries to find a way to transcend them through understanding. As entrepreneurs, they chose business models with little if any difference between shareholders and managers. They tend to be small businesses with an explicit focus on a social good—here, peace—so that when the business grows, new employees join the company with an understanding that the company is seeking both economic and noneconomic goals.

Although managers should maximize profit, they should also carry out the lawful directives of their shareholders. Some degree of economic return is likely to be important to just about every shareholder, but shareholders can have noneconomic desires that are also legitimate. Peace entrepreneurs have peace, as well as profit, as such a directive.

The Business for Peace Foundation in Oslo founded by Norwegian investment banker Per Saxegaard maintains that trustworthy business will be the coin of the twenty-first-century business realm and that business conducting itself ethically will constructively contribute to peace. The term Saxegaard uses to characterize this trustworthy model of commerce is *businessworthy*, symbolized by a handshake.[7] In annually awarding the work of individuals who see business as part of a wider society, the Foundation consistently identifies peace entrepreneurs. This book's appendix includes a list of award winners and a brief explanation of their work.

Saxegaard has articulated a way for business to foster peace along the same lines as the model Schipani and I propose. He has convened a set of Nobel Laureates in economics and peace to consider the best practices of businesspeople around the world. He has also partnered with major organizations such as the United Nations, the International Chamber of Commerce, and the *International Herald Tribune*, among others, so that his Business for Peace Foundation increasingly gains public attention not only for its work but for those businesses fostering peace.

Much like the work of Peace Through Commerce, the Path of Abraham, and MEDJI, the Business for Peace Foundation emphasizes the difference individuals make. Less focused on organizational conduct, these institutions realize that new models to address public ills and aspire to social goals may well come from individual entrepreneurs, who may be inspired in many different ways.

There are significant benefits with this focus. It is easier for us to admire the good work of an individual than it is to admire a massive company. One cannot help but be moved in reading Anael Harpaz's story and transformation, applaud the work of a famous negotiations expert like Bill Ury in creating a peace-making model, or be impressed with the massive time an investment banker like Per Saxegaard devotes to peace and trustworthy business practices. Without deifying any of them, we find that these individuals tend to be more compelling models to follow than companies; even when a company does do something well, our eyes train upward toward such leaders.

Another benefit is that these individuals demonstrate the importance of the normative. Recently, much has rightly been made about the "shared values" approach,[8] which argues that societal benefits and business benefits often cohere significantly so that notions of corporate social responsibility become both socially and strategically valuable.[9]

We must observe some caution, however, that the shared values perspective only goes so far. Businesses often look to benchmark "best practices" to guide their own behavior. What if best practices currently available are poor and society's values are deficient? Where do the values come from to lead to practices that are better than the best practices? The answer provided by these peace entrepreneurs is that, at least on some occasions, businesses could create new models for how business acts when they commit to normative goals.

In many ways, the notion that business can contribute to peace is in the same place as the notion of sustainability was thirty years ago, when the idea was laughed at in business schools and paid little heed in the C suite. Businesses that did emphasize sustainability were often leftover hippie kinds of fringe businesses (for example, Ben and Jerry's or Whole

Foods) with niche appeal. Yet it was exactly businesses like this that captured both public attention and a market. As increasing numbers of scientific studies showed that Earth's climate is changing, businesses responded with new green business models. Just about every dean and CEO now spout their institution's work in fostering sustainability. What entrepreneurs began in the area of sustainability became far more mainstream.

Although we may champion and support the courage of peace entrepreneurs, we cannot leave the fostering of peace to the entrepreneurs; that risks minimizing this work as niche, just as those working toward sustainability once were. Also, it's one thing to recognize an inspired businessperson's efforts to foster peace, but expecting others to do the same asks a great deal. Without some understanding of replicable models, legal support, and competitive environments, expecting that all businesses foster peace is premature. It might even be dangerous.

At a Peace Through Commerce conference hosted by the University of Notre Dame in 2006, I appeared on a panel with an economist who expressed concern over the notion of business contributing to peace. Although I did not agree with her willingness to keep institutions in their traditional sectoral roles, she did have a great point in cautioning that a business may significantly muddy sensitive waters when it gets involved in nuanced diplomacy. What training do businesspeople have in settling difficult disputes? Isn't there a reason why we train diplomats to handle sensitive negotiations? Even if well-intended, even an inspired business muddling around in sensitive conflict issues might make things worse.

As we saw in the previous chapter, businesses have made important contributions to peacemaking and peacekeeping. There is risk, however, should businesses clumsily wade into the intricacies of power politics, ethnic resentment, and religion/ideological beliefs. But perhaps there is less risk and potentially more value in the longer-term incremental contributions that businesses can make to peace building.

The Instrumental Business

Instrumental businesses provide more examples of how businesses have an impact on peace while still satisfying the needs of the enterprise itself. Holcim Philippines is featured by the United Nations as an example of a company that conducts itself admirably in a conflict-sensitive zone.

Situated within a country with poverty, religious conflict, instability, and environmental stress, Holcim Philippines traditionally used private security forces to protect its personnel and assets. Nevertheless, one of its plants was attacked in 2005 and incurred significant damage and theft. Holcim then increased its dialogue with the local community, prohibited its security personnel from carrying weapons, and conducted a human rights assessment of its operations. This calmed animosity toward the company, though the Holcim guards and employees were concerned by the lack of armed security. Despite that concern, the company extended its no-firearms policy to its other facilities around the country and exercised greater oversight of the forces within its general business operations. They also hired local residents as guards.[10]

A 2011 assessment implemented by Holcim Philippines[11] and the main company's sustainable development function held more than forty consultations with both internal and external stakeholders and included trade unions, NGOs, UN agencies, national officials, other business organizations, contract workers, employees, and local management. The recommendations resulted in a memorandum of understanding that called for additional intensive dialogue with local police stations (who needed to be ready to respond if security guards were unarmed), along with more involvement of Holcim's guards with the local community through sports activities, reading sessions with children, disaster relief services, and other community volunteering. The company also invited the local Commission on Human Rights to provide lectures to the guards in an educational format.[12]

The reported results are positive, with no armed attacks on the company since 2005 or any discharge of firearms by security forces. There was also much more collaboration among all the parties with respect to the firearm policy and the ongoing dialogue as a whole.[13]

Three important insights arise from this example that apply to other cases already presented. First, consistent with the UN approach and that of International Alert, strong emphasis was placed on engagement between the company and the local community; this conflict-sensitive approach has been advocated by other NGOs as well. How else could a company know the issues well enough to be able to dampen whatever flashpoints might result in violence? Unless a company has its own or allied (that is, governmental) power to crush potential opposition—which itself is likely only to cover resentment—its best recourse to stable relations is dialogue.

A second insight concerns motivation. Companies face quantifiable risks, whether it's the threat of an attack on a facility or the specter of economic collapse from loss of business. Such risks can motivate businesses to do something positive before the business suffers.

Finally, as calculating as an instrumental approach might be, the benefits of peace and stability might create an increased appetite for harmony with those one is working with. Following the lead of both peace entrepreneurs and instrumental businesses might lead to even more peace entrepreneurs.

William Shaw wrote that once people develop the habit of obeying the law, they often extend that habit even when the law is absent.[14] Similarly, dialoguing with angry constituents might encourage the same approach in other situations, something that may not have happened without a positive precedent. It is easy to laud peace entrepreneurs and to be more cynical toward instrumental businesses. But one may take steps toward social good in a variety of ways. It is best not to dismiss any of them out of hand, even the unintended actions of businesses that contribute to peace without ever knowing it.

A Positive Law of Unintended Consequences

Because attributes of nonviolent societies map well with generally accepted principles of business ethics, ethical businesses contribute to peace whether they mean to or not. Businesses may more mindfully practice ethics when they are aware of the potential good of their behavior, but regardless, ethical business behavior benefits peace.

Including these unwitting participants in the promotion of peace dramatically expands the number of companies contributing to peace. Although peace entrepreneurs set out to achieve a unique noneconomic good and instrumentalists understand that their businesses will be better off with stable peaceful relationships, ethical companies contribute to peace simply by doing what they are doing.

Ethics itself provides a useful analogy. Aristotle noted that we do not think about most of our actions that we would call "ethical." We do them by habit, and they are so much a part of our character that we do not consciously struggle whether to do them or not. We act that way because it is who we are.

I often illustrate this point with students by stopping twenty minutes or so into a class and asking why none of them has thrown his or her coffee, water, book bag, or something else at me. Fortunately, the thought has not seemed to cross their minds. There is an ethic of how to comport oneself in class that would not permit such action. Yet I do not think they struggle or wonder whether or not they should hurl something at me. Instead, they have internalized a set of ethical norms for how to act in a classroom.

The ethical values that lead to peace have a similar, habitual feel. Respect for coworkers, avoiding corruption, following the rules, gender equity (equity generally), and respect for rights are commonly identified traits of ethical companies as well as relatively nonviolent groups. Thus, if companies pay attention to ethical conduct, they are acting peacefully regardless of whether they seek to contribute to peace.

Becoming more aware of the positive effects of ethical actions reinforces people's enthusiasm for those good actions. When people see that respect for each other, avoidance of corruption, and productive work help create peace, they realize there is a larger impact than what they expected. Even though they may want to be ethical, if they see a bigger impact on peace, they will be more motivated to practice ethical behaviors, making an even greater contribution to peace and the gentleness of commerce. Thus, another way to encourage companies to contribute to peace is to acknowledge which companies already practice good ethics.[15]

Combined with peace entrepreneurs and instrumentalists, ethical companies add to the list of those that contribute to peace, which helps to mainstream the idea that business can foster peace. Even when peace is not the aim, it can still be fostered by ethical actions. The conscious pursuit of peace by a business may be unusual, but the contribution itself is not.

These examples are not as inspiring or as dramatic as Anael Harpaz's commitment to peace in Israel or Holcim's attempt to protect its property while harmonizing relationships with indigenous people. Hollywood is not going to make a movie about how a company routinely doing good work prevents a child in Sri Lanka from dying. Cummins Engines and Deere & Company's good work in the earth-moving and construction industry is as dull as dirt. Yet it is also real.

Businesspeople and businesses contribute to peace in different ways, as peace entrepreneurs, instrumental businesses, and in more latent ways that result from acting ethically. Peace entrepreneurs already believe that peace is a good thing and want their businesses to contribute to it. The instrumentalists may be aware of the benefits of peace for their businesses and recognize that it is smart business to practice gentle commerce. Businesses simply devoted to being good, ethical companies also contribute to peace even if they are unaware of their contribution because their ethical practices correlate with peaceful attributes. If such companies were more aware of the peaceful impact of their actions, they likely would practice their ethics even more seriously, creating more impact.

Motivations may differ, but we should not expect there to be any one way for business to contribute to peace. Structure matters too. An individual may be motivated to achieve peace, but the structure of a system or an institution has an impact on just how significant and how easily such a contribution can be made, which is the topic of the next chapter.

PART III

Policies for Peace

7   Little Brother Government Policy

There are many ways that law can make a positive contribution—a human rights law, an anticorruption treaty, or a free trade agreement may all support businesses' role in creating peace. One could further narrow the range to consider only those ways in which businesses engage in conflict-sensitive zones, but this narrows the scope of potential impact too much. This chapter seeks to strike a balance of proposals that foster businesses' contribution to peace but does not include all the stars of the Milky Way; yet it acknowledges that business activity has an effect on the cultural conduct that affects war and peace.

The first part of the chapter looks at some of current leading proposals, then moves on to a more focused elaboration of the aspects of open societies that provide hope for peace and yield four principles for government action. Those principles are then applied to map out four industries/sectors where businesses have a good opportunity to create a foothold for peace.

The Four Contributions to Peace Redux

In my work with Cindy Schipani, we identified contributions businesses can make to peace, specifically (1) economic development; (2) support of rule of law principles, especially with respect to avoiding corruption; (3) acting as a community, both externally as good citizens and internally by respecting human rights, gender equity, voice/democracy, and creating mediating institutions within companies; and (4) participating in multitrack diplomacy.

With the exception of multitrack diplomacy, these first three contributions are intertwined with governmental action. In our work, Professor Schipani and I made clear that business needs to take an active role to make these contributions rather than delegate them to government. Issues such as rule of law, human rights, and economic development are shared values to be pursued by multiple sectors.

The United Nations has also argued for how business can contribute to peace. The United Nations operates on two tracks with respect to business and peace. It has an active program that focuses on the ways in which business should act in zones of conflict[1] that correlate with Part II's emphasis on peacemaking and peacekeeping.[2] The United Nations also sponsors its "Global Compact," its code of corporate responsibility that is grouped according to themes of human rights, labor, the environment, and anticorruption.[3] Although the Global Compact has not been as explicitly tied to peace as UN work on zones of conflict, the two programs are of a piece as opposed to separate.

As with the Fort-Schipani principles, the Global Compact articulates a set of rights and duties that are commonly shared among all people and sectors. The Compact also articulates a vision of corporate responsibility. Both approaches assume that business and government share a commitment to peace; for example, although businesses should avoid corruption and support gender equity, government should as well. So a governmental proposal for fostering businesses' contribution to peace would not only encourage businesses to avoid bribery and gender discrimination but also recommend laws that reinforce those aims.

In addition to the Fort-Schipani and UN models, a third approach comes from the Institute for Economics and Peace, whose annual "Global Peace Index," including both quantitative and qualitative measures selected by an expert group of panelists, ranks countries according to their peacefulness each year.[4] Indicators include:

- Relations with neighboring countries
- The number of external and internal conflicts
- The perceived presence of criminality
- Levels of violent crime
- Number of homicides

- Number of police/internal security officers, jailed population, armed services personnel
- Exports of conventional weapons per 100,000 people
- Financial contributions to UN peacekeeping missions
- Political terrorist scales[5]

Here again, there is an assumption that government and business are both interested in peace and that their self-interests are affected by peace; not surprisingly, a quest for peace is also of (perhaps even more) interest from civil society.

All of these lead to a bigger question as to the underlying, foundational structure that contributes to peace. Does peace look the same for an open, democratic society as it does for a closed society? Are there qualitative differences between peace in each of these societies? These questions need to be acknowledged even if they can be only partially answered at this point. They raise important, if uncomfortable, issues that force us to consider whether some societies are, for lack of a better word, better than others, a consideration fraught with potential controversy.

First, these questions have normative dimensions. Peace may be a shared value—even a hypergood[6]—but what kind of peace are we thinking of? Societies with open political and economic systems, rule of law, and discipline from civil society and transnational organizations produce less violent behavior. A claim of this chapter is that some systems are better than others in reducing the likelihood of violence and therefore are morally preferred. Yet, in today's world, such claims often make people wince because they reek of imperialism. After all, we are supposed to be inclusive, open, and nonjudgmental. Taken to the extreme, however, such a position leaves us unable to ever improve. We really don't believe we should be nonjudgmental toward slavery or torture or discrimination; our progress toward overcoming such practices depends on maintaining the capacity to judge. If the cost of reducing bloodshed and other human suffering is the charge of imperialism, then tolerating such an epithet seems well worthwhile. I do want to approach this notion with caution, however.

Michael Strong has made the point that those who advocate social change on moral grounds are also the most prone to violence and torture. This should sober those who strongly and morally advocate for changes in societies to produce peace, lest they end up practicing exactly the things they oppose. One strong advocate for peace, theologian Stanley Hauerwas, often argued that peaceableness required such an exacting degree of nonviolence that religious organizations might just want to ignore engagement in the public realm and instead focus on their own community's practices.[7] Another religiously devout thinker and leader—Ghandi—took a different approach insofar as he actively engaged in social change, but, as he famously put it, "Be the change you seek to make." The change one attempts to make may end up proceeding by evolution rather than by revolution.

The second important issue is that seeing how these changes might be made requires us once again to take stock of where we are in the evolutionary moment of human history. Behaviors do follow structures, so we must consider how to move political economies toward a structural model that is more likely to enhance peace. We must also balance the claims that business contributions to peace are highly specific and context dependent and that dialogue and awareness tend to be driving forces of constructive business contributions to peace.[8]

Natural States versus Open Access Societies

In their 2009 book, Nobel Prize–winning economist Douglass North, along with Barry Weingast and John Wallis, argues that there have been two dramatic social revolutions in human history. The first started 10,000 years ago and the second 250 years ago with the rise of industrial technologies.[9] As with Pinker, Fry, and others, these dates appear as significant moments in human history. More akin to Pinker's work, North's centers on the creation of "open societies."[10]

North argues that "natural states" or "limited access societies" began 10,000 years ago and moved society beyond hunter-gatherers,[11] whose interactions were very personal.[12] North contends that these natural states used the political system to regulate economic competition and to create surpluses for the elite, who then controlled violence and established cooperation through ordered relationships.[13] These natural orders maintained strong interpersonal relationships among the elites but expanded the size and scope of society. Not wanting to share the spoils of such arrangements too widely, the elites limited access to key business, political, and religious leadership and thereby also constrained economic growth.[14]

Drawing from history, North lists medieval England as an example; to-day's examples would include Nigeria, Kenya, Argentina, Mexico, and Russia.[15]

Natural states come in three general forms. A few powerful individuals occupy power and organizations with access to economic rents in *fragile* natural states; examples include Iraq, Sudan, and Somalia.[16] In a *basic* natural state, there are an increasing number of differentiated organizations, but they remain closely tied to the central state; examples include Egypt, Nazi Germany, and Saddam Hussein's Iraq.[17] *Mature* natural states have not only even more differentiated organizations within the society but the beginnings of the concept of rule of law as well as some independent control over the military. There is also an increasing distinction between public and private organizations; examples include Argentina, Brazil, India, and Mexico.[18]

Open access societies, on the other hand, maintain peace through competition that reduces surpluses. They feature property rights and impersonal exchange.[19] These societies provide opportunity for nearly all members of society to compete economically. Judicial systems function as do property rights and basic notions of the rule of law of which we have seen to be traits of relatively nonviolent societies.[20] Open access societies also tend to be more economically vibrant, another trait of relatively nonviolent societies.[21] North claims that natural order societies have dominated most of human history and continue to be the structural approach for 85 percent of the world.[22]

Here lies the beginning of our challenge. A business contributing to peace by avoiding corruption is a great idea, but its effectiveness may depend on rule of law. Creating more economic development, and with it jobs, does seem to reduce the possibilities for violence, but who does the development makes a difference given these variations of economic and political order. If the political and economic order depends on elites for maintenance, what might be the role for things such as voice of the wider population, human rights, and gender equity?

Open access societies do better than natural order societies in fostering peace, and the business contribution to peace may be more effective within an open society than within a natural order society. Or to put otherwise, the foreign policy practiced by a company in a natural order society is likely to be that of deference to the elites that hold the levers of economic and political power. To the extent those elites are challenged, a company has a major navigational challenge of knowing what, exactly, to risk. This was true of Google and Twitter in Egypt (a natural order society) as it was with the *grupos* in Columbia. Confronting Mubarak in defense of free flow of information was dangerous; tacking back and forth between the Colombian government, the West, and narco-traffickers was similarly dangerous for the *grupos*.

Although economics has its importance, however, it is secondary to the agreements arrived at by governments in defining borders, treaties, and other geopolitical relationships.[23] To take this a step further, governmental structure has much to do with the ways in which business might foster peace. Moreover, businesses themselves do have a power unlike what they have held in the past because of their size, cross-border reach, technological capabilities, and ability to communicate, which allows companies to compete with nation-states in terms of message and loyalty, again demonstrated by Google and Twitter in Egypt. Along with diplomatic agreements, the very structure of political societies makes a difference to peace as well as to business and to governments.

But how does a society move from a natural state to an open society? North argues that it is very difficult and is the result of a long process. He proposes three "doorstep" conditions necessary to make the transition. In other words, what puts these societies in a position to move from natural order societies to open access societies?

The first occurs when elites extend property rights to a wide segment of the population, which they might be willing to do, North argues, if they see there are more market opportunities. As an example, he refers to fifteenth- and sixteenth-century England and the East India Company, where elites benefited by allowing nonelites to buy shares of stock in companies that increased capitalization and market reach.[24] This condition does mandate not that elites give up their wealth but instead that others gain access to wealth. The rich may still be rich, but poor aren't as badly off.

The second doorstep condition pertains to the institutions that can take advantage of expanding markets. If a business is solely dependent on a given individual, then that business has a problem when the person dies. However, corporations do not die; their ownership simply passes to the next investor, providing for perpetual life. A longer-range perspective is thus institutionalized, which creates further incentives for long-term investments.[25]

The third doorstep condition results when the military breaks free from control of elites who use it to retain power. The state will still need to control the military, but, to the extent a frustrated elite can no longer use the military to overthrow a regime and install a more favorable dictatorship, the military becomes more independent and less of a coercive threat to an open access society.[26]

North emphasizes that all three of these conditions must occur for a society to move beyond the natural state; this confluence does not often happen. It is a long, gradual process often not understood by policy makers today.[27]

What we face—both in terms of this transformation of orders as well as with respect to the contributions business can make to peace—is another kind of balance of power. The balance I've described thus far has looked at a tension between economic, political, and moral factors. In addition to this push and pull, there is also a tension between the autonomy of local governments, businesses, and NGOs on the one hand and, on the other, an overarching set of national and transnational rules applicable to everyone. The mix of these various governing mechanisms requires a multilayered combination of institutional responsibility.

Polycentric Governance and Four Principles Applicable to Business and Peace

Business (even if a monolithic entity itself) can no more wave its magic hand to transform natural order societies into open order societies than can the World Bank, the United Nations, or the G-7. That does not mean, however, that there is not a role for it to play and a way that governments can use businesses to structure the conditions necessary to achieve the open society model that is more akin to peace. Sketching the way in which that might happen leads us to consider another Nobel Prize–winning economist.

Elinor Ostrom focused much of her work on the issues of the commons—what we share rather than what any individual or institution owns; in particular, the environment. Ostrom searched for a governance mechanism that avoided the problems of decentralization, where issues of overuse of a commons still arise, and high-level regulation, which tends to not take into account local issues.[28] Moreover, she complained that much of economic theory posits two ideal forms of property ownership, one where there is government control and the other where there is private control.[29] Private individuals would seem to have little ability to address collective action problems, which include environment, public health, and peace.[30]

At the same time, Ostrom also demonstrated that local governments in North America (vis-à-vis both Canada and Mexico[31]) have found significant success in addressing reforestation issues. She further extends the range of problem solving of environmental issues to "research institutes, NGOs, community organizations, farmers, and local and national governments."[32] The impact of centralized governments, she concludes, is often "mediated, enhanced, or determined through actions conducted by a diversity of other actors."[33]

Ostrom proposes "polycentric governance, which seeks to integrate the benefits of the small scale with the large scale because [a]llowing citizens to form smaller-scale collective consumption units encourages face-to-face discussion and the achievement of common understanding." Larger units also can more effectively cope with the goods and services that have large-scale effects and real economies of scale.[34] To put this thought into this book's terms, polycentric governance may provide a way to blend the relatively pacific (Fry-documented) experience of small groups with the relatively pacific (Pinker-documented) experience of large institutions.

Although Ostrom addressed her work to environmental issues, four of her eight principles for designing the interaction between small-scale and large-scale institutions are directly relevant to my argument.[35]

REFLEXIVE GOVERNMENTAL REGULATION

The first of Ostrom's principles that can be used to create an optimal governance mechanism to allow business to foster peace is reflexivity, the notion that governments create enforcement incentives but leave the implementation of the policy aims to the efforts of individual corporations.[36] Reflexive corporate governance regimes have proliferated over the past quarter-century. For example, in an effort to encourage good corporate behavior, in 1991 Congress amended the Federal Sentencing Guidelines[37] to enable greater consistency in sentences and to prevent sentences from becoming too lenient. Section 8—the Organizational Amendments—was added[38] to create an incentive for companies to become serious about institutional attention to attend to ethics issues.

The bargain Congress proposed was that if companies established effective corporate compliance programs that rooted out illegal behavior, even if they did violate the law, sentences from convictions of federal crimes (such as insider trading or Medicare fraud) would be reduced. Several elements are required for an effective program, including a mission statement or code of conduct, a high-level official to oversee the program, self-reporting of violations of the law, and a way to safely report misconduct, such as an ethics hotline.[39] Although there was no requirement that companies adopt these programs, the fines that could result from not having them were so significant that courts have held that the absence of such compliance programs could itself be grounds for a shareholder derivative suit.[40] Thus, although not coercively mandated per se, the incentives made it highly advantageous to develop the programs.

In the aftermath of the Enron, WorldCom, and other corporate scandals, the guidelines were further amended in 2004 to state that companies should aim to create organizational cultures that lead to ethical as well as legal compliance.[41] Of course, in creating legal and ethical cultures, a good deal of autonomy[42] would be necessary for individual companies to design programs that fit their particular culture.

A reflexive, polycentric model recognizes the power of small groupings with face-to-face interaction, which have been anthropologically recognized as hallmarks of peaceful societies. Yet, as we have seen, small groups also need to be monitored.

Monitoring efforts provide a second level of reflexivity. Studies assessing how well companies implement compliance policies found that regardless of what policy was to be implemented, a key factor in employees trusting the program was consistency of enforcement.[43] This is a sense of procedural justice and also a common denominator in both North's and Ostrom's work. With North, the defining transition from natural order to open access societies occurs when elites give up their monopoly on power. They do so only when there are procedures to shield their investments, such as through protection of their property and contract rights and through the ability to settle disputes through adjudication or negotiation rather than through violence.[44] Such protections give rise to trade that itself gives rise to the ongoing relationships that are associated with peace. If elites can recognize that they will receive more overall wealth through an open society, they'll be more likely to give up monopolies.

So, how would reflexivity apply in terms of peace building? If we know that there are certain attributes already associated with peaceableness, then governments could provide incentives for companies to achieve such attributes. We already have a sense of what those attributes are and know that they are associated with generally accepted ethical business practices. Further, there are already laws—the Federal Sentencing Guidelines being among them—that reflexively "require" companies to conduct their affairs in certain ways. Governments would not then need to construct new, reflexive policies for companies; they would simply need to continue to follow the lead of these extant approaches.

MAINTAINING LONG-TERM PERSPECTIVES AND POLICIES

A second principle emphasizes the importance of maintaining a long-term perspective toward both politics and economics. As North argues, the existence of perpetual economic enterprises fundamentally orients a society toward open access so that long-term investment can occur. Yet there are more benefits to long-term perspectives; multiple studies show that good corporate conduct tends to be financially rewarded, but only over the long term.[45] In the short term, it is very difficult to place an economic value on elusive concepts such as social capital, reputation, or goodwill, but companies do so regularly with respect to long-term balance sheet statements.[46] The moral practices identified in Part I also have their greatest value and impact when considered on a long-term basis.

A long-term orientation is necessary to optimally build in peace-related activities. Indeed, one could look at both the principle of the Global Compact and the Institute for Economics and Peace's (IEP's) emphasis on things such as education, infant mortality, and incarceration of criminals as having their greatest value in a long-term rather than a short-term perspective. Pinker, too, emphasized the long-term, incremental approach.

It follows then that governments should suggest business-related practices that promote long-term approaches, such as requiring holding periods for executives to exercise stock options. In this way, decision makers are encouraged to follow long-term strategies rather than to game the stock market on the short-term.

More controversially, although there are disadvantages to differential tax rates on long-term capital gains,[47] a lower tax for such long-term holdings does encourage a longer-term investment perspective. Other tax-related strategies that shape incentives may be possible as well.

Financing provides another angle. Local governments create tax incentives for investments in their community. Governments must structure long-term incentives to combat companies' impulse to leave town shortly after harvesting a short-term financial aid benefit, which leaves governments and the people they represent in the lurch.[48]

In short, as with reflexive models, long-term policies are hardly revolutionary. There are existing models and activities that government's use that can be adapted to support the attributes of businesses contributing to peace. Indeed, many studies show that, over the long term, ethical business practices tend to have an economic payoff, so government insistence on protection of human rights, gender equity, and avoidance of corruption benefit long-term ethics, long-term performance, and long-term peace.

A CIVILIZING DIMENSION TO REGULATION

A third principle concerns the ways in which behaviors become more civilized. As we have seen, over the centuries behavior became more couth through cultivation of tastes and behaviors among elites that trickled down to the masses and passed down through government action.

Both civil society and governments have a role in civilizing behavior. Governments do, after all, legislate morality; if they did not, we would still have racial, ethnic, and other discrimination in our society.[49] Governments also prohibit sexual harassment now in a way unheard of even thirty years ago.[50]

What is particularly important here is that encouragement of ethical business behavior is also influenced by governmental action; such encouragement of civilizing business conduct is well within the reach of government to influence.

Gender-related issues provide a good example. Women have often suffered poor treatment in the workplace. Even as late as the 1990s, tremendous debate erupted over sexual harassment. Although stamping out harassment still has miles to go, there is far greater awareness of the issue than existed a generation ago. Why the change? In large part, through court decisions, legislation and executive orders, government punished—or allowed victims to sue through the court system—harassers.

THE USE OF RHETORIC

A fourth principle is rhetorical, in a positive way. Even when governments do not pass laws per se, they do have access to microphones. The bully pulpit belongs to the president as well as others in government. Lincoln, the Roosevelts, Kennedy, and Reagan all moved people in the country to see the world differently, aside from particular legislative or executive acts. Franklin Roosevelt's greatest contribution as president arguably may have been to calm the country in the middle of the Depression. Ronald Reagan took a country gripped in a "malaise" and talked about a shining city on a hill. Indeed, much good has come from leaders articulating their support and reasons for more respectful, less discriminatory, more responsible behavior, regardless of the laws themselves.

There is no reason why presidents and other governmental leaders cannot talk of achieving peace, just as John F. Kennedy talked about putting a human being on the moon. Eloquently advocating for a just and peaceful society is as relevant now to government leaders as it was to Abraham Lincoln.

These four principles reach different levels of society in different ways. Government already uses each of the principles in different forms, so advocating that they be used in a way oriented toward peace is not a great stretch from currently existing practices. In other words, apart from passing new regulations, government leaders can rhetorically champion the contribution business can make to peace. Governments can create reflexive laws that provide autonomy for businesses to reach prescribed legal goals without specifically mandating the particular ways in which business must achieve such goals. Similarly, laws can be enacted that encourage a long-term orientation of business strategies, which itself will help to align such business conduct with peace building practices. Finally, governments can mandate ethical practices that make businesses more civil, more like gentle commerce. The next question is how these ideas might translate into particular policies.

Polycentric Policies Applied to Industries

Leadership makes a difference, which is one reason why peace entrepreneurs are so important; they see things differently. If they can demonstrate that vision and show a way in which their efforts can be successful, others emulate it. Industries matter too. It may well be that some industries will be more open to the idea of peace building than others because of where they do their work or simply because peace building might resonate with the businesses' customers.

Several years ago, I had lunch with a member of the staff in charge of economic development in the just-conquered heart of Baghdad. He said that when corporate representatives got off the plane, they had three questions:

1. Does my cell phone work? If so, then there is communications capability.

2. Does my ATM card work? Now I can move capital.

3. Is there a good hotel from which I can operate? Now I have a head-quarters for operation.

Telecommunications, finance, and tourism: three industries from which to start building peace. Natural resources could be a fourth. We can place these industries/sectors within a matrix with the four polycentric principles to demonstrate how those principles apply to these four sectors (see Table 7.1).

NATURAL RESOURCES

Many question how an extractive business can constructively contribute to peace when it evokes such negativity. Frankly, my primary hope for the role of extractive industries in fostering peace lies in the realm of "do no harm." Extractives don't have the best history with peace-related practices, except for a few examples like Freeport McMoran Copper and Gold, which, as noted earlier in this book, has a long-standing reputation of practicing gentle commerce in the extractive industry. Alien tort statute lawsuits have been filed on many, including Chevron,[51] Unocal,[52] Shell,[53] and Exxon,[54] among others.

Moreover, some scholars have written that one of the best predictors for a civil war is if the main export product of a county is an undifferentiated commodity.[55] Because land is not the predominant source of wealth in countries with capitalist peace, control of a particular piece of real estate is not crucial to a country's well-being. Nothing could be further from the case than with extractive countries, where the very source of wealth is in the ground. This makes control of that real estate crucial; with such

Table 7.1. Polycentric Principles and Key Industries to Affect Peace

	Reflexivity	Long-term	Civilizing	Rhetoric
Natural resources	Transnational Accords; EITI; World Bank	Long-term holdings; stock options and incentives	Importance of protecting human rights of stakeholders in production and distribution	Articulating the need for extraction in a humane way that does not fall prey to resource curses
Finance	Basel and Internal Central Banks	Long-term lending requirements and practices	Importance of stakeholders in financial lending; equity and opportunity	Changing the tone of money from that of accumulation to developmental capability with the change in practical focus associated with that rhetoric
Telecommunications	New governance arrangements that monitor and make practices transparent while continuing Internet freedom	Long-term holdings; infrastructure development	Awareness of how practices are viewed and experienced by others	The (oft-worn) language of connection and commonality
Tourism	UN World Tourism Organization; government incentives for responsible tourism practices	Long-term holdings; stock options; agreements with local populations	Building of cultural awareness, practices, and traditions	Opportunity for a different kind of dialogue of engagement

focused attention on access to and exploitation of that land come opportunities for corruption and brutal oppression of those surrounding the land who might object to the company's work.

Nevertheless, a reflexive, transnational architecture that provides incentives for companies to act responsibly is viable, even though attempts such as the Kimberly Protocol have had mixed results.[56] Others, like EITI, have had more success and obtain support from companies to attend to issues such as human rights in their work.[57]

Governmental incentives for companies to take a long-term orientation have prima facie potential. To the extent long-term market holdings encourage any company to have a longer-term perspective, there is
potential for long-term values to play a role in corporate strategy. At the
same time, a multinational company may still have the incentive for a
short-term stripping of assets in a country. If a commitment to an area is
long term—say an oil field that has decades of potential—the long-term
approach may outweigh the short-term advantages if a field has just a
few years. Stronger regulatory pressures may be needed in order to assure
good corporate behavior.

Indeed, the partnership of governments to develop the EITI and other
transnational protocols stands as another example of a reflexive approach.
Governments negotiate a set of standards with industry leaders and companies and are then able to join the protocol, providing some guarantees
of proper behavior to the public. Such an approach also stands as an example of a civilizing function of government. Proper behaviors are identified and levers found to encourage those behaviors from those in the
industry without resorting to outright regulation.

Finally, if there is one thing that governmental leaders seem willing to
do, it is to rhetorically set out expected conduct by extractive companies.
Whether in terms of environmental spills (for example Exxon in Valdez or
BP in the Gulf of Mexico), it has long been good politics to rhetorically
bash oil companies to demand that they engage in responsible behavior.
More proactive possibilities exist as well, but the full force of these government levers certainly can be seen in the extractive industry.

FINANCE

Although it seems that extractives may be more concerned with responsible actions—perhaps on their own and perhaps dragging and kicking—
than they were fifty years ago, it is not so clear that finance is headed
in the right direction. The Main Street values my student asked Chairman Bernanke about in Chapter 4 are highly relational. They emphasize
honesty, integrity, compassion, accountability, and a profound sense of
solidarity with one's neighbors, in part because of the multiple kinds of
relationships with those neighbors.

Markets, on the other hand, largely exist to allow utter strangers to interact with each other. The division between relational and transactional,

however, is not so neatly made. Relationships are important on the trading floor of a stock exchange or within the corridors of the Fed itself, and distant transactions are important for the success of a bank teller's 401(K). Yet these two worlds—these two ways of looking at the world—clash frequently and cause deep misunderstandings, distrust, and even contempt among any number of participants in the economy.

I would like to suggest that a postwar supportive integration of values and economics withered under pressure from several sources. The first was the product of global politics, where notions of free enterprise were at (usually Cold War) odds with alternative conceptions of socialist economics. One was either a freedom-loving capitalist or a Communist. In that political context, concern for "employees" could be polemically transformed into a Marxist concern for the proletariat. Even today, issues of workplace ethics are occasionally denounced as being socialist.

Next, the increasing urbanization of American society left a Main Street, neighborhood-like policing of businesses to the side in favor of the pursuit of self-interest and devoid of an Adam Smith–like moderating feature. This is why the 1960s witnessed an attempt to revive a traditional understanding of business citizenship—an essential feature of any small-town Main Street business—in the guise of "corporate social responsibility," a concept inconsistent with the market approach and intellectually fragmented because it was yanked out of its traditional moral context.

Third, although traditional sources of morality—religious belief and education—flourished during this time, they also came under attack from multiple directions that in turn weakened both as institutions for reining in misconduct and as sources for individual ethical belief. The result was a polarity of economics versus regulation without the triangulating force of civil society to intermediate.

Finally, technology ushered in a new kind of globalization that allowed anyone with a television set to observe different cultures. The mix of foreign cultures, religions, and other behaviors made attempts to define a common good seem, at best, quaint. These four factors offered little to reframe an understanding of the ethical limits of business.

During the Great Moderation, which essentially coincided with the Federal Reserve leadership of Alan Greenspan, the mutually supportive relationship between values and finance did not cause particular difficulties because the economy largely flourished. To be sure, there were scandals such as Lockheed-Martin bribery, the S&L crisis, and Enron/MCI, but after the scandals things returned to normal, and in the mid-1990s technology ushered in a greater awareness of corporate responsibility via the Internet, which returns finance more toward Main Street because everyone can watch what is going on. However the Internet also made the clash between Main Street and Wall Street all the more dramatic, especially during the 2008 crisis.

The 2008 financial crisis laid bare the differences between transactional and relational approaches to the determination of appropriate behavior. From the helplessness one felt watching events unfold, to the anger that arose when large institutions were bailed out while friends lost their houses, to the amazement at the magical creation of money, the 2008 crisis exposed raw divides in ideas of fairness and trust. These concerns about fairness and trust remain relevant even if the actions of the Federal Reserve, Treasury, Congress, and the White House were, on the whole, correct and prevented a catastrophic worldwide meltdown, which would have gone far beyond economics. Even if necessary, these actions seemed indicative of a system off track.

Central banks remain in a good position to propose a set of actions, mostly likely through a G-20 kind of umbrella, which might reintroduce a set of policies that do integrate notions of fairness and trust with finance. Moreover, we already have a model of how to approach such a proposition through the four polycentric levers and through the four contributions businesses can make to peace.

With this in mind, the four levers mentioned seem readily available to encourage the kind of behaviors that contribute to peace. Financial institutions are already well within the framework of reflexive models of behavior and, perhaps more than some, may be affected positively by incentives for long-term capital holdings. The conduct of major financial institutions increasingly draws fire as decidedly uncivilized behavior, thereby using both civilizing and rhetorical angles.

Perhaps two of the better things that could happen to further promote good conduct within the financial industry revolve around central banking itself. Bernanke may have had both fans and critics, but one strong positive was his tireless effort to make the working of the central banks more transparent. This itself provides a model for his successors, other central bankers, and still others within the financial industry itself. Further, people pay close attention to central banks, which have a keen interest in stability and factors that lead to stability such as issues of unemployment, interest rates, and emergency lending practices to keep economies humming. Using central banks as a forum to discuss—without regulation per se—other factors that also contribute to peace and stability would be advantageous as well.

TELECOMMUNICATIONS

One can differentiate between telecommunications and Internet-based companies, but for our purposes they will be grouped together. Arguably, after all, it is the joint impact of these kinds of companies that has made such a dramatic change in the world. The Internet and telecommunications allow individuals from around the world to easily connect with each other, thus producing new kinds of cross-cutting associations and community building with individuals that can mitigate violence.[58] Telecommunications and the Internet also open new border-crossing economic opportunities that provide for further economic development.[59] They promote transparency and information flow, which themselves are tools used to battle corruption and other problematic behavior.[60] They provide voice for populations that often do not have significant voices.[61]

Although the Internet does not lack stakeholders, it remains relatively unregulated, especially in any kind of international context. Challenges in this industry result from the fast pace of the industry and its truly global nature. Four international supervisory bodies are of particular note: ICANN, Internet Engineering Task Force, International Telecommunications Union, and Internet Governance Forum.[62] These transnational bodies attempt to bring some common rules to the Internet.

Yet here again, the four polycentric principles—reflexivity, long-term orientation, civilizing behavior, and rhetoric—guide governments as they enact policies for the telecommunications/Internet industry. This industry requires some autonomy to allow for its pace of change, so rather than direct regulation, governments tend to create specialized entities—such as ICANN and others—to address issues.

A long-term orientation is as available to this industry as any other. Although the pace of the industry may make it seem very short-term oriented, there is little doubt that this industry has a vibrant long-term future that demands looking ahead rather than simply at quarterly profits. Tax incentives for long-term holding of stock ownership could apply to

Internet and telecommunications companies as easily as they could to any other company.

Can the Internet be civilized? Well, it certainly can encourage and capture uncouth behavior, but it also allows people from around the world to interact with each other and learn. Such interaction always encourages higher levels of understandings, which is foundational for respectful relationships. In this regard, the Internet at least has the potential for promoting civilized behavior.

Government itself, of course, has a microphone to the Internet, just as everyone else does. Government leaders are thus in a position to promote peacemaking and peacekeeping as well as the practices of gentle commerce that build peace.

TOURISM AND HOSPITALITY

Few industries "get" the notion of how business can foster peace more than the tourism industry does. Like telecommunications, this industry is in the business of bringing people together, which is a key reason for why it provided several of the peace entrepreneurs identified in Chapter 6.

It is hard to find many countries, outside of a few reclusive places like North Korea, that do not welcome an increase in tourism. Again, as with all of these industries, strategies for reflexivity and a long-term orientation are available for government engagement but, perhaps more so than any of the other industries, the opportunity to model civilizing behaviors and rhetorically encourage exchanges, dialogue, and understanding is available in the hospitality industry.

One of my partners in running conferences on business and peace is the International Institute of Peace through Tourism. Simply by reviewing some of their partnerships and affiliations, we can see these dimensions of reflexivity, long-term orientation, civilizing conduct, and rhetoric. Professional associations, for instance, have long been noted as places where member companies and business people learn from each others' experience, network, and undertake causes for a common good, not unlike what we saw in earlier chapters with respect to Columbia and El Salvador.[63]

In the 1950s, President Eisenhower championed the notion of citizen ambassador, using tourism to promote the good of goodwill, peace, and understanding. Because the program also "taught" people how to be respectful tourists, this ambassador program also had a civilizing dimension to it as well. Because building tourist accommodations and relationships tends to have a long-term orientation, the very practices such businesses engage in have the potential to align with the peace-building practices discussed throughout this book.

This should not be surprising. The very nature of tourism is to connect people and places that normally do not associate with each other. Whether it is a cultural exchange, an educational trip, or a visit to another geographical space, tourism has the opportunity to constructively build understanding among people. That is not to say that there are always positive impacts; like any other industry or sector, there is the opportunity for exploitation and insensitivity. Yet, these reflexive principles significantly enhance the opportunity for such exchanges to be peace building

In short, the tourism industry is well placed to be a place that can build peace, especially if it does its work in a way respectful to all involved and with a long-term orientation.

Conclusion

Governments will always have a crucial role in peacemaking, peacekeeping, and peace building. After all, they are the ones with the guns. Figuring out when to fire them and when not to stands as one of the essences of peace. In that regard, settling of borders and providing security become fundamental to establishing the playing field within which business can operate.

There are also, however, more subtle ways in which governments can actively promote peace without a heavy hand. By taking a polycentric approach, peace building can introduce ways in which to encourage the creation of more open societies, which have been shown to be more peaceful. Invading a country to establish an open society brings with it great risks, as has been seen in the twenty-first century.

This does not mean, of course, that government must stand to the side. Governments can encourage businesses to demonstrate to those within natural states that there are advantages to becoming more open through increasing economic opportunity. How governments encourage businesses (and elites within the country) to be more open to such activity is important. In particular, governments can encourage peaceful attributes reflexively by encouraging a long-term orientation, civilizing behaviors, and using rhetorical opportunities uniquely available to political leaders to foster peaceable practices.

To be sure, government is not alone in this effort. Just as North argued that all of the doorstep conditions must be at work to allow a country to make the transition from a natural state to an open state, so too must government, business, and civil society be operating in a way to encourage business contributions to peace. The next chapter addresses how civil society might help this process as well.

8   A New Great Awakening

For over twenty years, I have talked to my students about Garret Hardin's classic vignette, *Lifeboat Ethics*. Hardin supposed that 150 people found themselves shipwrecked at sea. A lifeboat could hold fifty people; one might squeeze in an extra ten, but that would test the engineering capacity of the lifeboat. Hardin used the vignette to talk about rich nations versus poor nations, how luck placed one in either geographical location, and how we might navigate life together on this planet.[1] I use it, instead, as an example of corporate self-interest.

Imagine the choices people on the lifeboat face if those in the water start to swim toward the boat.[2] In the short term, it would seem best to crack those in the water over the head with an oar to keep them out of the boat. Or perhaps those in the boat might paddle away quickly. Those in the water may not be in a great position, but they still may still be able to attack the boat; if those on the boat prove unsuccessful in paddling away or hitting people over the head, their own survival might be at risk. We often protect short-term self-interest quite well through these fight-or-flight strategies. But a long-term survival plan would recognize the great risks posed by such strategies and would be better served by finding ways to get people to hang onto the side of the boats, using natural human buoyancy and a small portion of the boat's capability. One might build that into time sharing on the boat or other ways to enhance one's own survival. Yet long-term self-interest and short-term interest conflict.

Long- and short-term interests may also conflict in business and peace. In the short term, peace does not seem to be of business's concern; it's up to government and perhaps some NGOs promoting peace. At the same time, businesses can find customers who value peace; when this happens, business might even profit from their aspirations for peace. Oddly, while some argue that business does better with peace, the same proponents see little role for business to actively promote peace behaviors. That strategy is very short-term oriented.

How does business learn to see this? Certainly there are peace entrepreneurs who can demonstrate new ways of doing business. There may also be times and places when the public spotlight shines on a corporation whose self-interest (foreign policy) projects it into the limelight: Google and Twitter during the Arab Spring, for instance. Both companies took political stands and did so in a nonviolent way. It will also be the case, however, that civil society will provide the ideas and opportunities for new development for increased understanding of peace strategies, as is the case with the academic and NGO contributions I have referenced throughout the book.

Civil Society

Civil society has long been fundamental to democracies, which themselves receive plaudits for being more peaceful than closed or natural-state societies.[3] Civil society can be broadly defined as the sector of society that is separate from business and government and comprised of families and NGOs, especially that sector of society where individuals volunteer their time and resources for nonpolitical and nonbusiness interests. Institutionally, this sector is comprised of religious, educational, charitable, and other advocacy organizations. These associations also provide a critical check on whatever regime is in political power, fosters voter education and turnout, and advocates for better governance generally. Without its presence, even in nominally democratic countries, "the power-brokers, economic exploiters, and warlord . . . tend to predominate in conflict-ridden weak or failed states, and may even capture the electoral process."[4] Some scholars argue that civic virtues such as tolerance, acceptance, honesty, and trust arise from civic associations, regardless of their purpose, and provide the social capital that undergirds democracy.[5]

The very presence of civil society will have a positive impact on peace building. Moreover, agencies devoted to democracy and peace building often use these intermediary organizations as vehicles to provide services and build capabilities. They enable international agencies to provide help to people coming out of conflict and to deal with the trauma of violence. Such organizations also support a population's reintegration into communities and participate in reconciliation processes. They often play a leading role in advocating for rule of law practices, including protection of human rights, dispute resolution mechanisms, legal reform, victim group advocacy, legal aid in poor communities, and organization of legal volunteers.

NGOs, sometimes also referred to as civil society organizations (CSOs), may take a leading role in issues related to security, including mine clearance programs, such as the International Campaign to Ban Landmines. CSOs often coordinate security reform efforts and small arms collection programs, as we saw in El Salvador.[6] CSOs also provide a natural way for cross-border efforts to bring people of otherwise conflicting agendas together.

Although there is a strong consensus that an active civil society is beneficial to peace, what impact can civil society—and the organizations that comprise civil society—have on supporting the business role in contributing to peace?

In fact, there is a foundation on which CSOs can rely. For example, CSOs play a role in economic issues, ranging from research and strategies recommendations for poverty reduction; employment promotion, especially among youth; natural resource management, microfinance programs, and providing public services when a failed or struggling state is unable to do so.

CSOs also affect how business may contribute to peace by partnering with businesses so that both better understand the nature of issues in a particular conflict-sensitive area.[7] To be sure, businesses may partner with various social service agencies merely in an attempt to provide cover for corporate affairs. If one is partnering with Oxfam, doesn't one get some halo protection?

Companies often discover, however, that NGOs remain open to working with corporate partners only if they retain the capacity to critique their corporate partners. I once spoke with an executive from a Fortune 500 company that had partnered with an NGO on a human rights issue. The NGO had then blasted the company in the press, which made them an even more valuable partner to the company. If an NGO withholds criticism, it may appear to have been bought off, and the NGO's very credibility will be called into question. But if the NGO is willing to take on the company, even while partnering with it, the company's efforts will most likely be enhanced because they appear to have an authentic, independent partner.

Having said this, *civil society* is a broad term. The organizations that comprise it are many and varied. Which of them might be most likely to be key allies to assist in the effort to support businesses' contribution to peace?

Key CSO Allies in Supporting Businesses' Contributions to Peace

PEACE CONTRIBUTORS

That paradigmatic resource for knowledge these days—Wikipedia—lists 289 peace organizations in the world today.[8] There may well be more. The notion that business could be a possible partner is strange and even angering to many involved in peace organizations because businesses are often seen as greedy obstacles to peace, not potential allies. Yet there are ways in which it makes sense for business to be interested in peace building, as we have already seen.

The profile of public–private partnerships has increased significantly over the years, as governments and NGOs fashion responses to disease, natural disasters, and war.[9] Too often, however, businesses are looked to as a source of funds for these partnerships. Although there may be a legitimate purpose for bankrolling charity, businesses can offer more than money, as some partnerships have found. When major transportation needs arise, a fleet of UPS, DHL, or Federal Express planes comes in as handy as a donation; so too, does such companies' logistical coordination capability.[10]

Too often, the notion of partnering with a peace organization may seem far afield from the radar screens of certain companies. But who better than civil society organizations to reach such companies? CSOs sit outside a company's competitive markets and also are separate from the political, so they are more likely to be perceived as honest brokers. And if peace is the raison d'être for peace organizations, the burden is fairly placed on these organizations *to actively initiate the conversation with business.*

Though conversations may falter, an old baseball adage states that you'll still end up with a Hall of Famer even with a 70 percent failure rate. A 30 percent success rate would build peace in a way that may not be matched by any other means.

ETHICS CONTRIBUTORS

If ethical business behavior correlates strongly with attributes of relatively nonviolent societies, then organizations that advocate for and foster corporate responsibility make a contribution to peace as well. Organizations such as the Aspen Institute Business & Society Program,[11] Business for Social Responsibility,[12] Ethisphere,[13] and others are naturally in the business of building bridges between successful business and corporate responsibility and may not be as adverse to business interests as peace players are. Their continued work, as well as that of academics and other activists, promotes peace whether they are consciously aware of it or not. To the extent that they and the businesses who embrace such conduct recognize that there is a pacific payoff for their efforts, they may become even more serious and mindful in their efforts, thereby creating a virtuous cycle in which the enhanced importance of their conduct reinforces and extends that conduct, making it even more impactful.

RELIGIOUS CONTRIBUTORS

Although Steven Pinker recognizes the valuable contributions religious believers can make to humanitarian efforts of many kinds, including peace, he treads carefully when it comes to religion. The fact that religion has a very checkered history in which zealots justified not only violence and killing but hideous torture as well makes him hesitant to suggest much a role for religion in the future.[14] Although understandable, this is a mistake.

Spirituality as part of human nature is ubiquitous throughout human history, though I use the term *spirituality* advisedly. One can differentiate between religion and spirituality, with religion pertaining more to a set of beliefs arising from some degree of affiliation with a group of people bound by common beliefs, whereas spirituality tends to be more of an individual recognition that something—the cosmos, human solidarity, mysticism—exists beyond our biological selves but is also connected to us.

Some biologists have gone as far as to argue that religion/spirituality is an evolutionary advantage; it becomes destructive when individuals act wholly for their immediate, hedonistic enjoyment without regard for anyone else in society.[15] To orient such self-interest into something that benefits society, religion offers up eternal life and membership in a group in exchange for deferring self-gratification.[16] That reorientation of self-interest transforms selfishness into citizenship.[17]

To be sure, religion is ambivalent. It can be the source of horrific atrocities, and it can also motivate inspiring humanitarianism. In claiming a potentially positive role for religion (and spirituality), some checks and balances are necessary to foreclose its dark side.

A similar analysis can be applied to government or business. A key reason that CSO organizations are often skeptical—sometimes downright outraged—at the notion that businesses might positively contribute to peace is that businesses *do* exploit children and pollute the environment. They *do* corrupt the government and act as agents of colonialism, two charges that also make us skeptical of how much we should trust government. Yet, both business and government can contribute positively as well. The notion of ambivalence could be applied to just about any human activity, which is why moral thinkers from Aristotle[18] to the Buddha[19] advocated moderation or a *middle way* so as to avoid the dark extremes of any human activity.

The former head of the Human Genome Project, Francis Collins, argues that his spiritual commitments are grounded in the evidence that humanity shares a moral sense.[20] Collins's optimism lays in his observation that, at the core, religious and philosophical systems tend to largely agree on what is morally appropriate. Although recognizing that there are differences among religions, Collins argues that the fundamental of faiths reflect an ethical basis of human identity. Given his leadership and expertise in the genetics that is core to evolutionary theory, Collins's commitment to a religious understanding stands as an example of how deep religion is in our nature as well as providing a thoughtful way to integrate religion and science. Indeed, it is exactly that shared moral sense that also captures our peaceful sense and connects ethical business behavior to the possibilities for businesses fostering peace.

Regardless of whether business likes it or not, commercial affairs bump into religious beliefs and believers, whether in the workplace (via employees) or in the market (via customers). If that is true, it is because of our evolutionary spiritual nature; then businesses must find ways to deal with such beliefs. In my previous work, I've suggested how businesses can create a model that allows its constituents to speak about their beliefs in order to be true to their identities. However, that model best works when there is a degree of spiritual literacy so that others can hear spiritual speech without turning it into spiritual attack or reacting as if under spiritual attack.

Not every kind of business can do this; indeed, those that can are open to the kind of difficult ethical dialogue that must occur to deal with such issues. Yet, if a business, which may well draw on a great deal of diversity in a global market, can do this, it can make a profound contribution to peace and to religious understanding.

Central, then, to that organizational commitment to spiritual literacy would be a *widely* shared theological virtue of hospitality to strangers, an ethic that would go a long way in diffusing some of the conflict flash points we see today.[21] In global business, we encounter strangers. Business has a reason for wanting those strangers to work together, and so openness to someone "other" carries with it this sense of hospitality while also capturing the benefits strangeness—even diversity—holds.

A second precept would be an articulation of our human connectedness. This is a sustainability argument, and it is one that has direct relationship to peace as well. If we are connected as fellow beings sharing a planet, it is harder to conceive of murdering each other than would be the case if we see other human beings as nonhuman.

The third is a sense of detachment, of moderating some of the material needs that drive the world in a direction that leads to violence. Are material goods or the political power really worth bloodshed? If we learn the lessons of detachment, the rationale for spilling blood falls apart.

CULTURAL CONTRIBUTORS: ARTS, SPORTS, AND EDUCATION

Rather than relying on religion to foster a culture that moves the needle along the road of peace, Pinker is enthusiastic about the arts.[22] I'm in full agreement. Like religion and business, the arts reach a wide range of individuals and allow for a larger possibility of transforming cultural attitudes toward peace, which includes attitudes that can be carried over into business. Although Pinker finds great potential in satire, I'd expand that and propose that television and film in general stand as crucial contributors to peace. Hollywood and television are businesses, of course, rather than members of civil society. Still, there are plenty of civil society organizations devoted to each, such as the documentary film producers recognized at the Sundance Film Festival, as well as nonprofits who can act as their own kind of peace entrepreneurs in fostering this model.

Sports are yet another vehicle to use to promote peace. Although the violence of football or ongoing replays of hockey fights send violent messages, sports provide the best way for violence to be contained in a way that minimizes harm. Just as I recognize that religion is part of our human nature, I believe we have aggressive, violent aspects to us as well; attempts to extinguish them aren't likely to be successful. We need to find ways to express our aggression as safely as possible and find the texture of an event that goes beyond the violence itself. Football may be a violent sport, but there is also speed, strategy, surprise, misdirection, and pageantry that make the game about more than just the big hit of the night.

Like television, sports are big businesses; because their popularity is so dependent on television, the combination of the two risks appealing to the lowest common denominator rather than to something more complex and uplifting. Again, there are civil society organizations oriented to this kind of task within sports as well, such as The Center for Sports, Peace, and Society in the United Kingdom, the Soccer for Peace Foundation in Florida, the Football for Peace Foundation in Israel, and Peace Players International in Washington, D.C. Peace Players International, for instance, runs sports programs for children at risk, providing them with constructive activity as well as mentoring and role modeling. They have also developed a curriculum for nonviolent conflict resolution so that kids in the programs learn how to resolve disputes peacefully.

It's not surprising that, as an academic, I conclude this section with praise for the possibilities of education. Beyond research, books, and classes, however, everything mentioned in the preceding pages provides education in a way. The business and peace movement is about educating civil society, as well as businesses and governments, of the possibilities of peace.

BUSINESS CONTRIBUTORS

Some business organizations figured out the relationship between business and peace long ago. Rotary International, which began in Chicago in 1905, was founded in part to help businesses foster peace "through a world fellowship of business and professional persons united in the ideal of service ."[23] Throughout its history, Rotary has been a vehicle for what we now call corporate social responsibility by fighting disease, awarding exchange scholarships, creating literacy programs, supporting international studies programs, and forming a Rotary Community Corps.[24] Among its programs are Peace Centers and Peace Fellowships that promote conflict resolution skills that both resolve disputes within companies and also offer ways to resolve disputes in places where businesses do their work.[25] Businesses can then also teach others how to resolve disputes peacefully. Rotary does this not simply to do good but because of its belief that public spiritedness is good for business as well.

The International Chamber of Commerce is another prominent organization whose members aim to be "merchants of peace."[26] The Chamber has promoted an open trading system that hopes to reduce the likelihood of violence.[27] It has had, therefore, a long history of members actively serving on transnational organizations to promote the elimination of barriers to free trade. It was also one of the primary founders and supporters of the Business for Peace Foundation, whose work has been profiled throughout this book.

Of the nearly 1.5 million charitable organizations in the United States, approximately 365,000 of them are chambers of commerce, civic leagues, and fraternal organizations.[28] These organizations have long been places business people looked to for information, increasing their political power, networking, and other benefits. These organizations provide a key service in sifting through the millions of ideas floating through the market (economic, political, and social) and relating those directly pertinent to association members through speeches, newsletters, and other services. As *business* associations, their work is to provide a forum for businesses to be able to do their work better, through networking and the sharing of ideas and research. Some of these associations are formed with a particular public spiritedness in mind with the implicit claim that being public spirited is also good business. They are, in short, a potentially key ally in helping businesses learn how their self–interest is fostered by promoting peace and that peace helps to create the stability for good business.

With these examples in mind, the notion that business might be an instrument of peace seems hardly new. Neither is the notion that businesses would advocate alongside governmental and transgovernmental organizations for free trade and other economic policies or that businesses would band together to combat public issues in a way we often describe as new—CSR—but that is very traditional. Frankly, much of what I ask for in this book is to reclaim a civic-minded business approach that embraces engagement in public life.

Further, we have seen how business associations can make a difference in peace building, peacemaking, and peacekeeping. Efforts in Northern Ireland, South Africa, Cyprus, and Sri Lanka stand as good examples.[29] Sometimes these efforts were made as part of a formal business association, whereas other times they were more informal; clearly, business associations have worked toward peace both generally and in specific situations.

Yet we must not be overly naïve. I say "overly" because without some degree of idealistic naiveté, I doubt much social progress is ever made. After all, it was an active business association that attempted to bring peace and stability to Colombia by opposing an administration tied to the drug trade while some of its members supported the same administration, thereby undercutting the associations' efforts.[30]

Perhaps the same charge of naiveté might be leveled at Rotary or the International Chamber of Commerce or Football for Peace or many other organizations that champion the cause of peace. Fortunately, there some who are willing to accept such charges to change the way in which the world works and to make it less violent. This includes business associations that can and have served as direct vehicles for businesses to promote peace and therefore stand as assets that could be constructively used in the future.

Our Baboon Moment

"The Forest Troop" was a group of baboons that lived on the edge of a tourist camp in Africa. Their social organization was dominated by a small set of aggressive alpha males who ate garbage left over from the tourists. The rest of the troop was able to get its share of food only after the aggressive males had had their fill. After tuberculosis swept through the camp and killed the aggressive males, the remaining less aggressive males and the females became more of a sharing culture and far more pacific.[31]

When a new set of aggressive males came to the Forest Troop to breed, they did not fill the vacuum and dominate as alpha males. Instead, the more pacific culture continued, and the aggressive alpha males changed instead. This more pacific culture has persisted for several generations.[32]

Cultures change both for humans as well as baboons. Switzerland and Sweden, now painted as peaceful oases, were not so peaceful a few hundred years ago. Germany and Japan look quite different than they did seventy years ago. If baboons and countries can change, so can business. Even central banking can change by recognizing the moral foundations that lead to prosperity and peace.

Peace? Yes. It is possible to achieve peace in today's world; by doing so, prosperity will flourish. If one thinks peace is not possible to achieve, consider slavery.

To be sure, gruesome slavery still exists in our world today, especially with respect to the sex trade.[33] But slavery has dramatically declined and has even been legally abolished in every country in the world.[34] The same can be done with war.

Business does indeed flourish with peace and stability. It also has contributions to make and, like lifeboat ethics, business needs to be able to see its long-term self-interests and practice them in the short-term. Otherwise, the pressures of conflict may swamp the lifeboat itself. The pressures of modern weaponry are too acute and the access many have to that weaponry too easy to defer to others or to a later time. Government can help business foster peace. So, too, can civil society. But, in the final analysis, business has to take up the cause itself, an idea we will explore in the next chapter.

9 Why a Peace-Oriented Corporate Foreign Policy Is Smart Business

Why does the Internet change everything? Because any person can use the information it provides to make assessments using values more likely to be drawn from Main Street than from any other avenue with a historically important return address. Fundamental changes in societal structures and information moved us from an agricultural to an industrial age.[1] And now the telecommunications/Internet age brings us into a time when, unless censors fully control the apparatus of the Internet and other means of communication, it will be harder for values to be kept to the side.

For business, this raises some important issues. First, a businessperson in the twenty-first century will be managing in a complex environment that requires executives to bring to bear questions more than template strategies.[2] How do we succeed?[3] What makes this environment complex?[4] How do our operations interact with the environment?[5] Are we meeting our responsibilities?[6] Are we disciplined about asking questions?[7] Are we working well with others?[8] Is our own house in order?[9] Who should be asking these questions?[10]

These are management questions to elicit information, always critical for any leader but even more crucial for businesspeople in complex environments, which increasingly comprise a good deal of the world. In an age when terrorism can reach across borders, global financial markets can affect prices anywhere, and messages and cultures can enter homes and businesses regularly, there are fewer and fewer simple environments. Perhaps there was a time when businesses could ignore these swirls of global activity, but telecommunications, the Internet, free markets, and capital flows make our view of those days more nostalgic than realistic.

The Internet itself is simultaneously transparent and permanent. Given the ubiquity of cell phone cameras and the ease with which one can post a picture, a video, or a podcast in a matter of seconds and have billions of views, the transparency of the Internet makes it more difficult to get away with things. What's more, once something is on the Internet, it is difficult to get rid of it.

The Internet also democratizes information, which is available not just to powerful political and business leaders but to anyone with an Internet connection. Such empowerment has its dark side to be sure—because anyone can be a "journalist," one can pass as one without any sense of journalistic integrity[11]—but it also turns everyone into a deputy sheriff who can battle wrongdoing.[12]

Because of these factors, to be successful in the coming years, businesses must be "businessworthy," which is much like creditworthiness; it stands as a trust-marking identity that ensures ethical behavior. This term, coined by the founder of the Business for Peace Foundation, Per Saxegaard, stands for the notion that an Internet-moderated environment demands trustworthy—ethical—business conduct in the twenty-first century. That same behavior is the basis for business's contribution to peace.[13] It will be smart business to be ethical as well as interested in and contributing to peace. My bigger concern is how companies that are more instrumental in their practices can be shown the benefits of peace building and to be recognized for that work as well.

Corporate Foreign Policy

To have a foreign policy, there has to be a domestic starting point. Domestic issues tend to follow with country rather than corporation. One gets to be an American or an Australian by being born in the country or moving there. One gets to be an Apple employee by getting a job; even if one extends the Apple "family" to those who buy the company's products, the identification is hardly the same. Thus, while it is easy to understand that France has a foreign policy, it seems a bit strange to say that Peugeot does.

Yet, companies do have policies that resemble those typically associated with nation-states, and they negotiate with nation-states on topics ranging from customs to taxes to regulation to promotion to labor issues to campaign contributions and many other issues. Companies often have significant power that can place pressure on a country and its policies.[14]

Multinational companies (MNCs) bring with them enormous power and influence.[15] Often, they will move into an emerging, conflict-sensitive market to obtain natural resources for their products, use lower-cost labor, or position themselves in a geographic area to launch into nearby markets. When a multinational moves into such a market, it must protect its own integrity and reputation. This may lead to an active corporate citizenship role. It might also improve local infrastructure—improved sewage treatment, better security—with positive visible effects for the community. More subtle issues can play an even larger role, such as when companies insist that local suppliers meet certain standards to maintain a contract to supply the company.

Motorola, for instance, can be said to have a peace-spreading impact because it requires its suppliers to participate in quality management processes.[16] In so doing, Motorola has a wider impact on the local economy, as those suppliers adapt to its insistence on high-quality products and services, humane treatment of employees, strong accounting practices, and leadership training. The same beneficial impact can occur because of anticorruption and human rights practices, which also both further peace.

Ford Motor Company is another corporation that has had an impact on local practices by pledging to apply the same human rights standards throughout its global supply chain, which earned it a 100 percent rating from the 2008 Human Rights Campaign Corporate Equality Index. According to Ford's manager for social sustainability, "That commitment strengthens our ability to weather economic storms by building stronger, trusting relationships with our suppliers, their employees and communities. The mutual commitment and alignment of values created reduce risks, improve access to markets and boost resilience and innovation during tough economic times."[17]

A small or medium-size company can also have strong peace practices, but in a different way. Voice and say in governance are themselves practices of nonviolence[18] and a key characteristic of peaceful societies, where members interact face-to-face[19] and have a say in how group actions will affect them. Empowering employees to have a voice in a large multinational corporation may be hard (which is not to say that it should be avoided). But in a smaller organization, interactions among shareholders, employees, and customers are more likely.

A state-owned enterprise can implement policies that aim to address social ills, something that may be hard for a for-profit business to do. In the 1990s, Hydro-Québec was faced with resistance from Cree and Inuit Indians over the construction of a hydroelectric dam in the tribes' traditional hunting grounds. Hydro-Québec, owned by the province of Québec, was able to address many concerns of the native peoples. The company also lowered infant mortality rates, built educational and medical facilities, and, in the words of the Cree themselves, made life change "only for the better."[20] That is not to say that all dialogue between Hydro-Québec and the native peoples was easy; there were difficult discussions, but the important aspect is that there was dialogue.[21] When the state that owns the enterprise is committed to resolving issues in this way, a SOE can be a significant contributor to peacefulness.

Regardless of whether a company is an MNC, SME (small or medium enterprise), or SOE, there are at least two important factors that are worth adding to the mix of this analysis and that make a difference in the strategies companies have available to them in creating their own foreign policies with an eye toward peace. Those factors concern a company's own narrative and, conversely, how companies are perceived.

Self-Narrative

At a gathering of corporate leaders at the Council of Foreign Relations in Washington, my colleagues and I were struck by the disconnect between what companies are actually doing and what the leadership thinks of as the identity of the company. Many participants at the event endorsed the need to assess the political landscape as a core component of the development of their business strategies. A few even had full-blown computer-generated "war-gaming" scenarios that were constantly updated. Others were not as sophisticated but understood the push-pull between business and government, assessing when to challenge or even defy government and for what reasons, and seeing their business as an actor in a multipolar world. They just didn't call it corporate foreign policy. Instead, they referred to it as "risk management" or simply "strategy."

Others at the gathering saw aspects of what they do—especially those actions that would garner public support—as corporate social responsibility. Yet, corporate foreign policy has a different feel than CSR or corporate citizenship (CC), a more recent term.[22] Many companies address corporate citizenship as part of their corporation's identity and assert that the business firm is not simply a collection of individuals or an extension of the government. Instead, the company is articulating a sense of its own corporate self that has citizenship as part of its self-narrative. Such narratives provide the driving identify of corporate culture.

In pushing CC beyond CSR, some scholars argue that, as nation states lose power because of corporate-led globalization, corporations take a larger role in carrying out what typically are governmental functions.[23] Others suggest that companies address "public health, education, social security, and protection of human rights while often operating in countries with failed state agencies."[24] Under these conceptions, businesses step in when government steps out; this is particularly true in foreign settings where businesses bring "a special capacity to help resolve underlying tensions."[25]

In the business consulting world, the admonition that "culture eats strategy for breakfast" stands as a jumping-off point for various culture-building sales pitches.[26] The phrase reputedly hangs in a prominent area of Ford Motor Company as emblematic of the idea that no matter how far reaching a vision or strategy might be, nothing will happen without the right kind of supportive corporate culture.[27] There is, in short, more to business purposes and actions than strategy. Corporations bring with them history and culture. They are "real entities," a term that not is only casually descriptive but also plays into a relevant legal theory about corporations.

When it comes to interactions between a corporation and various other political, economic, and NGO actors, strategy is certainly an aspect of the mix, but so too are the company's history and culture, just as they are for nation-states. A change in tactics resulting from a new election or even from a change of executive mind may well be a strategic move, but it will be contextualized within a larger history and culture. Calling corporate interactions on a global scale "strategy" captures part of what a company is doing, but not entirely.

That is even more true with risk management. Risk calculations embed themselves in every political and economic decision, but the determination of what risks to take, when to "roll the dice," or how to factor in nonmeasurable values also factors into many, if not all decisions. As with strategy, risk management crucially informs corporate foreign policy, but neither fully accounts for it. Calling what corporations do as "corporate foreign policy" seems to offer a more accurate characterization for those who make corporate decisions because ultimately "risk" and "strategy" are guided by a company's own narrative, which tells it how to interact with the world.

Perceived Identity

One might ask if calling risk management, strategy, or CSR something else—corporate foreign policy—is simply semantics. Yet, corporate foreign policy is a way to describe a corporate identity from an outside perspective. In the Council of Foreign Relations meeting previously mentioned, one executive claimed that his company had no foreign policy because it studiously separated itself from local political matters. All his company was doing, he said, was executing a strategy of providing a business service while minimizing risk by keeping the company's head low in volatile markets. Yet, he agreed that an even better characterization of the company's strategy was that of a "foreign policy" of "political neutrality." That outside perceived identity more aptly captures the company's self-narrative. Indeed, I suspect that companies will find this characterization of their work as "foreign policy" resonates with their own narrative and culture, even if they had not perceived it that way before.

Just as countries have identities they are known for, so do companies. Just as companies follow competing ideologies, so do companies. We don't expect China to have the same goals as Norway, so why would we think we can lump all corporations together monolithically? Yet, this simple reframing of what corporations do in the world today may help in them also seeing that, as foreign affairs actors, their work has an impact on issues of peace and diplomacy.

This is also important because institutions always face issues of legitimacy. Why does society allow them to exist in the first place?[28] Some have noted that corporations are artifactual; their existence relies on social constructs that provide them with their own identities, protections, and opportunities.[29] Individuals naturally group together for many different reasons, but they don't receive benefits of limited liability, free transferability of ownership interests, continuity of life, or centralized management without some kind of social endorsement, typically through the legal system.

Companies that stay within their own domestic borders may not be faced with as many issues of corporate foreign policy as those that cross borders, though that may not be as certain, given the way the Internet allows even a tiny business to do business globally. What choices do companies have when they go overseas?

Five Choices

In arguing beyond a conventional model that emphasized government–government interactions, Joseph Montville defined such traditional models as "Track I" diplomacy but added Track II diplomacy as the "unofficial, non-structured interaction between members of adversarial groups or nations that is directed toward conflict resolution by addressing psychological factors,"[30] an approach that others built on in stressing that Track II diplomacy might also influence public opinion in a way that could resolve conflict.[31] Whereas business has a role in contributing to peace, so do religious group interaction, the media, and others. Academic communities and activist groups can also help business foster peace just as business can help nongovernmental professionals foster peace.[32] Institutions working toward peace are allies, not enemies.

When companies expand beyond their traditional home-country borders, they must deal with issues of narrative, perception, and their own foreign policy. In a 2003 article, Thomas Dunfee and I offered a typology to describe five basic alternatives companies have in crafting their foreign policy.[33] The first approach is the *corporate imperialist* approach, in which the company has a clearly thought-out identity and waves the corporate flag rather than that of any home country; it truly has a multinational identity. Though the word *imperialist* has bad connotations, this kind of company is typically championed by ethicists because such a company would apply the same standards around the world. A pharmaceutical company would have the same drug testing policies no matter what an individual country, perhaps with more lax standards, would allow. Labor practices would follow the same rule as well.[34]

The second approach is the *corporate nationalist*. Here, the company would be closely identified with its home country. Its identity would be that of a Japanese company or an American country and would not have its own independent policies per se but would apply its home country policies aboard.[35]

The third approach would be the *corporate chameleon*, which would follow the law of the host country—a *when in Rome, do as the Romans do* approach. Although this could be the approach of a very humble, respectful guest, this kind of company could also lack a moral backbone and do whatever it could get away with.[36]

The *corporate opportunist* simply follows whatever strategy allows it to make the most money,[37] whereas the final approach, the *corporate integrationist*, is an ideal rather than an existing example. These companies would have strong, moral identities that apply wherever they go without losing a sense of their country of origin. They also respect the norms of the place where they do business.[38]

Getting to that final approach requires more than business sense and integrates economic, political, and moral knowledge and commitments. It's not adequately captured by risk management. Strategy might encompass it, as would corporate social responsibility, but only if those terms were also widened beyond what they typically mean. It seems that corporate foreign policy does capture the complexity of moral identity, political maneuverability, and economic vitality. Which term is used, of course, is incidental. What is important is that companies see that all these factors become necessary to successfully navigate a twenty-first-century global and technologically connected business world.

It may well be true that the Internet changes the capability of anyone to oversee the actions of businesses and make them accountable for their actions. Together with the five foreign policy frameworks already mentioned, this accountability leads to a larger point: Companies may be forced into having a foreign policy—whether related to peace or not—to navigate the twenty-first century. Or to phrase it another way, companies navigating on the global scene are often perceived as having a foreign policy; embracing that notion may help the company connect its self-narrative and its identity as well is its strategy, risk management, corporate social responsibility, and other functional areas into a more explicit notion of foreign policy.

Peace tends to arise from a balance of power that is in equilibrium, and a long-term balance of power is one grounded in ethics and justice that goes beyond keeping totalitarianism or ruthlessness at bay; it foments a justice-based peace that is sustainable. Corporations, of course, can enter into balance of power formulations in any kind of society. There is money to be made under the guises of repressive regimes just as there is in open societies. But companies will do better, again, in the long run, if they do their business in open societies. In those societies, they also have an opportunity, indeed an obligation, to constructively contribute to peace, justice, and openness. They do this by creating their own equilibrium, balancing issues of profit, compliance, and ethics.

These anchors recur because they are fundamentally rooted in our nature. Thus we see them in our politics and corporations but also in our deep, anthropological roots. Although it is true that a business contribution to peace will depend on the specifics of the context, it is also true that there are fundamental themes coursing through these issues. Recognizing and aligning one's work with these themes provides the best chance for businesses to contribute to peace and to establish a smart corporate foreign policy that makes for good business.

Societies change, but certain themes endure. Both Pinker and Fry make a strong argument for why the future holds good prospects for peace.[39] Gartzke shows how a capitalist peace holds potential,[40] whereas various economists demonstrate that thriving economics—and by extension, thriving business—is more than a push-and-pull match between markets and government; things like ethics and trust matter.[41] North and Ostrom point to a model in which open societies that create accountability, wealth, freedom, and responsibility.[42] Saxegaard articulates a hardheaded, purposeful strategy and operational conduct that will thrive in the twenty-first century.[43] In each of these—where our best hopes lie—we see the recurring tripartite theme. The table seems set. The previous chapters have set out a way in which gentle commerce is a crucial ingredient to foster peacefulness in the world, in part by asking business to draw on some deep history of peaceful societies prior to the agricultural and industrial revolutions.

If the name of the game for business peace building is trust and if the potential for smart business similarly depends on trust, then it would make sense to conclude this book with a model for how businesses can fashion a foreign policy on the basis of trustworthiness. I propose that there are three dimension of trust: *hard trust*, *real trust*, and *good trust*.

A Trust Model for CFP-Peace

Hard trust is about coercively requiring corporations to adhere to standards.[44] It is about law and public opinion. An outside third party provides assurances to the public that business will obey certain standards under the threat of punishment if they do not. Hard trust is about rules. It is about making clear what is permissible and what is not. When you work in a mobile work force, with people from all different cultures moving to a new job every few years in a global economy, a company needs to fairly alert everyone of the rules they are expected to know and abide by.[45]

This is old stuff for companies by now. In large part because of the 1991 federal sentencing guidelines, companies have adopted all kinds of codes of conduct, mission statements, and values statements.[46] These compliance programs attempt to get everyone at a company to abide by relevant laws and help create organizational cultures that lead to ethics and compliance, yet studies show that paper programs don't work very well. If a company writes a program but does little to implement it, obviously the program will be ineffective. Even if a company does try to implement a compliance program, if there is no top-to-bottom accountability,[47] it will likely flounder. Everyone knows that lower-level workers are accountable to people at the top. But if top-level people aren't accountable at least to a code of behavior that everyone from top to bottom must follow, then companies create great cynicism and undermine trust.[48]

Enron had a very well thought-out conflict of interest policy so that high-level executives could not hold ownership interest in related companies. Yet, according to the report of the independent members of Enron's board of directors, the board formally suspended its code of conduct three times to allow Andrew Fastow to obtain lucrative ownership interests in special purpose entities designed to remove Enron debt from its books and provide a financial windfall for him at the same time.[49] One can imagine the message this sends.

Companies may be powerful entities, but they still face the issue of complying with the laws in the countries where they do business. If they don't, they can expect prosecution, regulation, and punishment. Thus, for CFP, a company will earn a level of trustworthiness if it follows the laws of the country in which it is working.

But what if the law is unjust? A law has some degree of legitimacy if it follows lawful processes agreed on in a democratic society. Even if a company disagrees with congressional legislation, executive orders, or a Supreme Court decision, it is most likely to obey the law because it followed proper procedure. There may be some times when, even in following such procedures, the law is viewed as deeply immoral, as was the case with slavery. Then, there are times when both process and substance seemed to be on troubled grounds. This is the situation in which Google and Twitter found themselves during the Arab Spring. They opposed dictatorially imposed censorship. In such situations, businesses are confronted with a choice. The companies chose to support freedom of speech and democratic voice. The fact that they *chose* is important. They could not execute a foreign policy of neutrality; even a choice to not become involved becomes, in fact, a choice.

How does a company choose? If markets and wealth grow through obedience to just laws and by attention to human rights and to gentle commerce, then companies choose well when they align themselves with these peace-building values. Of course, in the short term, a business may jettison such considerations, but the long-term interests of companies would seem, from what we have seen, to benefit from allying with peace-building values.

Law is a coercive weapon to make sure companies behave. So is public opinion. Both emphasize an accountability based on toughness. Violate the law and be punished. Violate public opinion and be vilified. As we've discussed, it is very easy to capture incriminating behavior. Cameras and communications (social media, blogs, television) can turn public opinion against companies very easily, which is why companies today have developed public relations programs that emphasize corporate responsibility.[50]

Yet cameras are the tip of the technological iceberg. Technology can also make unethical behavior impossible; for example, companies can now prevent employees from accessing pornographic websites at work. Technology and public opinion (like the law) are double-edged swords, but their toughness can be used to force business to abide by standards found by many to build peace.

REAL TRUST

Real trust is what most people think of when they imagine trust in business. Real trust is about the business case for building social capital, reputation, and good will through ethical behavior. It's also about aligning rewards and incentives and garnering the confidence of stakeholders because you keep your word, tell the truth, and produce high-quality goods and services. It is about putting your money where your mouth is so that, when crunch time comes, you deliver on ethics rather than weaseling out of commitments. It is about making sure that, when conducting business, you don't trample on the interests of stakeholders who can't protect themselves that well and who trust a company not to harm them.[51]

Internally, real trust is about aligning incentives and rhetoric. It is one thing for a company to claim it values integrity but quite another to structure its affairs to actually reward that integrity. I frequently teach a case I call "the bug-infested cookie case," which tells the story of a recent MBA graduate working in a department store's gourmet food section, selling cookies wrapped in sealed foil. Some customers claim that there are bugs crawling on the cookies. The manager of the food section instructs the grad to get rid of the cookies, and she thinks that means throwing the cookies away. The manager, however, knows of a store in the inner city that will take the potentially infested cookies, sell them for cents on the dollar, and get back some of the department store's investment.[52]

There are a number of things wrong with this scenario, but from a certain twisted standpoint, it makes sense. The manager's annual bonus was based on a formula of profitability per square foot; her annual allocation of floor space was based on the same formula. All the company's incentives encouraged her to do exactly what she did: squeeze every cent of profit she could from the product. I'm sure the store did not want to be known as the bug-infested-cookie-store, but that's exactly what its incentives were leading to.[53]

In this case, as in most, ethics isn't about personal integrity (although it would have been good for either the recent graduate or the manager to take a firmer stand against the sale of the cookies), and it isn't about applying a refined philosophical principle. It's about designing a "bad food" category on the accounting books so that the manager wouldn't be punished for doing the right thing. This example demonstrates that ethics in business is a management issue, not a personal integrity issue.

A company is in its strongest position when its core constituents fully support it, just as holding one's base is central for political regimes. Twenty-first-century corporate foreign policy needs to align its rhetoric, strategy, and operations so that it maintains its integrity with its core internal constituents: employees, customers, shareholders, and, in many cases, creditors. This is not to jettison other constituents, but these internal stakeholders are essential. Moreover, these stakeholders breathe the air and drink the local water; thus, an environmental stakeholder will have some representation if employees have a voice in business affairs. The same logic holds true of local communities and political organizations, whose constituents may also be stakeholders of the company. A business will never be able to focus on every stakeholder affected by its actions, but it can give its internal stakeholders a voice in a practicable way and, in doing so, will end up with a broad range of perspectives.

GOOD TRUST

All the legal rules, empirical connections, and philosophical principles in the world only go so far. If people don't care about ethical behavior in the first place, nothing is likely to happen. Business ethics often neglects to address how to get people to care about ethics, but engaging the affective dimension is important. We tend to rely on external legal rules to guarantee trust and want to find a business case for why trust pays. Those are well and good. But the heart of ethical behavior in business hinges on how to nourish a sense of caring about the behavior in the first place.[54]

There are some companies for whom being ethical means following the law. There's something to be said for that. There are others who align their incentives with their rhetoric. There is even more to be said for that. But there are some companies for whom ethics is so much part of their identity and the reason people come to work that people and companies become passionate for moral excellence. In these companies, ethics is discussed on a regular basis, and people get good at making morally driven decisions. They build a culture so that most ethical problems are headed off before they become problems, and, even if they do, people in the company, like those at Johnson & Johnson in the Tylenol case, knew how to choose the right path.[55]

Philosophical and legal principles have their merit, but the most natural way for people to connect with ethical behavior is through telling stories. The first assignment I give my students is to tell me a story about something they witnessed that was "good" in business. Then they have to define what "good" is. The assignment is just a two-pager, but it is a difficult one. Many students struggle to remember something good, preferring to write about something bad instead. That's too easy. What's more interesting, and harder, is to define what you think is good. The story helps connect them to what's in their heart. Then they are challenged to articulate their idea of good so that others can evaluate and internalize it themselves.

Another way to build good trust is to take into account our hardwired, biological propensities for interacting with groups and maximize the expression of our innate moral sentiments.[56] Within the natural law tradition, there is a long-standing belief that human beings form their moral character in "mediating institutions."[57] These are small organizations where there are significant face-to-face interactions and people experience, in one form or another, the consequences of their actions. They are family, neighborhood, religious, and voluntary organizations, and potentially business, too. No matter how much a sibling may make you mad, you have to figure out a way to get along, to be a good citizen of the family. In these structures, our actions become habits, and we develop our moral character.[58]

At the same time, more than sentimental caring is needed. Caring sometimes gets limited to other members of the group and precluded from outsiders. Caring needs accountability (hard trust) and pragmatic fairness (real trust), just as hard trust needs pragmatic fairness and emotional commitment and just as real trust needs accountability and emotional commitment. They check and balance each other and make themselves stronger as a whole.[59]

Of course, the final aspect of good trust is peace itself. People will trust another more if they believe that person is truly committed to a good. In getting people to care about ethics at work, I believe that if they see a good that can be achieved by being ethical—peace or sustainability—they will be more mindful of their actions and more committed to those goods.

Peace is a hypergood.[60] Every society values peace. Every religion valorizes it. To be sure, martial values demonstrated in battle are also glorified, but as anthropological research shows, it is empirically inaccurate to say that human beings are prone to violence and to war. Most of our human history has been peaceful. When it has not been peaceful, violence has tended to be individual and episodic rather than organized as in war. Those who believe in a life after death rarely look forward to eternal war but instead look forward to rest and peace. In the final analysis, we yearn for peace. We are getting better at being more peaceful. Commerce has had some positive role in that development, and gentle commerce can play an even bigger one.

Per Saxegaard provides one more reason for why the notion of business and peace—or businessworthiness—is so fitting for the future. Although people do like to make money, there is a decreasing, marginal return to it. To be sure, making money to feed a family produces happiness. But once those Maslovian needs are satisfied, the marginal utility of money decreases.[61] What does increase happiness if not more money? Research increasingly shows that happiness comes from the quality of relationships—both personal and social—that we have. At some point, businesspeople will also realize that they will find greater happiness by improving the quality of their relationships and those of the society in which they live.

We have already seen that peace entrepreneurs and ethical businesses can provide such leadership. The more leadership that can come from others who have been financially successful and who therefore can be more easily observed around the world, the better. We simply ought to celebrate any business that sees how to align its work with peace building.

The good news is that the notion that businesses can contribute to peace is not so novel any more. Academics are writing about it, international organizations actively promote it, and governments are recognizing that "it's been under our noses for a hundred years and we've missed it." Increasingly, businesses are seeing the advantages of peace building and often peacemaking and peacekeeping. My prediction and hope is that in 2050 our progeny will just shake their heads at what took us so long to figure this out.

Appendix

Appendix: Winners of Award for Corporate Excellence and Oslo Award Winners

Winners of Award for Corporate Excellence

2013 Taylor Guitars, Cameroon
      Fruit of the Loom, Honduras
      Plantronics, Mexico
2012 Sorwathe, Rwanda
      Intel Corporation, Vietnam
2011 Sahlman Seafoods, Incorporated, Nicaragua
      Procter & Gamble, Nigeria
      Procter & Gamble, Pakistan
2010 Cisco Systems, Israel
      Mars, Ghana
      Denimatrix, Guatemala
2009 Trilogy International Partners, Haiti
      TOMS Shoes, Argentina
2008 Cargill, China
      SURevolution, Colombia
2007 G.E., Indonesia
      Transnational Automotive Group, Cameroon
2006 General Motors, Colombia
      Goldman Sachs, Chile
      Sambazon, Brazil
2005 Cisco Systems, Jordan
      Lapa Rios Ecolodge, Costa Rica
2004 Motorola, Brazil
      FIJI Water, Fiji

2003 Chevron/Texaco, Nigeria
      U.S. Steel Corporation, the Slovak Republic
2002 Coca-Cola, Egypt
      Chindex International, China
2001 Ford Motor Company, South Africa
      SELCO, Vietnam
2000 Motorola, Malaysia
      Rayonier New Zealand
      Land O'Frost, Uruguay
1999 Xerox, Brazil
      F. C. Schaffer & Associates, Ethiopia.[1]

Oslo Award Winners

Margaret Mussoi L. Groff, Brazil, Chief Financial Officer of ITAIPU Binacional, the world's largest hydropower station in terms of power generation. She
has been engaged in motivating female employees to seek professional development, which resulted in an increase of female managers from 10 to 21 percent
in nine years, in ITAIPU Binacional. Groff has also established ITAIPU's policy
and guidelines for gender equality based on the UN Global Compact Women's
Empowerment Principles Leadership Group, contributing to more gender-equal
societies.

Connie Hasemann, Denmark, founder and CEO of Telehandelshuset AS. Ms.
Hasemann is a strong advocate for social change through sustainable business.
With a mission to help disabled people show they are a valuable labor resource
on equal standing with others, Hasemann established what is now one of the
leading social enterprises in Denmark. Her drive and dedication break down
barriers and are appreciated across national borders. Connie Hasemann has developed a business model that demonstrates a new concept of comprehensive
rehabilitation of disabled people, where the outcome is employment. This business model is both scalable and adaptable across sectors and national borders.

Arif Masood Naqvi, Pakistan, Founder and Group Chief Executive of the
Abraaj Group. Mr. Naqvi is a leading investor operating in Asia, the Middle
East and North Africa, Turkey and Central Asia, sub-Saharan Africa, and Latin
America. In 2012, he was invited by UN Secretary General Ban Ki-moon to
become part of the UN Global Compact Board. His work in promoting responsible business practices by looking at the stakeholder, rather than exclusively a
shareholder approach, is pioneering in the private equity industry. The Abraaj
Group devotes the time of its employees and resources to mentoring social, cultural, and economic entrepreneurs. The Abraaj Group, under the leadership of

Naqvi, has partnered with best in class organizations focused on entrepreneurship and job creation, health care, education, and community engagement.

Dean Cycon, USA, founder and owner of Dean's Beans Organic Coffee Company. Mr. Cycon has worked for more than twenty-five years on development issues in indigenous communities, including coffee-producing villages around the world. He created Dean's Beans to prove that businesses can promote positive economic, social, and environmental change in developing countries and be profitable at the same time. The company designs and funds people-centered development projects in coffee-producing areas in partnership with growers and returns a percentage of profits to the growers as a "social equity premium." Mr. Cycon is a cofounder of Coffee Kids (a nonprofit development group) and of Cooperative Coffees, the world's first fair trade roaster's cooperative.

Nadia Al-Sakkaf, Yemen, the Chief Editor of *Yemen Times.* The *Yemen Times* is the country's first and most widely read independent English-language newspaper, a leading voice in Yemen on issues of media, gender, development, and politics. During the May 2011 leadership crisis in Yemen, Ms. Al-Sakkaf and her organization were vital in reporting the news and putting the political situation in context for international readers. Under Ms. Al-Sakkaf's leadership, the *Yemen Times* has also created several publications—including publications to advocate for women's participation in politics, such as *Breaking the Stereotype,* a book on Yemeni women's experience as political candidates in elections.

Ibrahim Abouleish, Egypt, founder of the comprehensive development initiative SEKEM. During a journey through Egypt in 1975, Dr. Abouleish was overwhelmed by his country's overpopulation and its pollution, particularly from the use of chemical pesticides. SEKEM has been a leader in developing and spreading biodynamic farming methods in Egypt. The organization's commitment regarding innovative development has led to widespread use of biodynamic methods in pest control and to the improvement of yields. SEKEM means "vitality from the sun," and remarkably Dr. Abouleish has stated: "I had a vision of a threefold project that would allow me to contribute to community-building, humanity, and healing the Earth. The desert was like the canvas of a painting, but without a frame."

Eduardo Eurnekian, Argentina, president of Corporacion America. Mr. Eurnekian has a strong commitment to peace and reconciliation and advocates genuine restoration and reconciliation between Turkey and Armenia, with the consolidation of bilateral relations between the two countries. He is a prominent advocate of ethical business practices who sold all his media holdings when diversifying into other sectors of the Argentinian economy so as not to have privileged access to the media "in a manner that would imply unfair competition with other companies." As honorary chairman of the Raoul Wallenberg Foundation and as Vice President of the Argentinian Chamber of Commerce, as well as a member of the B-20 group that advises the G-20 nations, he is able to spread his business wisdom globally and significantly.

Vladas Lasas, Lithuania, CEO/Founder of Skubios siuntos UAB Kaunas & UPS/Lithuania. Dr. Lasas is an inspirational business leader who is helping drive awareness of how technology, cooperation, and synergy can provide important solutions to pressing global problems. He is cofounder of the Carbon War Room, the global nonprofit initiative by entrepreneurs to implement market-driven solutions to climate change. His numerous involvements and initiatives all have as a common goal to bring together resources from a number of fields and disciplines, across established boundaries, to find ways to make the world a better place. In a play on his last name, which means "drop of water" in Lithuanian, his business card declares, "Every drop counts."

David W. MacLennan, USA, President and Chief Operating Officer at Cargill, Inc. Under Mr. MacLennan's guidance, Cargill has developed management systems and policies to ensure environmental compliance, prevent pollution, and continually improve performance on criteria relevant to their business and operations. The group's commitment in this area has led the way for others by showing that it is possible to have a proven social responsibility record and also be a leader in profitability and growth. The Ethical Guiding Principles developed for the group under MacLennan's stewardship can serve as a guideline for all businesses.

Reginald A. Mengi, Tanzania, founder and chairman of the IPP Group. From humble beginnings, Mr. Mengi's company today ranks among the largest private companies in Tanzania. Mr. Mengi has consistently advocated the need for business to actively engage with communities and take responsibility for their development. He promotes initiatives that assist the disadvantaged and infirm and is seen to be in the forefront in fostering national unity as a leading advocate for peaceful coexistence. He indiscriminately contributes to all religious faiths and helps finance the construction of schools. The examples of social responsibility set by Mr. Mengi are widely emulated in the Tanzanian business community. Mengi's business peers have shown their trust by voting him "most respected CEO in East Africa" for three successive years.

Latifur Rahman, Bangladesh, Chairman and CEO of the Transcom Group. The group's growth has taken place under adherence to ethical and responsible business practices that serve as a guideline for other businesses in the region. The group is one of the highest corporate tax, VAT, and import duty payers in Bangladesh, with a clean bank record. The companies in the group also adhere to labor standards and industrial laws. Other businesses in the region look up to Mr. Rahman for leadership and guidance for his integrity, ethical standards, and business acumen—well illustrated by his reelection as chairman of the Metropolitan Chamber of Commerce and Industry for a total of seven terms.

Ratan Tata, India, chair of the Tata Group, India's largest conglomerate. Mr. Tata has more than once declared that his group is not driven to grow "over everybody's dead bodies." His personal view is that the group's sense of social responsibility does not collide with the creation of shareholder value. The Tata Group gives away on average 8 to 14 percent of its net profits every year through dedicated philanthropic programs.

Stef Wertheimer, Israel, founder and honorary chair of Iscar Metalworking Company, one of the world's largest manufacturers of carbide cutting tools. Mr. Wertheimer employs an integrated workforce of Arabs, Jews, and Christians. In his company, employees work side by side toward a common goal, shedding the stereotypes so prevalent in the Middle East. Mr. Wertheimer believes in the importance of quality technical education as a basis for a better society. To this end, he has initiated the Aramb-Jewish Executive Development program, bringing together Jews and Arabs in intensive courses on entrepreneurship.

Francis Yeoh, Malaysia, managing director of the YTL Corporation Berhad, Malaysia's leading integrated infrastructure conglomerate. Mr. Yeoh believes that a sustainable business means one that can thrive in the long term and that true sustainability has four equal components: social, economic, environmental, and cultural.

Roberto Servitje Sendra, Mexico, chair of Grupo Bimbo, a multinational baking enterprise. Early in its development, Mr. Sendra stated that the group's goal was to be *"altamente productiva y plenamente humana"*—highly productive and truly humane. Grupo Bimbo has a significant social responsibility program that is tightly related to health, the environment, society, poverty and food distribution, and the well-being of its workers. In terms of health, the group has been making serious efforts to promote exercise as a way of life. On the environmental front, it has set a leading example through its efforts to recycle and to reduce water consumption while supporting a major reforestation campaign in Mexico.

Venkataramani Srivathsan, Nigeria, managing director of Nigerian operations at Olam, a leading global supply chain management company for agricultural products and food ingredients. Mr. Srivathsan has created the rice extension farming and out-grower program in collaboration with farmers' organizations and NGOs. This program has allowed Olam Nigeria to increase overall returns to rice farmers through enhanced productivity, improved quality, and the guaranteed buy-back of crops.

Emily Cummins, UK. Ms. Cummins designs products to improve the quality of life in developing countries. She designed and created a multibucket water system to transport water effectively across southern Africa. Her sustainable fridge uses solar heat to provide refrigeration cheaply and easily. Ms. Cummins has selflessly given her designs away because she wanted as many people as possible to build their own sustainable refrigerators. Her product is now serving the everyday refrigeration needs of countless families across southern Africa.

William Rosenzweig, United States, managing director of Physic Ventures, whose purpose is to invest in companies that create value through delivering innovative solutions for preventing disease, promoting consumer-driven health, and ensuring a sustainable planet for future generations. Mr. Rosenzweig's vision achieves a union of business performance with a higher purpose by creating strong clusters of experienced enterprises working with companies in developing countries to create an ultimate benefit that goes far beyond bottom-line considerations.

Anders Dahlvig, Sweden. Mr. Dahlvig started working for IKEA in 1984 and assumed his current position as CEO in 1999. Under his leadership, IKEA has placed sustainability at the heart of its product development and supply strategy. "The IKEA Way of Purchasing Home Furnishing Products" (the IWAY) is a code of conduct that defines what suppliers can expect from IKEA and what IKEA requires from its suppliers in terms of legal requirements, working conditions, the active prevention of child labor, environmental protection, and forestry management.

Mo Ibrahim, Sudan. Dr. Mohamed "Mo" Ibrahim is a Sudanese-born British mobile communications entrepreneur. He is currently on the board of the Mo Ibrahim Foundation and is a member of the Africa Regional Advisory Board of London Business School. In 2006, the foundation launched the Prize for Achievement in African Leadership. The prize is awarded to African heads of state who deliver security, health, education, and economic development to their constituents and who democratically transfer power to their successor. With a $5 million initial payment, plus $200,000 a year for life, the prize is believed to be the world's largest, exceeding the $1.3 million Nobel Peace Prize.

Mohammed Jameel, Saudi Arabia, President of Adbul Latif Jameel Co., Ltd. A great philanthropist as well as a respected businessman, Mr. Jameel has developed several community programs promoting job opportunities for thousands of young Saudi men and women each year. Jameel has been the driving force behind the Grameen Jameel Pan Arab Initiative, which aims to reduce poverty through microcredit. In addition, he opened the first Bab Riza (Gateway to Prosperity) Jameel Center in June 2007 in Jeddah for creating employment opportunities for women and offering financial support for start-ups and loans for vocational training in both the public and private sectors.

Jeffrey R. Immelt, United States, Chairman of the board and Chief Executive Officer of the U.S.-based conglomerate General Electric since 2000. Under Mr. Immelt's leadership, G.E. implemented a new initiative, under the name of "ecomagination" to ramp up development of clean technologies and lighten the company's environmental footprint. GE committed itself in 2005 to double its research-and-development investments in eco-friendlier technologies from 2004 to 2010, more than ten times the 2005 federal U.S. R&D budget for solar and wind combined. In 2007, G.E. announced that it was expanding its ecomagination strategy, committing to reduce its global water use by 20 percent by 2012.

Josephine Okot, Uganda, founder and Managing Director of Victoria Seeds, a full-line seed company in Uganda. Ms. Okot founded Victoria Seeds for the purpose of delivering quality seeds to "small holder" farmers who produce over 90 percent of agricultural output in Uganda. Her goal is to reverse the decline in agricultural productivity in Uganda and other countries of the region to which Victoria Seeds is exporting.

Jiang Jianqing, China. Mr. Jianqing served as Governor of the Shanghai Bank and the Pudong Subsidiary Bank before becoming the Head of the Investment and Commercial Bank of China (ICBC). Under the leadership of Mr. Jianqing, the ICBC became the first Chinese bank in the country's domestic banking to introduce and apply the notion of "Green Credit," strictly constraining credit inputs for heavily polluting and/or high energy-consuming corporations. For the ICBC, the environmental protection compliance serves as the ultimate determinant to reject or accept any projects and business entities requesting loans.

Zhengrong Shi. The Chinese–Austrialian solar scientist Dr. Zhengrong Shi is the founder, Chairman, and Chief Executive Officer of Suntech Power, one of the leading solar energy companies and the largest solar module manufacturer in the world. When he decided to start his own company in 2001, he was acutely aware of the growing need for renewable energy, and he wanted to be part of the solution. Now he is considered to be one of the world's leaders in the development and commercialization of renewable energy technology Dr. Shi guided Suntech into designing and providing low-cost solar generators to allow even the disadvantaged to afford clean energy. His idea and vision is to bring environment-friendly power to the world.

Notes

Preface

1. David Fabbro, "Peaceful Societies: An Introduction," *Journal of Peace Studies* 15 (1977) 8: 67.
2. Raymond Case Kelly, *Warless Societies and the Origin of War* (Ann Arbor: University of Michigan Press, 2000).
3. Fabbro, *Peaceful Societies*.
4. Kelly, *Warless Societies*.
5. Jane Nelson, *The Business of Peace: The Private Sector as a Partner in Conflict Prevention and Resolution* (Cambridge, UK: Prince of Wales Business Leader Forum, 2000).
6. Virginia Haufler, *A Public Role for the Public Sector: Industry Self-Regulation in a Global Economy* (Washington, DC: Carnegie Endowment, 2013).
7. International Chamber of Commerce, "History" (Paris: Author).
8. Rotary International, "Merchants of Peace" (Evanston, IL: Author).
9. Ian Morris, *War! What Is It Good For?* (New York: Farrar, Straus, and Giroux, 2014).

Chapter 1

1. Drawn from Tim Fort and Stephanie Hare, "Foreign Policy Joins Corporate Toolkit," February 15, 2011; available at www.oxan.com/display.aspx? ItemID=DB166187 and used with permission of Dr. Hare and Oxford Analytica.
2. Timothy L. Fort and Alexandra Cristina, "Corporate Foreign Policy," *QFinance* (2014). Available at www.financepractitioner.com/corporate-governance-best-practice/corporate-foreign-policy?full.

3. Stephanie Hare and Timothy Fort, "Corporate Foreign Policy," work in progress, *Academia.edu*; retrieved on June 25, 2014, from www.academia .edu/2092025/Corporate_Foreign_Policy.

4. Andrew Hammond, "U.S. Surveillance Underlines Importance of Corporate Foreign Policy," *Japan Today*, August 29, 2013; retrieved on June 25, 2014, from www.japantoday.com/category/opinions/view/u-s-surveillance-underlines-importance-of-corporate-foreign-policy.

5. S. Prakash Sethi, David B. Lowry, Emre A. Veral, H. Jack Shapiro, and Olga Emelianova, "Freeman-McMoran Copper & Gold Inc.: An Innovative Voluntary Code of Conduct to Protect Human Rights, Create Employment Opportunities, and Economic Development of the Indigenous People," *Journal of Business Ethics*, 103: 1–30, 2011.

6. Michelle Westermann-Behaylo and Kathleen Rehbein, "Corporate Diplomacy," presentation at the Annual Meeting of the Academy of Management, Orlando, FL, August 11, 2013.

7. "Secretary of State Award for Corporate Excellence," U.S. State Department; retrieved on June 25, 2014 from www.state.gov/e/eb/ace/.

8. Timothy L. Fort, *Business, Integrity, and Peace: Beyond Geopolitical and Disciplinary Boundaries* (New York: Cambridge University Press, 2007).

9. Timothy L. Fort, *Prophets, Profits and Peace: The Positive Role of Business in Promoting Religious Tolerance* (New Haven, CT: Yale University Press, 2008).

10. Walter Russell Mead, "America's Sticky Power," *Foreign Policy*, March 1, 2004; retrieved on June 25, 2014, from www.foreignpolicy.com/articles/2004/03/01/americas_sticky_power.

11. Fort, *Business, Integrity, and Peace*.

12. Joseph S. Nye Jr., "The Benefits of Soft Power," *Harvard Business School Working Knowledge*, August 2, 2004; retrieved on June 25, 2014, from http://hbswk.hbs.edu/archive/4290.html.

13. Phillip Bobbitt, *The Shield of Achilles* (New York: Random House, 2002).

14. Cooperatives, for example, are legally set up to be organizations where there is shared governance among those, including customers and employees, who wish to become members of the organization and thereby obtain a vote in the work of the cooperative.

15. Of course, there are journals devoted to the topic of business ethics and corporate responsibility, but increasingly one now sees both special issues and articles in mainline academic journals such as the *Academy of Management Review* and in presentations at meetings of the Academy of Management and the Academy of Marketing.

16. One can make differentiations between CSR and business ethics, but I think the distinctions tend to be rather arbitrary, and so I will use them interchangeably. The same applies to other monikers such as "corporate citizenship."

17. Edward Freeman, *Strategic Management: A Stakeholder Approach* (Pitman Publishing, 1984; reprinted Cambridge, UK: Cambridge University Press, 2012).

18. Reuven Avi-Yonah, "Taxation, Corporate Social Responsibility and the Business Enterprise," July 30, 2009; retrieved on June 24, 2014, from http://papers.ssrn.com/sol3/papers.cfm?abstract_id=1440884, 5–6.

19. Ibid., 6.

20. Ibid.

21. Ibid.

22. Thomas Donaldson, *Corporations and Morality* (Englewood Cliffs, NJ: Prentice-Hall, 1982), 37.

23. Freeman, *Strategic Management*.

24. Amitai Etzioni, *The New Golden Rule* (New York: Basic Books, 1996).

25. William C. Frederick, *Values, Nature, and Culture in the American Corporation* (New York: Oxford University Press, 1995).

26. Ann Rynd, *Atlas Shrugged* (New York: Penguin Press, 1957).

27. Milton Friedman, "The Social Responsibility of Business Is to Increase Its Profits," *New York Times Magazine*, September 13, 1970.

28. Norman Bowie, "A Kantian Theory of Capitalism," *Business, Science, and Ethics* 1 (1998): 37.

29. Aaron B. O'Connell, "The Permanent Militarization of America," *New York Times*, November 4, 2012; retrieved on June 25, 2014, from www.nytimes.com/2012/11/05/opinion/the-permanent-militarization-of-america.html?pagewanted=all&_r=0. It is worth noting the author's argument in this op-ed piece that, although the percentages do not appear large, the spiritual dimension is with a popular culture devoted to issues of the military.

30. Timothy L. Fort and Cindy A. Schipani, *The Role of Business in Fostering Peaceful Societies* (London: Cambridge University Press, 2004), 110–111.

31. Vincent Trivett, "25 U.S. Mega Corporations: Where They Rank if They Were Countries," *Business Insider*, June 27, 2011; available at www.businessinsider.com/25-corporations-bigger-tan-countries-2011-6?op=1.

32. Per Saxegaard, "Rebuilding the Trust Proposition between Companies and Society through Being Businessworthy," *Business for Peace*, 2011; retrieved on June 25, 2014, from http://businessforpeace.no/wp-content/uploads/2014/05/Rebuilding-the-trust-proposition.pdf.

33. Richard Behar, "Peace through Profits?," *Forbes Magazine*, August 12, 2013, 72.

34. I hosted twelve conferences on the topic between 2001 and 2011. Other conferences were held in the United States at the University of Notre Dame, University of Kansas, and University of San Diego. The Business for Peace Foundation, headquartered in Oslo, holds an annual conference on the topic as well.

35. Secretary of State Award for Corporate Excellence; available at www.state .gov/e/eb/ace/.

36. "Labour," U.N. Global Compact; retrieved on June 25, 2014, from www .unglobalcompact.org/AboutTheGC/TheTenPrinciples/labour.html. See also the work of the World Bank Institute.

37. "History," Rotary International; retrieved on June 25, 2014, from www .rotary.org/en/history; "The Merchants of Peace," International Chamber of Commerce, retrieved on June 25, 2014, from www.iccwbo.org/about-icc/ history/.

38. Fort and Schipani, *The Role of Business.*

39. African Centre for Economic Growth, "The Link between Corruption and Poverty," United Nations, 2000; retrieved on June 25, 2014, from http:// unpan1.un.org/intradoc/groups/public/documents/IDEP/UNPAN005215.pdf.

40. Caroline Moser and Jeremy Holland, *Urban Poverty and Violence in Jamaica,* World Bank, 1997; retrieved on June 25, 2014, from http://dx.doi .org/10.1596/0-8213-3870-6.

41. Paul Collier and Anke Hoeffler, *Greed and Grievance in Civil War,* World Bank, 2000; retrieved on June 25, 2014, from http://siteresources.worldbank .org/INTKNOWLEDGEFORCHANGE/Resources/491519-1199818447826/ multi_page2355.pdf.

42. "About," Kimberley Process; retrieved on June 25, 2014, from www .kimberleyprocess.com/en/about.

43. "What Is the EITI?," Extractive Industries Transparency Initiative; re-trieved on June 25, 2014, from http://eiti.org/eiti.

44. This became apparent to me about fifteen years ago. During the first ten to twelve years of my academic career, I often felt as if I needed to do a song and dance—sometimes literally—to convince students that a corporate responsibil-ity course was worth their time. But, around 1997 or so, things changed. It was not that deans and faculty became interested in issues of corporate responsibil-ity; it was the students. Often reporters ask me if various corporate scandals have sparked interest in my courses. I believe there may be some marginal impact, but there are two major products that I think sparked the interest of the students. One is technology (the Internet and cell phones) that are able to broadcast cor-porate deeds and misdeeds within seconds, and the other is the Nike sweatshop scandal, which brought home to campuses issues that were very relevant to their daily lives and purchasing choices.

45. Saxegaard, "Rebuilding Trust."

46. Fort and Schipani, *The Role of Business.*

47. Ibid.

48. "Collaborative Governance," World Bank Institute; retrieved on June 25, 2014, from http://wbi.worldbank.org/wbi/about/topics/governance.

49. Bribery and Corruption," OECD; retrieved on June 25, 2014, from www.oecd.org/corruption/; and "Monitoring Report of the G20 Anti-Corruption Working Group," G20; retrieved on June 25, 2014, from www.g20civil.com/documents/195/364/.

50. "Rule of Law," U.S. Institute for Peace; retrieved on June 25, 2014, from www.usip.org/ruleoflaw/index.html.

51. W. Edwards Deming, *Out of the Crisis* (Cambridge, MA: The MIT Press, 2000).

52. Stuart Weart, "Peace among Democratic and Oligarchic Republics." *Journal of Peace Research* 31 (1994): 299–316.

53. Amartya Sen, *Development and Freedom* (New York: Random House, 1999).

54. Daniel Griswold, "Trade, Democracy, and Peace: The Virtuous Cycle," Cato Institute, April 20, 2007; available at www.cato.org/publications/speeches/trade-democracy-peace-virtuous-cycle; and Nils Petter Gleditsch and Havard Hegre, "Peace and Democracy: Three Levels of Analysis," *Journal of Conflict Resolution* 41(2) (1997): 283.

55. The interesting question, then, is this: Could a corporation that uses management practices emphasizing employee voice provide an experience of self-governance that could spill over into the political sector, especially if that sector had not previously had experience with such democratic principles? That question has not been addressed, to my knowledge, but it would be a fascinating one to tackle. In the meantime, this remains a possibility at least.

56. Terry Dworkin and Cindy Schipani, "Linking Gender Equity to Peaceful Societies," *American Business Law Journal* 44(2) (2007): 391–415.

57. Michael Novak, "Catholic Social Teaching and These Changing Times," *CatholiCity*, March 8, 2011; retrieved on June 25, 2014, from www.catholicity.com/commentary/mnovak/08815.html; and Robert P. George, "He Threw It All Away," *First Things*, March 20, 2009; available at www.firstthings.com/web-exclusives/2009/03/he-threw-it-all-away.

58. Timothy L. Fort, *Ethics and Governance* (New York: Oxford University Press, 2001), 8–10.

59. Ibid.

60. Robin Dunbar, *Grooming, Gossip and the Evolution of Language* (London: Faber and Faber, 1996).

61. Dunbar, *Evolution of Language*, 182.

62. Ibid., 158.

63. Ibid., 101.

64. Tina Nielsen, "WL Gore," *Director Magazine*, February 2010; retrieved on June 25, 2014, from www.director.co.uk/magazine/2010/2_Feb/WLGore_63_06.html.

65. Fort, *Ethics and Governance.*

66. Putting this all together, my colloquial summary pertains to a wedding. There were four to six who had to be there: the bride, the groom, two witnesses, and an officiant. In planning the wedding, the bridge and groom probably thought of thirty people they would love to invite. They also might have thought of 150 whom it would have been great to have. But get above those numbers, and the betrothed may look at each other and ask: Who are they?

67. Fabbro, *Peaceful Societies,* and Kelley, *Warless Societies.*

68. Secretary of State Award for Corporate Excellence; available at www.state .gov/e/eb/ace/.

69. Gretchen Spreitzer, "Giving Peace a Chance," *Journal of Organizational Behavior* 28(8) (2007): 1077.

70. "A Better Tour Company for the World," MEJDI Tours; retrieved on June 25, 2014, from www.mejditours.com/about/.

71. Thomas Friedman, "Foreign Affairs Big Mac I," *New York Times,* December 8 1996; retrieved on June 25, 2014, from www.nytimes.com/1996/12/08/opinion/foreign-affairs-big-mac-i.html.

72. Jim Marshall, "Address at the Business for Peace Foundation Summit," Oslo, 2013.

73. Donald Kagan, *On the Origins of War and the Preservation of Peace* (New York: Doubleday, 1995); and Geoffrey Blainey, *The Causes of War*, 3rd edition (New York: Free Press, 1988).

74. Moises Naim, *Illicit: How Smugglers, Traffickers and Copycats Are Hijacking the Global Economy* (New York: Anchor, 2006); and Raymond W. Baker, *Capitalism's Achilles Heel: Dirty Money and How to Renew the Free Market System* (Hoboken, NJ: Wiley, 2005).

75. Oliver Williamson, *The Economic Institutions of Capitalism* (New York: Free Press, 1985); and Douglas North, *Violence and Social Orders: A Conceptual Framework for Interpreting Recorded Human History* (New York: Cambridge University Press, 2009).

76. Bobbitt, *The Shield of Achilles.*

Chapter 2

1. Randal Collins, *Violence: A Micro-Sociological Theory* (Princeton, NJ: Princeton University Press, 2009).

2. S. L. A. Marshall, *Men against Fire: The Problem of Battlefield Command* (Norman: University of Oklahoma Press, 1978), 50–55.

3. For an elaboration of the ideas in this section, see my book *Business, Integrity, and Peace: Beyond Geopolitical and Disciplinary Boundaries* (New York: Cambridge University Press, 2007).

4. William C. Frederick, *Corporation Be Good! The Story of Corporate Social Responsibility* (Indianapolis, IN: Dog Ear Publishing, 2006).

5. William C. Frederick, *Values, Nature & Culture in the American Corporation* (New York: Oxford University Press, 1995).

6. I have tweaked Frederick's work arguing for a more positive view toward power aggrandizement in several places, including in *Business, Integrity, and Peace*.

7. David Sloan Wilson, *Darwin's Cathedral: Evolution, Religion, and the Nature of Society* (Chicago: University of Chicago Press, 2002), 156.

8. Michael Novak, "Catholic Social Teaching and These Changing Times," *CatholiCity*, March 8, 2011, retrieved on June 25, 2014, from www.catholicity .com/commentary/mnovak/08815.html; and Robert P. George, "He Threw It All Away," *First Things*, March 20, 2009, available at www.firstthings.com/web-exclusives/2009/03/he-threw-it-all-away.

9. Walter Russell Mead, "Power, Terror, Peace, and War: America's Grand Strategy in a World at Risk," *Foreign Affairs*, November/December 2004, retrieved on June 25, 2014, from www.foreignaffairs.com/articles/60179/ michael-mastanduno/power-terror-peace-and-war-americas-grand-strategy-in-a-world-at.

10. Henry Kissinger, *Diplomacy* (New York: Simon & Schuster Paperbacks, 1994), 57–58.

11. For something as prevalent in human history, I cannot do full justice to the entire literature on this topic, but there do seem to be some key, identifiable themes. For a more detailed treatment, see Donald Kagan, *On The Origins of War and the Preservation of Peace* (New York: Doubleday, 1995); and Geoffrey Blainey, *The Causes of War*, 3rd edition (New York: Free Press, 1988).

12. Phillip Bobbitt, *The Shield of Achilles* (New York: Random House, 2002), 61.

13. Thucydides, *History of the Peloponnesian War: Chapter XVII*, (New York: Penguin Classics, 1974): retrieved on June 25, 2014, from www.mtholyoke.edu/ acad/intrel/melian.htm.

14. Carl von Clausewitz (trans. by Michael Howard and Peter Paret), *On War* (Princeton, NJ: Princeton University Press, 1989), 88.

15. Charles Krauthammer, "Bush's U.N. Speech Sent the Wrong Signal to Hussein at the Wrong Time," *Philadelphia Inquirer*, October 9, 1990, available at http://articles.philly.com/1990-10-09/news/25890690_1_iraq-and-kuwait-rumaila-oil-fields-hussein.

16. Ian Morris, *War! What Is It Good For?* (New York: Farrar, Straus, and Giroux, 2014).

17. Lord John Acton, "Letter to Bishop Mandell Creighton," 1887; available at http://history.hanover.edu/courses/excerpts/165acton.html.

18. Amy Chua, *World on Fire: How Exporting Free Market Democracy Breeds Ethnic Hatred and Global Instability* (New York: Anchor Books, 2003).

19. Ibid.

20. See, for example, Lawrence Keeley, *War before Civilization: The Myth of the Peaceful Savage* (Oxford, UK: Oxford University Press, 1997).

21. Konrad Lorenz, *On Aggression* (Orlando, FL: Routledge, 2005), 47–49.

22. Frans DeWaal, *Peacemaking among Primates* (Cambridge, MA: Harvard University Press, 1989).

23. Ibid.

24. Ibid.

25. Tony Brewer, *Marxist Theories of Imperialism: A Critical Survey* (London: Routledge, 2002).

26. Jonathan Haas, *The Anthropology of War* (Cambridge, UK: Cambridge University Press, 1990); and Douglas P. Fry, *Beyond War: The Human Potential for Peace* (Oxford, UK: Oxford University Press, 2009).

27. Morris, *War!*, 202–205.

28. Robert Higgs, "How U.S. Economic Warfare Provoked Japan's Attack on Pearl Harbor," *The Independent Institute*, May 1, 2006, available at www.independent.org/newsroom/article.asp?id=1930.

29. Geoffery Ingersoll, "80 Years Ago a Marine General Explained the Ugliest Truth about War," *Business Insider*, July 30, 2013, available at www.businessinsider.com/excerpt-from-marines-speech-proves-little-has-changed-in-80-years-2013-7.

30. One might make the argument that these three forces are present and describe individuals as well, but I will leave that argument to the side for now.

31. Scott Appleby, *The Ambivalence of the Sacred* (Lanham, MD: Rowman & Littlefield Publishers, 2000), 58–81.

32. Bobbitt, *Shield of Achilles*.

33. David Cook, *Understanding Jihad* (Berkeley: University of California Press, 2005).

34. David G. Chandler, *The Campaigns of Napoleon* (New York: Simon and Schuster, 2009), xl.

35. "Sadaam's Iraq: Key Events," BBC, retrieved on June 25, 2014, from http://news.bbc.co.uk/2/shared/spl/hi/middle_east/02/iraq_events/html/chemical_warfare.stm.

36. Raymond Case Kelly, *Warless Societies and the Origin of War* (Ann Arbor: University of Michigan Press, 2000).

37. Graham T. Allison and Philip Zelikow, *Essence of Decision: Explaining the Cuban Missile Crisis* (Boston: Little, Brown, 1999), 284.

38. NPR Staff, "Ike's Warning of Military Expansion, 50 Years Later," NPR, January 17, 2011, available at www.npr.org/2011/01/17/132942244/ikes-warning-of-military-expansion-50-years-later.

39. Alasdair MacIntyre, *After Virtue* (Notre Dame, IN: University of Notre Dame Press, 1981).

40. To be sure, there are some correlations that may be outside of our capacity to do much about. One of those is a recent study showing that the hotter the temperature becomes, the more we are inclined to violence. Early on in my work on business and peace, I interviewed a scholar who was highly skeptical of any positive contribution that business could make. He (seemingly half-seriously) said that to reduce violence, people should get more sleep and suggested that companies should make sure not to work their people so hard. He backed up his assertion with evidence that showed that, when short of sleep, people become crankier and more violent.

41. University of Michigan, *Correlates of War Project*, Ann Arbor, retrieved on May 8, 2015, from www.correlatesofwar.org.

42. Institute for Economics and Peace, *The Global Peace Index*, retrieved on May 8, 2015, from http://economicsandpeace.org last accessed May 8, 2015

43. Gretchen Spreitzer, "Giving Peace a Chance: Organizational Leadership, Empowerment, and Peace" *Journal of Organizational Behavior* 28: 1077 (2007).

44. Louis Ryan, "Top 10 Disadvantages to Capitalism," Listverse, January 16, 2010, available at http://listverse.com/2012/01/16/top-10-disadvantages-to-capitalism/.

45. Michael Medved, "Does Hollywood Bash Big Business?" in *The Moral Imagination: How Literature and Film Can Stimulate Ethical Reflection in the Business World* (Oliver Williams, ed.) (Notre Dame, IN: Notre Dame University Press, 1998).

46. R. Edward Freeman, "The Business Sucks Story," The Darden Graduate School of Business Administration Working Papers (Charlottesville, VA, 1996).

47. "War Production: The War at Home," PBS, retrieved on June 25, 2014, from www.pbs.org/thewar/at_home_war_production.htm.

48. Antonia Juhasz, "Why the War in Iraq Was Fought for Big Oil," CNN, April 15, 2013, available at www.cnn.com/2013/03/19/opinion/iraq-war-oil-juhasz/.

49. T. J. Stiles, "Cornelius Vanderbilt," *New York Times*, retrieved June 25, 2014, from http://topics.nytimes.com/top/reference/timestopics/people/v/cornelius_vanderbilt/index.html.

50. Moises Naim, *Illicit: How Smugglers, Traffickers and Copycats Are Hijacking the Global Economy* (New York: Anchor, 2006); and Raymond W. Baker,

Capitalism's Achilles Heel: Dirty Money and How to Renew the Free Market System (Hoboken, NJ: Wiley, 2005).

51. Per Saxegaard, "Rebuilding the Trust Proposition between Companies and Society Through Being Businessworthy," *Business for Peace*, 2011, retrieved on June 25, 2014, from http://businessforpeace.no/wp-content/uploads/2014/05/Rebuilding-the-trust-proposition.pdf.

52. Kim Cameron and Robert Quinn, *Diagnosing and Changing Organizational Culture: Through the Competing Values Framework*, 3rd Edition (San Francisco: Jossey-Bass, 2011).

53. Cameron and Quinn, "Organizational Culture Assessment Instrument," from ibid.; retrieved on May 31, 2010, from www.ocai-online.com/userfiles/file/ocai_pro_example_report.pdf.

54. Ibid., 5.

55. Ibid.

56. Ibid.

57. Ibid., 7.

58. Ibid.

59. Ibid.

60. Ibid., 6.

61. Ibid.

62. Ibid.

63. Ibid.

64. Ibid.

65. Ibid.

66. Countess Alexandra and Timothy Fort, "Catalyst, Obstacle, or Something in Between? Dealing with the Law in Building Ethical Corporate Culture," *Notre Dame Journal of Law, Ethics, and Public Policy*, 29 (2015), 101.

67. Cameron and Quinn, *Diagnosing and Changing Organizational Culture*, 92.

Chapter 3

1. Konrad Lorenz, *On Aggression* (London: Routledge, 2005); Robert Ardley, *The Terriortial Imperative* (New York: Atheneum, 1966); Helen Fisher, *The Sex Contract: The Evolution of Human Behavior* (New York: William Morrow & Co., 1982); and Irenäus Eibl-Eibesfeldt, *Biology of Peace and War* (New York: Viking Press, 1979).

2. Frans de Wall, *Chimpanzee Politics: Power and Sex among Apes* (Baltimore, MD: Johns Hopkins University Press, 1982); Frans DeWaal, *Peacemaking among Primates* (Cambridge, MA: Harvard University Press, 1989); and Frans DeWaal,

Good Natured: The Origin of Right and Wrong in Humans and Other Animals (Cambridge, MA: Harvard University Press, 1996).

3. Michael Nagler, "Ideas of World Order: The Map of Peace." In *Approaches to Peace: A Reader in Peace Studies*, edited by David P. Barash, p. 378. (Oxford, UK: Oxford University Press, 1999.

4. Lawrence Keeley, *War before Civilization: The Myth of the Peaceful Savage* (Oxford, UK: Oxford University Press, 1997).

5. William C. Frederick, "Nature and Business Ethics." In *A Companion to Business Ethics*, edited by Robert Frederick, p. 100. (Indianapolis, IN: John Wiley & Sons, 2008).

6. Douglas Fry is a highly regarded anthropologist at the University of Finland with an appointment at the University of Arizona as well.

7. Douglas P. Fry, *Beyond War: The Human Potential for Peace* (Oxford, UK: Oxford University Press, 2009) 3, 6.

8. Richard Wrangham and Dale Peterson, *Demonic Males: Apes and the Origin of Human Violence* (Boston: Houghton Mifflin, 1996).

9. Fry, *Beyond War*, 78.

10. Fry further argues that it is important to differentiate between nomadic hunter-gather societies and complex, sedentary hunter-gatherers. Simple hunter-gatherer societies are nomadic and egalitarian with no social hierarchy or well-defined positions of leadership and authority. By contrast, complex hunter-gatherer societies have partially given up the nomadic lifestyle and "may exhibit elaborate economic and political status differentiation systems, including rank distinctions and chiefs." Warfare is rare among the former and pervasive among the latter. Fry then relies on the work of a prominent anthropologist who agrees that for the 99 percent of human history dominated by hunter-gatherers, the "lack of archeological evidence for warfare suggests that it was rare or absent for most of human prehistory." Ibid., 63.

Looking at current Australian nomadic hunter-gatherers, South American Yanomamo, and Canadian Montagnais-Naskapi, Fry again finds warfare rare among the most basic of human organizations[o]. [o]Those who argue for man the warrior, Fry claims, come from primatology and evolutionary psychology and are far afield from actual hunter-gatherer research. Ibid., 131–147.

11. Ibid., 22.

12. Ibid., 65–67.

13. Ibid., 13.

14. Even more optimistically, Fry cites the work of Keith and Charlotte Otterbein, who found blood feuding absent in 56 percent of the sample they used and infrequent in 28 percent of others. Using the same sample as Embers, Karen Ericksen and Heather Horton found blood feuding in 34.5 percent of societies

and kin group vengeance not considered legitimate in 46 percent of societies; even where it was permitted, it wasn't always carried out. Ibid., 178.

15. Ibid., 16, citing Bobbi Low, "An Evolutionary Perspective on War." In *Behavior, Culture and Conflict in World Politics*, edited by W. Zimmerman and H. Jacobsen, page 13 (Ann Arbor: University of Michigan Press, 1993).

16. Fry, *Beyond War*, 17.

17. Ibid.,18.

18. Ibid., 21.

19. Ibid., 24.

20. Steven Pinker, *The Better Angels of Our Nature* (New York: Penguin Books, 2011), 345.

21. Ibid, 25.

22. Ibid., 37–39.

23. Ibid., 483.

24. Ibid., 41.

25. Ibid., 43.

26. Ibid., 49.

27. Ibid., 60–63.

28. Ibid., 67.

29. Ibid., 69.

30. Ibid., 72.

31. Michael Barnett, *Empire of Humanity: A History of Humanitarianism* (Ithaca, NY: Cornell University Press, 2011), 49–76.

32. Pinker, *Better Angels*, 87.

33. Ibid., 88–89.

34. Ibid.

35. Ibid., 195.

36. Pinker says that great powers participated in 70 percent of wars that Wright included in his half-millennium data base, and four have been in at least a fifth of all European wars; it is also true that "zero" marks the number of times nuclear weapons have been used in conflict since 1945; the number of times Cold War superpowers fought, the number of interstate wars fought between countries in Western Europe, the number of interstate wars fought between major developed countries (except for invasion of Hungary in 1956), the number of times developed countries have expanded their territory by conquering another country, and the number of internationally recognized states that have gone out of existence through conquest. Ibid., 222–228.

37. Ibid., 279–282.

38. Ibid., 284–288.

39. Ibid., 288–289.

40. Ibid., 313. The Muslim world an exception, and they are about 20 percent of the world's population. Pinker argues that Muslim societies tend to not be democratic, not to embrace humanitarianism (for example, the presence of torture in these societies), and base much of their law and politics on a culture of religion and honor. Ibid., 362–363.

41. Fry, *Beyond War*, 233.

42. Ibid., 82.

43. Ibid., 200.

44. Ibid., 215.

45. Ibid., 216–217.

46. Ibid., 221–223.

47. Ibid., 611.

48. Pinker, *Better Angels*, 611.

49. David Sloan Wilson, *Darwin's Cathedral: Evolution, Religion, and the Nature of Society* (Chicago: University of Chicago Press, 2002), 98–100.

50. Timothy L. Fort, *Prophets, Profits, and Peace: How Businesses Can Become Instruments of Peace and Foster Religious Harmony* (New Haven, CT: Yale University Press, 2008).

51. Pinker, *Better Angels*, 572–573.

52. Ibid., 622–623.

53. Ibid., 633.

54. Gerald Schneider and Nils Petter Gleditsch, "The Capitalist Peace: The Origins and Prospects of a Liberal Idea," *International Interactions* 36 (2010): 107.

55. Ibid.

56. Eric Gartzke, "The Capitalist Peace," *American Journal of Political Science* 51 (2007): 166.

57. Charles A. Kupchan, "Enmity into Amity: How Peace Breaks Out," *Council of Foreign Relations*, April 2011, 4, retrieved on June 25, 2014, from http://library.fes.de/pdf-files/iez/07977.pdf.

58. Ian Morris, *War! What Is It Good For?* (New York: Farrar, Straus, and Giroux, 2014), 9.

Chapter 4

1. Michael Porter and Mark Kramer, "Creating Shared Value," *Harvard Business Review*, January, 2011, available at http://hbr.org/2011/01/the-big-idea-creating-shared-value.

2. The lectures were captured on tape. Bernanke's lectures are available on the Fed's website and the commentaries on George Washington University's website.

Bernanke's lectures became a book: Ben S. Bernanke, *The Federal Reserve and the Financial Crisis* (Princeton, NJ: Princeton University Press, 2013).

3. Louis Hyman, "How Did World War II End the Great Depression? Echoes," *Bloomberg*, December 16, 2011, available at www.bloombergview.com/ articles/2011-12-16/how-did-world-war-ii-end-the-great-depression-echoes.

4. This topic was explored at length in Chapter 2.

5. Bernanke, *Federal Reserve and the Financial Crisis*, 123.

6. "Johnson & Johnson History," Johnson & Johnson, retrieved on June 25, 2014, from www.jnj.com/about-jnj/company-history.

7. "Our Credo," Johnson & Johnson, retrieved on June 25, 2014, from www .jnj.com/sites/default/files/pdf/jnj_ourcredo_english_us_8.5x11_cmyk.pdf. The Johnson & Johnson Credo reads as follows:

> We believe our first responsibility is to the doctors, nurses and patients, to mothers and fathers and all others who use our products and services. In meeting their needs everything we do must be of high quality. We must constantly strive to reduce our costs in order to maintain reasonable prices. Customers' orders must be serviced promptly and accurately. Our suppliers and distributors must have an opportunity to make a fair profit.
>
> We are responsible to our employees, the men and women who work with us throughout the world. Everyone must be considered as an individual. We must respect their dignity and recognize their merit. They must have a sense of security in their jobs. Compensation must be fair and adequate, and working conditions clean, orderly and safe. We must be mindful of ways to help our employees fulfill their family responsibilities. Employees must feel free to make suggestions and complaints. There must be equal opportunity for employment, development and advancement for those qualified. We must provide competent management, and their actions must be just and ethical.
>
> We are responsible to the communities in which we live and work and to the world community as well. We must be good citizens—support good works and charities and bear our fair share of taxes. We must encourage civic improvements and better health and education. We must maintain in good order the property we are privileged to use, protecting the environment and natural resources.
>
> Our final responsibility is to our stockholders. Business must make a sound profit. We must experiment with new ideas. Research must be carried on, innovative programs developed and mistakes paid for. New equipment must be purchased, new facilities provided and new products launched. Reserves must be created to provide for adverse times. When we operate according to these principles, the stockholders should realize a fair return.

8. Thomas Moore, "The Fight to Save Tylenol (*Fortune* 1982)," *Fortune*, October 7, 2012, available at http://features.blogs.fortune.cnn.com/2012/10/07/ the-fight-to-save-tylenol-james-burke/.

9. Stephen B. Presser, "Thwarting the Killing of the Corporation: Limited Liability, Democracy, and Economics," *Northwestern University Law Review* 87 (1992): 148.

10. Alasdair MacIntyre, *After Virtue* (Notre Dame, IN; University of Notre Dame Press 1981), 31–41.

11. Joshua Daniel Margolis and James P. Walsh, *People and Profits? The Search for a Link between a Company's Social and Financial Performance* (New York: Taylor and Francis, 2001).

12. Ibid.

13. Alan Greenspan, "Testimony of Chairman Alan Greenspan before the Committee on Financial Services, U.S. House of Representatives," The Federal Reserve Board, February 27, 2002, available at www.federalreserve.gov/boarddocs/hh/2002/february/testimony.html.

14. Quantitative research, although certainly of great value, tends to crowd out ineffable moral values, which don't fit into statistical modeling very well. Ignoring values allows sophisticated statistical analysis to proceed. This makes for elegant models, but they surf—even free ride—on something they didn't create. Sumenta Ghosal, "Bad Management Theories Are Destroying Good Management Practices." *Academy of Management Learning & Education* 75–91 (2015).

15. Per Saxegaard, "Rebuilding the Trust Proposition between Companies and Society through Being Businessworthy," *Business for Peace*, 2011, retrieved on June 25, 2014, from http://businessforpeace.no/wp-content/uploads/2014/05/Rebuilding-the-trust-proposition.pdf.

16. For a more thorough examination of this concept, see Timothy L. Fort, *Business, Integrity, and Peace: Beyond Geopolitical and Disciplinary Boundaries* (New York: Cambridge University Press, 2007).

17. Greg Smith, "Why I Am Leaving Goldman Sachs," *New York Times*, March 14, 2012, www.nytimes.com/2012/03/14/opinion/why-i-am-leaving-goldman-sachs.html?pagewanted=all.

18. Adam Smith, *Theory of Moral Sentiments* (Charleston, SC: Biblio-Bazarre Reprints, 2008; originally published in 1759).

19. Athol Fitzgibbons, *Adam Smith's System of Liberty, Wealth, and Virtue: The Moral Foundations of The Wealth of Nations* (Oxford, UK: Oxford University Press, 1997).

20. Katherine L. Lemon et al., "Measuring the Effects of Corporate Social Responsibility: A Stakeholder-Based Approach," *The Conference Board*, April 2011, available at www.conference-board.org/retrievefile.cfm?filename=TCB%20DN-V3N7-11.pdf&type=subsite.

21. Ibid.

22. Aneel Karnani, "The Case against Corporate Social Responsibility," *Wall Street Journal*, August 23, 2010, retrieved on June 25, 2014, from http://online .wsj.com/news/articles/SB10001424052748703338004575230112664504890.

23. This is very much the point of Spanish economist Javier Aranzadi, who has done a wonderful job contrasting two forms of liberal economics, one from the Chicago School and the other from the Austrian School. He helps to clarify that there is more than one free market economics approach; we tend to fall into the trap of thinking that, and the Austrian School provides a far more robust space for ethics. Aranzadi's analysis shows that both arise from liberal notions of freedom and laissez-faire oversight, but although the Chicago School is much more comfortable with a transactional analysis, the Austrian School is much more dependent on a set of social institutions and supports that also emphasize notions of fairness.

24. F. A. Hayek, *The Fatal Conceit: The Errors of Socialism* (Chicago: University of Chicago Press, 1988), 34.

25. Ibid.

26. Oliver Williamson, *The Economic Institutions of Capitalism* (New York: Free Press, 1985); and Douglas North, *Violence and Social Orders: A Conceptual Framework for Interpreting Recorded Human History* (New York: Cambridge University Press, 2009).

27. Robert Frank, *Passions within Reason: The Strategic Role of Emotions* (New York: W. W. Norton & Company, 1988); Amartya Sen,, *Development as Freedom* (New York: Random House, 1999); and Hernando de Soto, *The Mystery of Capital: Why Capitalism Triumphs in the West and Fails Everywhere Else* (New York: Basic Books, 2003).

28. Immanuel Kant, *Fundamental Principles of the Metaphysics of Morals* (Radford, VA: Wilder Publications, 2008; originally published in 1797), 13.

29. R. Edward Freeman, *Strategic Management: A Stakeholder Approach* (Cambridge, UK: Cambridge University Press, 1984); Patricia Werhane, "Business Ethics, Stakeholder Theory, and the Ethics of Healthcare Organizations," *Cambridge Quarterly of Healthcare Ethics* 9(2) (2000): 169–181; and Norman E. Bowie, *Business Ethics: A Kantian Perspective* (Malden, MA: Blackwell Publishers, 1999).

30. Immanuel Kant, *Perpetual Peace* (New York: Filiquarian Publishing, 2007; originally published in 1795), 14–20.

31. Timothy L. Fort and Cindy A. Schipani, *The Role of Business in Fostering Peaceful Societies* (Cambridge, UK: Cambridge University Press, 2004).

32. Philip Nichols, "The Business Case for Complying with Bribery Laws," *American Business Law Journal* 49(2) (2012): 325–368.

33. Sen, *Development as Freedom*, 16.

34. Douglas P. Fry, *Beyond War: The Human Potential for Peace* (New York: Oxford University Press, 2009).

Chapter 5

1. Jan Joel Andersson, Tobias Evers, and Gunnar Sjöstedt, *Private Sector Actors & Peacekeeping: A Framework for Analysis* (Stockholm: Swedish Institute of International Affairs, 2011), 14–17.

2. Ibid., 16.

3. Canan Canan Gündüz and Nick Killick, *Local Business, Local Peace: The Peace Building Potential of the Domestic Private Sector* (London: International Alert, 2006).

4. Juliette Bennett, "Business in Zones of Conflict: The Role of the Multinationals in Promoting Regional Stability," UN Business for Peace, retrieved on August 23, 2014, from www.unglobalcompact.org/issues/conflict_prevention/meetings_and_workshops/Reg_stability.html.

5. Thomas Friedman, "India, Pakistan, and G.E.," *New York Times*, August 11, 2002, available at www.nytimes.com/2002/08/11/opinion/india-pakistan-and-ge.html.

6. Angelika Rettberg, "El Salvador: A Firm Grip on the Peace Process," in *Local Business, Local Peace: The Peace Building Potential of the Domestic Private Sector* (London: International Alert, 2006), 324.

7. Ibid., 324.

8. Ibid., 326.

9. Ibid., 326–327.

10. "Revolutionary Armed Forces of Colombia—People's Army," Stanford University, retrieved on August 21, 2014, from http://web.stanford.edu/group/mappingmilitants/cgi-bin/groups/view/89.

11. Alexandra Guaqueta, "Doing Business amidst Conflict: Emerging Best Practices in Colombia," in *Local Business, Local Peace: The Peace Building Potential of the Domestic Private Sector* (London: International Alert, 2006), 273, 274–275.

12. Mapping Militant Organizations, "Revolutionary Armed Forces of Columbia," Stanford University. Retrieved on May 1, 2015 from www.stanford.edu/group/mappingmilitants/cgi-bin/groups/view/89.

13. Guaqueta, *Business amidst Conflict*, 275–276.

14. Ibid., 278.

15. Angelika Rettberg, "Business vs. Business? Grupos and Organized Business in Colombia," *Latin American Politics & Society* 47 (2005): 31.

16. Ibid., 31.

17. Ibid., 33.

18. Ibid., 38.

19. Ibid., 38–39.

20. Ibid., 39–40.

21. Ibid., 40.

22. Ibid., 41.
23. Guaqueta, *Business amidst Conflict*, 279.
24. Ibid., 280.
25. Ibid.,
26. Ibid.
27. Ibid., 281.
28. International Alert, "The Confederation of British Industry and the Group of Seven: A Marathon Walk to Peace in Northern Ireland," in *Local Business, Local Peace: The Peace Building Potential of the Domestic Private Sector* (London: International Alert, 2006), 438.
29. International Alert, "Marathon Walk," 438–442:
    1. Nonsegregation of the races in all eating, comfort, and work facilities.
    2. Equal and fair employment practices for all employees.
    3. Equal pay for all employees doing equal or comparable work for the same period of time.
    4. Initiation of and development of training programs that will prepare, in substantial numbers, blacks and other nonwhites for supervisory, administrative, clerical, and technical jobs.
    5. Increasing the number of blacks and other nonwhites in management and supervisory positions.
    6. Improving the quality of life for blacks and other nonwhites outside the work environment in such areas as housing, transportation, school, recreation, and health facilities.
Working to eliminate laws and customs that impede social, economic, and political justice.
30. Ibid.
31. Andre Fourie and Theuns Eloff, "The Case for Collective Business Action to Achieve Systems Change: Exploring the Contributions Made by the Private Sector to the Social, Economic and Political Transformation Process in South Africa," *Journal of Corporate Citizenship* 18 (2005): 508–509.
32. Ibid., 509–510.
33. Ibid., 510.
34. Ibid., 510–511.
35. Ibid., 511.
36. The call for nominations is made each spring. Nominations are submitted by the chiefs of missions at U.S. embassies and cabroad. Eligibility requirements include the following:
    • Nominated firms must be American (having headquarters in the United States)
    • Each firm must have been operating in the host country/economy for at least one year.

- The activity for which a firm is nominated must have been in place for at least one year.

37. Richard Behar, "Peace Through Profits? Inside the Secret Tech Ventures That Are Reshaping the Israeli–Arab–Palestinian World," *Forbes*, August 12, 2013.

38. Ibid.

39. "Cisco Receives U.S. State Department Award for Corporate Excellence," Cisco, December 17, 2010, available at http://newsroom.cisco.com/dlls/2010/corp_121710.html.

40. 2013 Cisco Corporate Social Responsibility Report, retrieved on August 18, 2014, from www.cisco.com/assets/csr/pdf/CSR_Report_2013.pdf#page=33, C19.

41. Charmian Gooch, "The Kimberley Process," Global Witness, retrieved on August 23, 2014, from www.globalwitness.org/campaigns/conflict/conflict-diamonds/kimberley-process.

42. "Development Partnership with Private Sector: Mars Partnership for African Cocoa-Communities of Tomorrow," Mars, retrieved on August 22, 2014, from http://hespa.net/sites/hespa.net/files/mars-gtz-impact-en.pdf.

43. Ibid., 1.

44. Ibid., 1, 2.

45. "Cocoa," Mars: People, Planet, and Performance, retrieved on August 21, 2014, from www.mars.com/global/about-mars/mars-pia/our-supply-chain/cocoa.aspx.

46. "2000 Award for Corporate Excellence," U.S. Department of State, retrieved on August 24, 2014, from http://1997-2001.state.gov/www/about_state/business/cba_00award_motorola.html.

47. "Secretary of State's 2004 Awards for Corporate Excellence," U.S. Department of State, October 28, 2004, retrieved on August 24, 2014, from http://2001-2009.state.gov/r/pa/prs/ps/2004/37511.htm.

48. "2004 Ace Award Presentation to Motorola," U.S. Department of State, retrieved on August 24, 2014, from http://2001-2009.state.gov/secretary/former/powell/37732.htm.

49. "U.S. Secretary of State Bestows Award for Corporate Excellence: Embassies Nominated P&G Nigeria and P&G Pakistan for Improving Lives," Procter & Gamble, January 18, 2012, available at http://news.pg.com/blog/childrens-safe-drinking-water/us-secretary-state-bestows-award-corporate-excellence.

Chapter 6

1. John Mackey, *Conscious Capitalism: Liberating the Heroic Spirit of Business* (Boston: Harvard Business Review Press, 2013), 20.

2. William H. Clark Jr. and Larry Vranka, *The Need and Rationale for the Benefit Corporation: Why It Is the Legal Form That Best Addresses the Needs of Social Entrepreneurs, Investors, and, Ultimately, the Public*. Benefit Corporation Information Center, January 18, 2013, retrieved on August 25, 2014, from http://benefitcorp.net/storage/documents/Benecit_Corporation_White_Paper_1_18_2013.pdf.

3. "Anael's Amazing Story," Peace Through Commerce, retrieved on August 18, 2014, from www.peacethroughcommerce.org/SearchResults.asp?Cat=250. Material used with permission.

4. "Overview," Creativity for Peace, retrieved on August 23, 2014, from http://creativityforpeace.com/about/index.html.

5. "Projects: Path of Abraham," William Ury, retrieved on August 19, 2014, from www.williamury.com/projects/.

6. "A Better Tour Company for the World," MEJDI Tours, retrieved on June 25, 2014, from www.mejditours.com/about/. This venture was discussed in Chapter 1.

7. "Being Businessworthy," Business for Peace, retrieved on August 23, 2014, from http://businessforpeace.no/about-us/being-businessworthy/.

8. Michael E. Porter and Mark R. Kramer, "Creating Shared Value," *Harvard Business Review*, January 2011.

9. Ibid.

10. UN Global Compact, *Responsible Business Advancing Peace* (New York: United Nations, 2013), 29.

11. Technically the Phillipines subsdiary of Holcim Phillipines.

12. Ibid., 30.

13. Ibid., 32.

14. William Shaw, *Business Ethics: A Textbook with Cases* (Boston: Cengage, 2013), 16.

15. Please see the appendix for a 2013 ranking by Ethisphere of the Top 100 Ethical Companies in the world. The ranking is skewed to U.S. companies by the Washington-based NGO, but it still helps to get a flavor of these leading companies.

Chapter 7

1. UN Global Compact, *Guidance on Responsible Business in Conflict-Affected and High-Risk Areas* (New York: United Nations, 2010), retrieved on August 22, 2014, from www.unglobalcompact.org/docs/issues_doc/Peace_and_Business/Guidance_RB.pdf.

2. See Chapter 5.

3. "Overview," United Nations Global Compact, retrieved on August 22, 2014, from www.unglobalcompact.org/AboutTheGC/index.html. The Global Compact is governed by the Ten Principles, including:

Human Rights

- Principle 1: Businesses should support and respect the protection of internationally proclaimed human rights; and
- Principle 2: Make sure that they are not complicit in human rights abuses.

Labour

- Principle 3: Businesses should uphold the freedom of association and the effective recognition of the right to collective bargaining;
- Principle 4: The elimination of all forms of forced and compulsory labour;
- Principle 5: The effective abolition of child labour; and
- Principle 6: The elimination of discrimination in respect of employment and occupation.

Environment

- Principle 7: Businesses should support a precautionary approach to environmental challenges;
- Principle 8: Undertake initiatives to promote greater environmental responsibility; and
- Principle 9: Encourage the development and diffusion of environmentally friendly technologies.

Anti-Corruption

- Principle 10: Businesses should work against corruption in all its forms, including extortion and bribery.

"The Ten Principles," United Nations Global Compact, retrieved on August 22, 2014, from www.unglobalcompact.org/AboutTheGC/TheTenPrinciples/index.html.

4. "Global Peace Index," Institute for Economics and Peace, retrieved on August 22, 2014, from http://economicsandpeace.org/research/iep-indices-data/global-peace-index.

5. "Global Peace Index Methodology," Vision of Humanity, retrieved on August 23, 2014, from www.visionofhumanity.org/#/page/news/920.

6. Thomas Dunfee and Timothy Fort, "Corporate Hypergoals, Sustainable Peace, and the Adapted Firm," *Vanderbilt Journal of Transactional Law* 36 (2003): 563.

7. Stanley Hauerwas, *The Peaceable Kingdom: A Primer in Christian Ethics* (Notre Dame, IN: University of Notre Dame Press, 1983).

8. Anette Hoffmann, "Conflict Sensitivity: From 'Business as Usual' to 'Business for Peace,'" Netherlands Institute of International Relations, March 6,

2014, retrieved on August 23, 2014, from www.clingendael.nl/publication/%
E2%80%98business-usual%E2%80%99-%E2%80%98business-peace%
E2%80%99-unpacking-conflict-sensitivity-narrative.

9. Douglass C. North, John Joseph Wallis, and Barry Weingast, *Violence and Social Orders: A Conceptual Framework for Interpreting Recorded Human History* (New York: Cambridge University Press, 2009), 2.

10. Ibid., 2–6.

11. Echoing Pinker and contrary to Fry, North argues that violence within such societies was high as it was between such groups as well, perhaps thus conflating nomadic hunter-gatherer societies (which Fry and others argue are relatively pacific, especially within groups) with equestrian and settled banded societies, which were considerably more violent.

12. North, Wallis, and Weingast, *Violence and Social Orders*, 14.

13. Ibid., 15.

14. Ibid., 15–16.

15. Ibid., 140.

16. Ibid., 41.

17. Ibid., 43.

18. Ibid., 47.

19. Ibid., 2–3.

20. Ibid., 154.

21. Ibid., 12.

22. Ibid., xii.

23. Charles A. Kupchan, *How Enemies Become Friends: The Sources of Stable Peace* (Princeton, NJ: Princeton University Press, 2012).

24. North, Wallis, and Weingast, *Violence and Social Orders*, 151.

25. Ibid., 152.

26. Ibid., 153.

27. Indeed, North argues that this befuddles the work of major transnational organizations such as the World Bank. He cautions that although economics has powerful tools, they can't be uniformly applied because generalizations do not work anywhere and everywhere. Much is context dependent.

28. Harini Nagendra and Elinor Ostrom, "Polycentric Governance of Multifunctional Forested Landscapes," *International Journal of the Commons* 6(2) (2012): 104.

29. Ibid., 107.

30. Ibid., 108.

31. Ibid., 108.

32. Ibid., 109.

33. Ibid., 109.

34. Ibid., 115–116.

35. Elinor Ostrom, Governing the Commons: *The Evolution of Institutions for Collective Action* (Cambridge, UK: Cambridge University Press, 1990), 90–91. Ostrom articulated eight design principles related to climate change issues and resource use, including:
1. Clearly defined boundaries for the user pool . . . and the resource domain
2. Proportional equivalence between benefits and costs3
3. Collective choice arrangements ensuring that the resource users participate in setting . . . rules
4. Monitoring . . . by the appropriators or by their agents
5. Graduated sanctions for rule violators
6. Conflict-resolution mechanisms [that] are readily available, low cost, and legitimate
7. Minimal recognition of rights to organize
8. Governance activities . . . organized in multiple layers of nested enterprises.

36. Nina K. Cankar and Simon Deakin, "The Reflexive Properties of Corporate Governance Codes: The Reception of the 'Comply or Explain' Approach in Slovenia," *Journal of Law and Society* 37(3) (2010): 501.

37. "Federal Sentencing Guidelines," Ethics Resource Center, December 31, 2005, retrieved on August 22, 2014, from www.ethics.org/resource/federal-sentencing-guidelines.

38. United States Sentencing Commission, *Guidelines Manual* (1991), 347.

39. Paula A. Tuffin, "Effective Compliance and Ethics Programs under the Amended Sentencing Guidelines," American Bar Association, retrieved on August 23, 2014, from http://apps.americanbar.org/buslaw/committees/CL925000pub/newsletter/201007/tuffin.pdf.

40. In re Caremark International Inc. Derivative Litigation, 698 A.2d 959 (Del. Ch. 1996).

41. U.S. Sentencing Commission, *Amendments to the Sentencing Guidelines*, May 10, 2004, retrieved on August 22, 2014, from www.ussc.gov/sites/default/files/pdf/amendment-process/reader-friendly-amendments/20040430_RF_Amendments.pdf.

42. This is an argument I made at length in Timothy L. Fort, *Ethics and Governance: Business as Mediating Institutions* (New York: Oxford University Press, 2001).

43. Linda Klebe Trevino and Gary R. Weaver, *Managing Ethics in Business Organizations* (Stanford, CA: Stanford University Press, 2003).

44. North, Wallis, and Weingast, *Violence and Social Orders*, 149.

45. Josh Margolis and James Walsh, "Misery Loves Companies: Rethinking Social Initiatives by Businesses," *Administrative Science Quarterly* 48(2) (2003): 268.

46. Note that, in this context, goodwill refers to the ethical concept and not the accounting term used in mergers and acquisitions.

47. Mike Whalen, "Eliminate the Capital Gains Tax," *U.S. News,* September 28, 2012, retrieved on August 22, 2014, from www.usnews.com/opinion/blogs/economic-intelligence/2012/09/28/eliminate-taxes-on-capital-gains.

48. Louise Story, "As Companies Seek Tax Deals, Governments Pay Heavy Price," *New York Times,* December 1, 2012, retrieved on August 23, 2014, from www.nytimes.com/2012/12/02/us/how-local-taxpayers-bankroll-corporations.html?pagewanted=all.

49. Of course, we still do, but not to the level that occurred prior to the Civil Rights Act.

50. *Burlington Industries, Inc. v. Ellerth,* 524 U.S. 742 (1998).

51. *Bowoto v. Chevron Texaco Corp.,* 312 F. Supp. 2d 1229 (N.D. Cal. 2004).

52. *John Doe I, et al., v. UNOCAL Corp., et al.,* 395 F.3d 932 (9 Cir. 2002).

53. *Kiobel v. Royal Dutch Petroleum,* slip op. 10-1491 (U.S. 2012)

54. *Doe VIII v. Exxon Mobil Corp.,* No. 09-7125 (D.C. Cir. 2011).

55. Paul Collier and Anke Hoeffler, "Greed and Grievance in Civil War," *Oxford Economic Papers* 56 (2004): 563.

56. See Chapter 5.

57. "What Is the EITI?" Extractives Industry Transparency Initiative, retrieved on August 22, 2014, from http://eiti.org/eiti.

58. UNESCO, *Internet Universality: A Means towards Building Knowledge Societies and the Post-2015 Sustainable Development Agenda* (New York: United Nations, 2013), 2.

59. Joshua Meltzer, "The Internet, Cross-Border Data Flows and International Trade," Brookings, February 25, 2013, retrieved on August 22, 2014, from www.brookings.edu/research/papers/2013/02/25-internet-data-flows-international-trade-meltzer.

60. Ibid.

61. Pippa Norris, *Giving Voice to the Voiceless: Good Governance, Human Development and Mass Communications* (Cambridge, MA: Harvard University, John F. Kennedy School of Government, 2004).

62. Scott Shackelford, "Toward Cyber Peace: Managing Cyber Attacks through Polycentric Governance," *American University Law Review,* 2013.

63. For example, IIPT partners with the UN World Tourism Organization, which includes 150 ministers of tourism and a number of private sector and NGO organizations as affiliate members. The World Travel and Tourism Council (WTTC)—is a body of about 130 CEOs of the major travel/tourism private sector companies. Skal International is the largest organization of travel and tourism industry executives with 18,000 members in 450 cities in eighty-five countries. One of its projects is an IIPT/Skal Peace Towns/Villages project,

which aims to have 2,000 by November 11, 2018—the last day of the WWI Centenary commemoration. Other organizations include the Pacific Asia Travel Association (PATA), Caribbean Tourism Organization, European Travel Commission, Africa Travel Association, TIA, International Airlines Transportation Association, International Hotel and Restaurant Association, International Tour Operators Association, and Universal Federation of Travel Agent's Associations.

Chapter 8

1. Garret Hardin, "Lifeboat Ethics: The Case against Helping the Poor," *Psychology Today*, September 1974.

2. See LaRue Hosmer, in Timothy L. Fort, *Vision of the Firm: A Textbook on the Ethics of Organiztions* (St. Paul, MN: WestAcademic Publishing, 2014).

3. Jane Dudman, "Open or Closed Society Is Key Dividing Line of 21st Century, Says Hillary Clinton," *The Guardian*, April 17, 2012, available at www .theguardian.com/technology/2012/apr/17/open-closed-society-hillary-clinton.

4. Beatrice Pouligny, "Civil Society and Post-Conflict Peacebuilding: Ambiguities of International Programmes Aimed at Building 'New' Societies," *Security Dialogue* 36(4) (December 2005): 495.

5. Robert Putnam, *Making Society Work: Civic Traditions in Modern Italy* (Princeton, NJ: Princeton University Press, 1994).

6. Professionals in Humanitarian Assistances, "Peacebuilding Initiative," retrieved on May 1, 2015 from www.peacebuildinginitiative.org.

7. See the example of Northern Ireland in Chapter 5.

8. "Peace Organizations," Wikipedia, retrieved on August 22, 2014, from http://en.wikipedia.org/wiki/Category:Peace_organizations.

9. John Forrer et al., "Public–Private Partnershps and the Public Accountability Question," *Public Administration Review* (2010).

10. "FedEx, UPS and DHL Play Critical Role in Relief Efforts," Salvation Army, February 15, 2010, retrieved on August 21, 2014, from www.salvation armytexas.org/sanantonio/news/international-shippers-provide-in-relief-effort/.

11. "About the Institute," Aspen Institute, retrieved on August 23, 2014, from www.aspeninstitute.org/about.

12. "About BSR (Business for Social Responsibility)," Business for Social Responsibility, retrieved on August 23, 2014, from www.bsr.org/en/about/bsr.

13. "About," Ethisphere Institue, retrieved on August 23, 2014, from http://ethisphere.com/about/.

14. Steve Pinker, "Has Religion Made the World Less Safe?" *Washington Post*, December 27, 2011.

15. Ralph Wendell Burhoe, "War, Peace, and Religion's Biocultural Evolution," *Zygon* 21(4) (1986): 439, 457.

16. David Sloan Wilson, *Darwin's Cathedral* (Chicago: University of Chicago Press, 2003), 156.

17. Ibid., 155–157.

18. Aristotle, *Eudemian Ethics*, Book 2, 1227(b), available at www.perseus. tufts.edu/hopper/text?doc=Perseus%3Atext%3A1999.01.0050%3Abook%3D2% 3Asection%3D1227b.

19. "The Middle Way," Soka Gakkai International, retrieved on August 22, 2014, from www.sgi.org/buddhism/buddhist-concepts/the-middle-way.html.

20. Francis Collins, *The Language of God: A Scientist Presents Evidence for Belief* (New York: Simon and Schuster, 2008), 243.

21. Forrer et al., "Public–Private Partnerships."

22. Steve Pinker, *The Blank Slate: The Modern Denial of Human Nature* (New York: Viking Adult, 2002), 400.

23. Rotary International, *The 2013 Rotary Manual of Procedure*, retrieved on August 21, 2014, from www.rotary.org/en/document/468, 59. This work provides the following goals as the object of Rotary International:

1. The development of acquaintance as an opportunity for service;
2. High ethical standards in business and professions, the recognition of the worthiness of all useful occupations, and the dignifying of each Rotarian's occupation as an opportunity to serve society;
3. The application of the ideal of service in each Rotarian's personal, business, and community life;
4. The advancement of international understanding, goodwill, and peace through a world fellowship of business and professional persons united in the ideal of service.

24. "Rotary International," Wikipedia, retrieved on August 19, 2014, from http://en.wikipedia.org/wiki/Rotary_International.

25. "Support Peace Centers," Rotary International, retrieved on August 19, 2014, from www.rotary.org/myrotary/en/take-action/empower-leaders/ support-peace-centers.

26. "The Merchants of Peace," International Chamber of Commerce, retrieved on August 18, 2014, from www.iccwbo.org/about-icc/history/.

27. "The fundamental objective . . . is to further the development of an open world economy with the firm conviction that international commercial exchanges are conducive to both greater global prosperity and peace among nations." *Constitution of the International Chamber of Commerce*, retrieved on August 20, 2014, from file:///C:/Users/Jason/Downloads/ICC%20Constitution %20EN%20June%202012.pdf.

28. "Quick Facts about Nonprofits," National Center for Charitable Statistics, retrieved on August 22, 2014, from http://nccs.urban.org/statistics/quickfacts .cfm.

29. See discussions in Chapter 5.

30. See Chapter 5.

31. Natalie Angier, "No Time for Bullies: Baboons Retool Their Culture," *New York Times*, April 13, 2004, retrieved on August 23, 2014, from www .nytimes.com/2004/04/13/science/no-time-for-bullies-baboons-retool-their-culture.html.

32. Ibid.

33. Max Fisher, "This Map Shows Where the World's 30 Million Slaves Live," *Washington Post*, October 17, 2013, retrieved on August 23, 2014, from www .washingtonpost.com/blogs/worldviews/wp/2013/10/17/this-map-shows-where-the-worlds-30-million-slaves-live-there-are-60000-in-the-u-s/.

34. "Modern Slavery," BBC, retrieved on August 23, 2014, from www.bbc .co.uk/ethics/slavery/modern/modern_1.shtml.

Chapter 9

1. Douglass C. North, John Joseph Wallis, and Barry Weingast, *Violence and Social Orders: A Conceptual Framework for Interpreting Recorded Human History* (New York: Cambridge University Press, 2009), 2.

2. Brian Ganson, "How Do We Succeed in a Complex Environment?" in *Management in Complex Environments: Questions for Leaders*, edited by Brian Ganson, p. 11 (Stockholm: International Council of Swedish Industry, 2013).

3. Ibid., 11.

4. Achmin Wenmann, "What Makes This Environment Complex?" in *Management in Complex Environments: Questions for Leaders*, edited by Brian Ganson (Stockholm: International Council of Swedish Industry, 2013), 22.

5. Dost Bardouille-Crema, Diana Chicags, and Benjamin Miller, "How Do Our Operations Interact with the Environment?" in *Management in Complex Environments: Questions for Leaders*, edited by Brian Ganson, p. 58 (Stockholm: International Council of Swedish Industry, 2013).

6. Kathleen Hamill, "Are We Meeting Our Responsibilities?" in *Management in Complex Environments: Questions for Leaders*, edited by Brian Ganson, p. 94 (Stockholm: International Council of Swedish Industry, 2013).

7. Nicklas Svensson, "Are We Disciplined about Asking Questions?," in *Management in Complex Environments: Questions for Leaders*, edited by Brian Ganson, p. 130 (Stockholm: International Council of Swedish Industry, 2013).

8. Cecile Renouard in *Management in Complex Environments: Questions for Leaders*, edited by Brian Ganson, p. 166 (Stockholm: International Council of Swedish Industry, 2013).

9. Paul Hollesen, "Is Our Own House in Order?" in *Management in Complex Environments: Questions for Leaders*, edited by Brian Ganson, p. 206 (Stockholm: International Council of Swedish Industry, 2013).

10. Brian Ganson, "Who Should Be Asking These Questions?" in *Management in Complex Environments: Questions for Leaders*, edited by Brian Ganson, p. 238 (Stockholm: International Council of Swedish Industry, 2013).

11. Caitlin Dewey, "Why the Internet Is a False Idol," *Washington Post*, April 26, 2013, retrieved on August 23, 2014, from www.washingtonpost.com/blogs/innovations/wp/2013/04/26/why-the-internet-is-a-false-idol/.12 David Wolman, "Facebook, Twitter Help the Arab Spring Blossom," *Wired*, April 16, 2013, retrieved on August 24, 2014, from www.wired.com/2013/04/arabspring/.

13. "Being Businessworthy," Business for Peace Foundation, retrieved on August 23, 2014, from http://businessforpeace.no/about-us/being-businessworthy/.

14. Nicholas Carlson, "Google to 'Pressure' China over Censorship," *Business Insider*, January 29, 2014, retrieved on August 22, 2014, from www.business insider.com/google-will-apply-some-pressure-on-china-says-schmidt-2010-1.

15. For instance, if Walmart were a sovereign country, its 2012 gross revenues would have made it one of the twenty-five largest economies in the world. Vincent Trivett, "25 U.S. Mega Corporations: Where They Would Rank if They Were Countries," *Business Insider*, June 27, 2011, retrieved on August 22, 2014, from www.businessinsider.com/25-corporations-bigger-tan-countries-2011-6?op=1.

16. "Supplier Code of Business Conduct," Motorola, retrieved on August 23, 2014, from http://responsibility.motorola.com/index.php/suppliers/scoc/.

17. "Ford Motor Company Expert Makes Business Case for Human Rights," Bloomberg, November 30, 2009, retrieved on August 22, 2014, from www.bloomberg.com/apps/news?pid=newsarchive&sid=afhZC9NLSAPU.

18. Gretchen M. Spreitzer, "Social Structure Characteristics of Psychological Empowerment," *Academy of Management Journal* 39 (1996): 483–504.

19. Raymond Case Kelly, *Warless Societies and the Origin of War* (Ann Arbor: University of Michigan Press, 2000), 12.

20. LaRue Tone Hosmer, *Teaching Business Ethics* (New York: Kluwer Academic Publishing, 1997), 99.

21. Sam Howe Verhovek, "Power Struggle," *New York Times*, January 12, 1992, retrieved on August 23, 2014, from www.nytimes.com/1992/01/12/magazine/power-struggle.html.

22. Dirk Matten and Andrew Crane, "Corporate Citizenship: Toward an Extended Theoretical Conceptualization," *The Academy of Management Review* 30(1) (2005): 166.

23. Ibid., 171–173.

24. Andreas Georg Scherer and Guido Palazzo, "The New Political Role of Business in a Globalized World: A Review of a New Perspective on CSR and Its Implications for the Firm, Governance, and Democracy," *Journal of Management Studies* 48(4) (2010): 899.

25. Michelle Westermann-Behaylo, Kathleen Rehbein, and Timothy L. Fort, "Corporate Diplomacy: Operationalizing Political Corporate Social Responsibil-

ity to Overcome Global Governance Gaps in Conflict-Prone Regions." *Academy of Management Perspectives*, forthcoming.

26. Adam Levin, "Post-Target Data Breach: Culture Eats Strategy for Breakfast," *Forbes*, June 12, 2014, retrieved on August 23, 2014, from www .forbes.com/sites/adamlevin/2014/06/12/post-target-data-security-culture-eats-strategy-for-breakfast/.

27. Jeffrey McCracken, "'Way Forward' Requires Culture Shift at Ford," *Wall Street Journal*, January 23, 2006, retrieved on August 22, 2014, from http://online.wsj.com/news/articles/SB113797951796853248.

28. Guido Palazzo and Andreas Georg Scherer, "Corporate Legitimacy as Deliberation: A Communicative Framework," *Journal of Business Ethics* 66 (2006): 71.

29. Thomas Donaldson and Thomas Dunfee, "Toward a Unified Conception of Business Ethics: Integrative Social Contracts Theory," *Academy of Management Review* 19(2) (1994): 252.

30. Joseph Montville, *Conflict and Peacemaking in Multiethnic Societies* (Lanham, MD: Lexington Books, 1989), 535.

31. John W. Burton and Frank Dukes, *Conflict: Practices in Management, Settlement and Resolution* (London: Macmillan, 1990).

32. This multitrack notion of peace building has further expanded into nine levels that include:

1. Official government interaction
2. Nongovernmental policy experts
3. Business professionals and private sector corporate interactions
4. Citizen to citizen exchange programs (culture, arts, sports, youth exchanges)
5. Media education about other societies and ethnic groups
6. Learning and academic communities
7. Activist groups
8. Religious group interaction

Louise Diamond and John McDonald, *Multi-Track Diplomacy: A Systems Approach to Peace* (Bloomfield, Connecticut: Kumarian Press, 1996).

33. Thomas Dunfee and Timothy Fort, "Corporate Hypergoals, Sustainable Peace, and the Adapted Firm," *Vanderbilt Journal of Transactional Law* 36 (2003): 563, 599.

34. Ibid., 600–601.
35. Ibid., 601–602.
36. Ibid., 602–603.
37. Ibid., 603–605.
38. Ibid., 610–617.
39. See Chapter 8.
40. See Chapter 3.

41. See Chapter 3.

42. See Chapter 7.

43. See Chapter 2.

44. Adapted from Timothy L. Fort, *Business, Integrity, and Peace: Beyond Geopolitical and Disciplinary Boundaries* (New York: Cambridge University Press, 2007).

45. Ibid., 190–191.

46. Paula A. Tuffin, "Effective Compliance and Ethics Programs under the Amended Sentencing Guidelines," American Bar Association, retrieved on August 23, 2014, from http://apps.americanbar.org/buslaw/committees/CL925000pub/newsletter/201007/tuffin.pdf.

47. Gary R. Weaver, Linda Klebe Treviño, and Philip L. Cochran, "Corporate Ethics Programs as Control Systems: Influences of Executive Commitment and Environmental Factors," *The Academy of Management Journal*, 42(1) (1999): 41.

48. Fort, *Business, Integrity, and Peace*, 127.

49. Ibid., 185.

50. Ibid., 134.

51. Ibid., 8–11.

52. LaRue Tone Hosmer, *Moral Leadership in Business* (Burr Ridge, IL: Irwin Professional Publishing, 1994), 86–87.

53. Ibid., 87.

54. Fort, *Business, Integrity, and Peace*, 101–105.

55. Ibid., 9.

56. Timothy L. Fort, *Ethics & Governance* (New York: Oxford University Press, 2001), 46–48.

57. Timothy L. Fort, "Business as Mediating Institution," *Business Ethics Quarterly* 6(2) (1996): 149.

58. Fort, *Ethics & Governance*, 11–13.

59. Fort, *Business, Integrity, and Peace*, 210–213.

60. Dunfee and Fort, "Corporate Hypergoals," 588.

61. As noted by Jeremy Bentham, "The effect of wealth in the production of happiness goes on diminishing, as the quantity by which the wealth of one man exceeds that of another goes on increasing: in other words, the quantity of happiness produced by a particle of wealth (each particle being of the same magnitude) will be less and less at every particle; the second will produce less than the first, the third than the second, and so on." Jeremy Bentham, "Pannamonial Fragments," *The Works of Jeremy Bentham, Vol. 3*, (Chestnut Hill, MA: Adamant Media, 2005), 228.

Index

Printed and bound by CPI Group (UK) Ltd, Croydon, CR0 4YY